THE PRIZEFIGHTER AND THE PLAYWRIGHT
Gene Tunney and Bernard Shaw

THE PRIZEFIGHTER AND THE PLAYWRIGHT
Gene Tunney and Bernard Shaw

by Jay R. Tunney

with an introduction by Christopher Newton

FIREFLY BOOKS

A Firefly Book

Published by Firefly Books Ltd. 2010

First printing

PUBLISHER CATALOGING-IN-PUBLICATION DATA (U.S.)
Tunney, Jay R.
The Prizefighter and the Playwright :
Gene Tunney and Bernard Shaw / Jay R. Tunney.
[288] p. : photos. ; cm. Includes index.
Summary: The story of the unlikely relationship between
a champion boxer and an award-winning author.
ISBN-13: 978-1-55407-641-3 ISBN-10: 1-55407-641-2
1. Tunney, Gene, 1897-1978. 2. Shaw, Bernard, 1856-1950.
3. Boxers (Sports)—United States—Biography.
4. Dramatists, Irish—20th century—Biography. I. Title.
796.83092 dc22   GV1132.T8.T86   2010

LIBRARY AND ARCHIVES CANADA
CATALOGUING IN PUBLICATION
Tunney, Jay R.
The Prizefighter and the Playwright :
Gene Tunney and Bernard Shaw / Jay R. Tunney.
Includes index.
ISBN-13: 978-1-55407-641-3 ISBN-10: 1-55407-641-2
1. Tunney, Gene, 1897-1978. 2. Shaw, Bernard, 1856-1950.
3. Boxers (Sports)—United States—Biography.
4. Dramatists, Irish—20th century—Biography. I. Title.
GV1132.T8T85 2010   796.83092   C2010-900703-4

Published in the United States by Firefly Books (U.S.) Inc.
P.O. Box 1338, Ellicott Station, Buffalo, New York 14205

Published in Canada by Firefly Books Ltd.
66 Leek Crescent, Richmond Hill, Ontario L4B 1H1

Cover and interior design by Punch & Judy Inc., Stratford, Ontario
Printed in Canada

The publisher gratefully acknowledges the financial support
for our publishing program by the Government of Canada
through the Canada Book Fund as administered by the
Department of Canadian Heritage.

CONTENTS

Dedicated to my Parents,
whose Love of Language, Poetry
and Life Enriched us All

BERNARD SHAW ATTENDING A BOXING EXHIBITION IN LONDON IN 1929. "THE INTELLIGENT
PRIZEFIGHTER IS NOT A KNIGHT-ERRANT: HE IS A DISILLUSIONED MAN OF BUSINESS TRYING
TO MAKE MONEY AT A CERTAIN WEIGHT," WROTE SHAW (GETTY IMAGES).

So perhaps this is what he was really like. It's clear from Holroyd and all the other biographers that Shaw was a generous man. He was more than kind to Wilde when he was in trouble. He gave anonymously to so many good causes and to so many people who were hurt or sick or caught in circumstances over which they had no control, but to me the public voice always seemed unsympathetic, hectoring and dissatisfied. I have a fading memory of hearing Shaw on the radio when I was eleven or twelve. Because he was a famous, even revered, celebrity, my parents encouraged me to listen. Unfortunately my memory is of a voice complaining endlessly about something which didn't interest me.

Even the plays weren't particularly compelling. It was perhaps 1950 when I saw an amateur production of *Pygmalion* — a play by the great Bernard Shaw! Already fascinated by the theatre, by make believe, I needed to see this play which was done in modern dress by local amateurs. But there were too many words and I suspect that I was more intrigued by hearing someone use a swear word on stage than anything else. That was thrilling, but the rest paled in comparison and I gained an impression that I carried with me for years that his plays were simply animated lectures. And in this, of course, I was not alone.

My very first professional job — acting in *Saint Joan* and *Julius Caesar* with the Canadian Players — didn't change my mind. I was happy to be acting. I was happy to see all of Canada from Port aux Basques to Trail but on stage it was *Julius Caesar* that intrigued me not *Saint Joan*. I played at the Shaw Festival in the early days and again I thought I'd been caught up in a lecture not a real play, not an adventure that connected the audience with the stage. I played Henry Higgins with Nicola Cavendish in Vancouver but wasn't convinced. It was not until I first directed Shaw that I gained any kind of understanding of the plays. I realized after the first few weeks of rehearsal that he was a genuine playwright who could invent believable human beings. I began to think that all the Shaw plays I had either seen or acted in were mis-directed. I began to say: "When in doubt about Shaw, look for the sex." This helped, though I would probably now say: "Look for the love." Nevertheless after arguing — even in Ireland where there is a certain skepticism — that after Shakespeare, Shaw is the greatest playwright in the language, I still found him an almost impossible human being. I didn't like the man that I glimpsed behind the public persona and in my mind the ugly suburban house at Ayot St. Lawrence seemed to confirm the worst.

I had to be missing something. Dan Laurence used to talk to me about Shaw being like an onion. Every time you removed a skin, there was another layer underneath, and then another, and then the centre seemed to disappear. Well, Jay Tunney in this most attractive book about his father, the famous boxer, and his father's friendship with Shaw, has given me a revelation. Here is a glimpse of the centre. Here for a few brief moments is the man himself divested of that carping, public voice. The book has at its heart a vacation on Brioni, once a fashionable island resort in the Adriatic. Here, surprisingly, the highly literate Gene Tunney, ex-heavyweight champion of the world now a wealthy businessman, and his wife vacationed with the Shaws. Bernard and Charlotte Shaw found the Tunneys good company — good enough company to actually go on a holiday with them. And for that to be successful you must share interests and values.

Shaw always seemed to have a strong paternal streak in him. He helped and mentored the young Granville Barker. That wasn't really surprising. After all they were both in the theatre, both, even though Shaw was old enough to be Barker's father, were making their reputations. Gene Tunney appeared on the scene after the split between Barker and Shaw and he seemed to fill a need.

Of course, Shaw had always been interested in boxing. I would never imagine that Shaw could have been a team player. He needed an individual sport and boxing supplied it for him. He followed the boxing news. He read of Tunney's defeat of Carpentier in 1924 and was intrigued. When Tunney defeated Dempsey, he made an effort to meet the boxer. Eventually they made contact and Shaw was delighted with this oddly compelling, bookish young man. After all Tunney seemed like Cashel Byron brought to life: a pugilist who loved the arts, who married well and who had risen from a New York Irish working class background to become a major celebrity.

So here are the Tunneys and the Shaws on an island in the Adriatic. The press thought it must be a strange Shavian joke, but as Jay Tunney makes very clear, this just wasn't the case. I won't reveal the highly charged event that brought them so close. That's the heart of the book. But I can say that it moved me and more than anything else that I have read about Shaw, it described a man who I only half suspected might be there — the human being, the vulnerable and compassionate G.B.S.

At one point Jay Tunney writes about the similarity between his father and Shaw. They were both surprisingly private people. The boxer, after his marriage to an intensely discreet wife who hated to see herself even mentioned in the press, was particularly shy of reporters. And yet both men were celebrities and knew it. Shaw exploited this public interest. Tunney, pursued by reporters who never believed that a boxer could read for pleasure, did everything he could to avoid the publicity. Shaw, in private, became the politic and caring father that Tunney wished for, just as he had been the theatrical father that Granville Barker never knew.

This book has sent me scurrying around my own library looking up Gene Tunney in William Lyon Phelps' autobiography — there's a chapter devoted to him — finding a reference in Rupert Hart-Davis's life of Hugh

Walpole, realizing that we had a mutual acquaintance in Thornton Wilder. (My connection was fleeting.) A small but important association in the life of a major literary figure has come to life in a most remarkable way. And the story provides a source for incidents in two of Shaw's later plays and that's always of interest because ideas seldom occur in a vacuum. There are always connections.

Tunney and Shaw agreed on so many things, but they disagreed about Russia. Shaw, the old Fabian, had always been sympathetic towards the Soviet Union and Stalin. Tunney, the American businessman, was not. But he wanted to see for himself. There's a curious incident that resonated with me. In the '30s, Tunney on a visit to Russia arrived at a factory where thousands of church bells, many of them beautiful works of art, were being melted down to make armaments.

I think it was in 1990 — it was certainly the year when Leningrad reverted to its old name — when Cameron Porteous and I were in Russia. We'd spent a day in an artists' village outside St. Petersburg. In the evening we hopped on a suburban train and arrived at another village. It started to snow and when we got off the train, the Russians in our party suddenly stopped. "Listen. Listen," they said. We couldn't hear anything unusual. "Bells," said the Russians. "Bells. The lost sound of the Russian soul. We haven't heard bells for sixty years."

In every town we visited, they were putting the bells back into the churches.

This book is a bit like that. This story of the boxer and the playwright has helped to put the soul back into an author who hid his humanity behind a screen of words. It is a particularly personal book. At times I felt the same fear of intrusion that Jay Tunney's mother must have felt during all those public years with his father. It is an odd and intriguing book about an odd friendship and a strange and intriguing event.

CHRISTOPHER NEWTON
ARTISTIC DIRECTOR EMERITUS, SHAW FESTIVAL

GENE TUNNEY READING A NEWSPAPER IN CHICAGO,
FOLLOWING HIS DEFENSE OF THE CHAMPIONSHIP
IN 1927 (CHICAGO HISTORY MUSEUM).

The heiress, once a great beauty, was now 100 years old. She moved in slow but deliberate steps toward the straight-backed chair set up in front of the windows. The chair was facing out, so that from her second-floor bedroom, she could see across the treetops and down onto the rolling lawn which sloped away from the house to the rock garden she had planted so many years ago. With help, she sat down and reached toward the back of the chair for a sweater, which was handed to her. Her hair, once a glowing chestnut, was gray and pressed against her head under a hair net. Her hearing was still sharp, but her eyes were watery and clouded.

Somehow, she managed to see the distant trees she had presided over for three quarters of a century, trees that Daniel Chichester, the farmer who had built the house in 1735, may have planted himself. She had always loved trees, as if they were family. She had learned that from her mother. She could tell you about the tall tulip tree near the garden, the dogwood trees that spilled their white petals around the pond, the great oak, the sycamore, the elms and the old hickory so near the house she said it seemed to whisper to her in the wind. She was blessed with hundreds of trees, and when she needed more after Gene died, she started a Christmas tree farm in one of the meadows. That was in 1978, and some of the blue spruce and cedar had grown so large, they could never grace the inside of a home for the holidays.

"Love, love, love," she used to say when she left voice messages. And then, "Good-bye, good-bye, good-bye."

"Mr. Shaw used to do it," she said, her mouth curling upward with pleasure at the memory of it. "He used to have a little wave, and he always said 'Good-bye, good-bye, good-bye,' and I kind of picked it up. It sounded so sincere, you know. Like a little song. I loved it."

She smiled and looked over at the dozens of photographs on the bureau next to the bed, pictures of her four children and their children, pictures of a wedding, the schooner *Endymion* in full sail, and an old black-and-white image of a young Gene holding a rosary. Her eyes came to rest on a photograph from the 1920s that showed two men standing together deep in conversation as late-afternoon shadows fell languidly across their path.

"Let's talk about Brioni," she said. "It was a beautiful time. I'm the only one left, you know. I'm the only one who can remember."

It was her favorite story, and she wanted to start at the beginning.

GENE'S FIRST COMMUNION, 1907 (MARY
AGNES MCINTYRE ANDERSON COLLECTION).

CHAPTER I

The Altar Boy

"In the home of my rearing, prayer was regular and fervent."
GENE TUNNEY

It was the last weekend in May 1907, and Gene was doing what he always did in his spare time, sitting at the kitchen table reading with his head down, dark unruly curls falling over his ears, his arms flung over the sports section of the paper and legs dangling off the side of an old wood chair. Today, a Saturday, was his tenth birthday, and there was, praise God, no school and no Mass. A Saturday meant he had time to pore over Bob Edgren's column in the *New York Evening World* and the big, bold, black-and-white drawings of fighters punching and whacking, each one labeled with details to memorize.

Gene read slowly, mouthing each word quietly to himself, following the type to the end with his fingers, then methodically going back again and again to make sure he understood it perfectly, each word, each phrase. It took him a long time, but he knew he was good at it. Once he understood a passage, he remembered it, and when he wanted to feel the sound of the words in his mouth, he could beckon them back into his mind. The priests said he was their best altar boy because he memorized the liturgy, and the nuns told his mother he liked to use words that other boys hadn't learned. His chest swelled with pride. Once Gene read something, he tried hard never to forget it.

Sisters and brothers dashed in and out of the small kitchen as Nana tried to feed the youngest, baby Agnes. Papa had been up late drinking and had yet to leave for work. Papa was a longshoreman who did a little boxing at Owney Geaghan's club in the Bowery. Old man Tunney, they said, could "fight like the dickens!" On evenings when he indulged in his home-brewed gin, Papa liked to debate loudly and vigorously the merits of one fighter versus another. There was nothing young Gene wanted more than to please his tough, opinionated Irish father, and there was no one who seemed harder to satisfy. Papa didn't ruffle Gene's hair as a show of affection as the priests did, and he seemed moody or distracted. Gene was often frightened of him.

For Irish lads from the poor, working-class Lower West Side of Manhattan in the early 1900s, there were two constants in life: the church, for its unchangeable rhythms and innate order and promise of hope, and boxing, for its signature of manhood. Pugnacity took precedence over romance, and the Irish had long used boxing as a way to elevate themselves from lives of grinding poverty. When the men crowded around the long brass railing at O'Connor's Columbia Hotel Garden on Christopher Street for whiskey and beers and they weren't talking about the "stinkin' bloody limeys" or raising funds for "Holy Irish" revolutionary causes, they were bragging about exploits with their fists. Generations of Irish found fights at village smokers or saloons where amateurs could do battle for a ham sandwich, a ginger ale or a couple of bucks. Sometimes, if they got enough wins and attracted enough notice, they could enter boxing contests, maybe even get good enough for a fight at Sharkey's Athletic Club, a firetrap of a loft uptown. The boast of the two-fisted drinker John L. Sullivan that he could whip any man in the house was what every Irishman hoped to emulate.

"James," he heard her say. "Come. Papa is leaving!" Nana, as he referred to his mother, was the only one who called him by his Christian name. Since he had started school, he had been "Gene," a nickname picked up from his younger brother John, who pronounced his name as "Geeme." In an Irish Catholic neighborhood where the name James was commonplace, the Gene stuck.

He walked into the parlor to find Nana at the piano wearing her apron, smiling and leading a chorus of "Happy Birthday," and on the settee, there was a parcel with twine wrapped around it. The last thing Gene could have expected was a birthday present. With nine mouths to feed, and after giving something to the priests and the church at Christmas, there was never money left over. He didn't expect a gift. In fact, Gene could not remember ever having received one.

He approached the brown paper package with his usual wariness, thinking perhaps it was a practical joke, like those he played on others. He picked up the bundle. The package gave in to his squeeze, and he saw what looked like shoestrings attached to leather mitts. With his wide-eyed brothers and sisters watching, Gene ripped off the paper and his heart seemed to stop. Slowly, carefully, he reached into the wrapping to pick out a pair of second-hand leather boxing gloves, holding them so tightly that the laces cut into the soft flesh of his fingers. The priests promised that if you told the truth, worked hard, attended confession and said Hail Marys, you would be rewarded. For a skinny ten-year-old boy, the worn brown mitts were a talisman, a treasure transforming him instantly into a muscular contender in the ring. In a flash of childhood fantasy, he felt that his life had forever changed. He had studied Edgren's column. He knew a right cross from a left hook and a haymaker from a rabbit punch. Elated, he thundered down the stairs to show the neighborhood his prize.

The birthday boy spent the rest of the day exchanging playful blows with his brothers, sometimes sharing the gloves with other boys on the block. "I was in complete, utter ecstasy," he later remembered. "I was filled with confidence and a young boy's dreams." Papa said he had given Gene gloves to teach him to be a man, a mensch, to learn some respect, to take punches as well as give them. Gene went to bed determined to show his father how good he could be, and he took the bruises, swollen lip, black eye, and severe headache as a sign of manhood. "Even that early in my career, the conditioning process of becoming a prizefighter had begun."

He punched boxes, pillows, piles of trash, shoes hanging by shoestrings and even a turkey crop from dinner, which he tied from the transom between two rooms and used as a makeshift punching bag. The birthday gloves were almost worn out by summer's end, but Gene was just beginning.

Around the same time, in London, England, one of the greatest wordsmiths of the era was annoyed to discover that upstarts in the American theatre were showing fresh interest in a boxing novel he had written years earlier. He was George Bernard Shaw, one of England's most combative and audacious playwrights, a middle-aged man who was still easily recognizable for his long, springy strides and a face with a red beard that one acquaintance described as an "unskillfully poached egg." To Shaw's irritation, former heavyweight boxing champion Jim Corbett had twice in five years staged a New York play based on Shaw's novel, *Cashel Byron's Profession*, forcing the playwright to do his own stage adaptation of the book to protect his English dramatic rights.

The boxer-actor Corbett, who had defeated the great Sullivan, was young Tunney's hero. Gene identified with the well-spoken former bank clerk, a stylistic prizefighter the fans called "Gentleman Jim." Gene followed every detail he could find about the former champion in the newspaper, including Corbett's interest in Shaw's fictional boxer.

Shaw could not have known then that the story of Cashel Byron would inspire a boy who would later become a world boxing champion. The boy and the playwright would not meet for almost 20 more years.

"Where ye from?" the Tunneys were asked.

"From County Mayo."

"From County Mayo — oh, oh, God help us!"

John Tunney, Gene's father, was the youngest of 13 children. He had been born in 1859 on the heels of the potato famine, on a hardscrabble piece of sheep land in western Ireland — the poorest, roughest ground in a poor, rough country. His family said his fair complexion and ginger-colored hair marked him as a descendant of the Vikings. Some said the Tunneys had been stone carvers in the 16th century, expert at effigies of knights and apostles. And indeed, an O'Tunney had signed a 1526 tomb at the Cistercian Abbey at Kilcooley and another at Kilkenny Cathedral. Some said the Tunneys were weavers who had escaped from the hills of County Tyrone in Northern Ireland, a reckless lot of Catholics who had lost to the better-armed Protestants in the famous Battle of the Diamond in 1795.

Flight was the motif of their lives, and for more than a century, the tradition of resisting authority had been deeply ingrained. When John Tunney was still too young to walk, his parents, poor tenant farmers, were evicted over a few farthings and forced with thousands of their starving countrymen to beg for passage across the Irish Sea. They sailed by cattle boat to Liverpool, where the uprooted Irish were booed and hissed in a reception that toughened their resolve.

Legends repeated at the dinner table when Gene was a boy were stories of emasculated peasants dragging themselves on the ground for crumbs, of stirring tales of revolt and conspiracy, of men on the run, and of great-uncle Martin, who played a violent part in one of those tragic Irish rebellions and fled with a price of one hundred British pounds on his head. Papa used to talk about Patsy Tunney, a fighter who, it is said, once fought 267 rounds in the old bare-fist days in England. Who knows, Papa mused, Patsy may have been an ancestor.

A character sketch of Papa would show a calloused laborer with bulging muscles, covered with sweat and grime from bruising hours on the wharves six days a week, holding a cigarette in one hand and a drink in the other. He was the sort that other men didn't mess with, especially when his dark Irish temper flared. Papa felt his youth in England gave him an edge and made him smarter and more sophisticated than the typical Mick who stepped off the boat straight from a bog. He favored the literature and poetry he had learned in a British grammar school, and he was proudly self-assured of his good memory for facts and quotations. In this, he was "intensely English," Gene once told a reporter. "He had a natural predilection for all things British."

When he was 11, John Tunney joined the British Merchant Marine, first as a cabin boy, then as a mariner, sailing to Argentina and Australia and around the Horn of Africa. By 18, he was feisty, hard-drinking, stubborn, quick with an opinion and fast with his fists, especially if another sailor seized on the color of his hair and dared call him "Red." "I'm an Irishman, sir!" he shouted at police in Buenos Aires, after he and two sailors were imprisoned for fighting and drunkenness at the gates of the presidential palace.

Almost a million Irish had moved into New York in the wake of the potato famine, their overcrowding exacerbated by unemployment, alcoholism, violence, prostitution, gang warfare and crime. Protestants and Anglo-Saxon "Yankees" were in charge, and Irish Catholics were despised as foreigners. "Dogs and Irishmen not allowed," proclaimed tavern signs. Police vans used to collect troublemakers were so jammed with Irish that they were nicknamed "paddy wagons" after Patrick, Ireland's patron saint. But John Tunney saw opportunity, and when he got a chance to ship to the United States, he took it.

More than half of the Irish immigrants were single women sent by their families to get jobs and mail money home. So it was that in 1889, at a church social, the sailor Tunney met his match in Mary Jane Lydon, a spirited, strapping, take-charge young housekeeper with brown curly hair and bright blue eyes. At 6 feet, she was almost 2 inches taller than John. Mary Jane hailed from Kiltimagh, mere miles from John's own birthplace, and was the daughter of a clan who had so angered the local parish priest that none could get jobs. Four years later, in November 1893, John and Mary Jane were married under the Tiffany windows of the Church of the Holy Cross on Forty-second Street. He was 34, a union man working the docks. Mary Jane, who had wooed him by playing the piano and concertina, mending his shirts and feeding him apple pie and chicken and dumplings, was 28.

Their first son was born James Joseph on May 25, 1897, the third child in an eventual family of seven, three boys and four girls. Five months later, the family moved from West 52nd Street in Hell's Kitchen to the Irish Catholic working-class section of Greenwich Village. For most of Gene's boyhood, the family lived in a cramped, cold-water walk-up with a copper-plated gin mill in the only bathtub and wood crucifixes on the walls. The flat was situated over a general store at the corner of Perry and Washington Streets, a block from the Hudson River on Manhattan's West Side.

The neighborhood streets and alleyways were often sinister and dangerous, controlled by the Hudson River Dusters and the Gophers, murderous mobs made up largely of Irish youth who robbed delivery wagons and terrorized local merchants with fists, rocks and knives. Donnybrook, the name of a notoriously rowdy village near Dublin, became shorthand for street fights between surly young men with cigarettes dangling from their lips and God-fearing youths carrying rosaries. Gene found his first sanctuary outside of home in the local firehouse, under the protection of a toughened Irishman, Michael F. McCaffrey, a taciturn veteran of the Spanish-American War. In the beginning, Gene stayed at the firehouse after school, sequestered in a corner soaking up the camaraderie while he worked his way through schoolwork. Later on, he "took his gloves down to the station and put them on with some of the firemen." "He was an unusually polite boy," McCaffrey remembered, "a boy with three library cards and a vocabulary."

For a youngster growing up, the great, open expanse of the Hudson offered new horizons. With its constantly moving ships and barges, the river was an ever-changing panorama of light and motion, an invitation to adventure and a hideout from an apartment too small and too loud. To stand on the cobblestones at the intersection where Perry Street faced the Hudson was to make believe the city was far away. To the north and the south, the curves of Manhattan were visible, but the tall buildings, the racket of bustling carriages, wagons and wheelbarrows, and the clatter of vendors and deliverymen were almost nonexistent. Late in the afternoon, when shadows had fallen over the apartment house, the perches along the river remained sunny. A boy could watch scudding gray clouds billow and race into the orange sunset and sense the nearby sea and the brooding emptiness of the ocean. "I embrace

FOR MUCH OF HIS GROWING UP, TUNNEY LIVED IN A COLD-WATER FLAT ABOVE
THIS GROCERY STORE IN GREENWICH VILLAGE. "WE DIDN'T THINK OF OURSELVES
AS POOR," HE SAID, "WE WERE LIKE EVERYONE ELSE" (TUNNEY COLLECTION).

solitude," Gene used to say, "and even as a youngster, I sought out the quiet places."

With his friends and younger brothers, Gene swam off the piers and decks of ships, played baseball on the dockside staging areas and raced through smelly horse stables dubbed "the pig farm." Scuffles and fistfights were common. Yet early on — and despite the fact that he enjoyed boxing with gloves — Gene showed little interest in purposefully hurting other boys unless called upon to defend himself or his two younger brothers.

"I felt it didn't pay to pick fights," he said. "But I bitterly resented being punched around by the bullies of the neighborhood. My first interest was in self-protection. I thought less of hitting somebody than of not being hit."

Nana coped with most things through prayer. She taught her seven children to kneel on the cold, hard floor and pray, hands positioned fingertip to fingertip, every morning and night. Photographs of first communions were placed on the piano as a reminder that the church was central to her life and should be to theirs. During grace at meals, she preached that morality was next to Godliness, that to be honest, upright and loyal was the only way to gain God's grace, and that character was the embodiment of the soul. Chastity was expected, and she believed celibacy and pursuing the Lord's work were the highest goals one could attain. She didn't drink, didn't swear and expected her children to do the same. She nursed a deep yearning for respectability and acceptance in her new homeland.

Gene said that his mother gave him a character and a spirituality that he liked to think was particularly Irish. But she also encouraged his learning. "It was always his mother," recalled his eldest son, also named Gene. "His mother was the one who encouraged him to educate himself, to read the dictionary, to learn and to build up his vocabulary." While doing chores, Nana quoted poetry, such as "A Psalm of Life" by Longfellow: "In the world's broad field of battle / In the bivouac of Life / Be not like dumb, driven cattle! / Be a hero in the strife!"

"Say it again, Nana!" begged one of the children. And she did. She quoted all of it.

"Time and tide wait for no man," proclaimed Nana regularly. "You must get up and get out and get on with life to make something of yourself!"

As Gene grew older, his mother worried when he came home with bruises or a bloodied nose from fighting in the streets. One after-school battle went into a third day before a policeman stepped in and broke it up. "I was considered rather incorrigible by my parents, because no matter how much they punished me after each scrap, I continued to get into them at the slightest provocation," he admitted years later.

The hard necessity of helping with the family finances forced Gene to go to work at age 12. His bossy oldest sister, Rose, bragged that she had made the most money because she was earning pennies as an errand girl by the age of 7. By the time they were 11 or 12, the age when their father had gone to sea, all the children would have jobs, with every nickel handed over to Nana for household expenses.

Gene worked as a butcher's boy at John McNamara's meat market for $2.50 a week, taking orders from customers in the morning and making deliveries after school. When he showed up late for class, which was most days, the nuns wielded their rulers like scimitars, rapping his knuckles until they were raw. But waiting on stoops for the various McTigues, O'Sullivans and Duffys to find dimes for beef allowed the altar boy to see neighbors in provocative undress and using language that he had never found in a dictionary.

One day, Gene slipped and fell, slashing open his leg on a butcher's knife. Summoned from home to help, Nana wrapped her son's bleeding leg in her petticoats, hoisted him across her broad shoulders and, breathless, raced six long city blocks to the hospital emergency room.

"I'm Dr. Van Vliet," said the man in a white jacket. "And what shall I call you, young man?"

Dutch-born Dr. Frederick Van Vliet, the most highly educated man Gene had ever met, dazzled him with information and the prospect that, like a storybook hero, Gene could find a path out of his humble beginnings. Gene went to work for him as a messenger and carried the doctor's medical bag on calls. In becoming his first trusted teacher, the doctor gave much-needed direction to Gene's life.

"It was the books, all those treasured books that captured me, full of words and ideas. I couldn't read fast enough, couldn't get enough of them." Four walls of the doctor's office had bookshelves, not just medical books but novels, historical fiction, travel books, short stories and tomes on modern and ancient history. When the doctor was busy, Gene sat alone in a big leather chair with the sound of a ticking clock and a veritable library stacked beside him on the old, wide-plank floors. Van Vliet encouraged him to ask questions and to challenge himself. "The doctor exposed me to a broader world," Gene said, "and he had the education, time and enthusiasm to talk about ideas. He championed dissent and debate, discussed literature and music." He urged Gene to educate himself, and against Gene's parents' wishes, he also encouraged the young man's boxing aspirations.

"Gene reveres the memory of Dr. Van Vliet," recalled a friend a half century later. For many years after the doctor's death, Gene walked by his house to remind himself of the mentor who had taught him that a library was the chart room of knowledge. Gene began to see writers as confidants, and he memorized words and passages from books, hoping that he, too, might become as erudite as those who had written them.

Apart from his pranks, Gene was considered by his friends to be something of a prig, almost a stereotype of the perfect altar boy. He didn't drink or smoke, and he regarded swearing as crude and sacrilegious, turning away when another boy told a suggestive or an off-color story. Early on, he liked to use big words he'd picked up from reading, words that he wrote down in notebooks stashed beneath his bed like treasures. "In a way, Gene was as out of place as a fish in a park lane, and yet somehow, we didn't seem to think it anything unusual that he could be one of us and yet so different," said his childhood classmate, Eddie O'Brien Jr. "If some other boy had been such a stickler in the matter of language and deportment, he would have been in danger of getting his head punched."

Facts learned from reading and conversations with the doctor also gave the maturing Gene grist for his increasing defiance at the dinner table where Papa dominated. If someone read a book, Papa had read it first. If someone had a quote, he corrected it. If someone knew an historical incident, he cited the dates. (To try to get a word in edgewise and impress his father, Gene's youngest brother, Tom, memorized the births and deaths of the English kings.) Papa was practiced at using ridicule, belittling his seven children to make a point, and was unwilling or unable to display affection or to acknowledge that their schooling matched his as they grew older. The hard man from the docks also refused to tolerate complaints or whining. If he detected infractions in behavior or received a report of lack of discipline at school, whether it was true or not, he meted out punishment harshly.

For his oldest son, fear came at night. "Bring the BELT!" shouted Papa.

Gene was made to bend over a kitchen chair with his pants pulled down to his ankles. He closed his eyes, gripped the chair with all his strength and struggled to hold back the tears that he knew his father saw as a sign of weakness. He recalled hearing the frightful hiss of the leather winging through the air, warning him of the pain to come. He tried to block it out, tried to forget that he had been flogged before and that it would inevitably happen again. The impact of the belt raised red welts on the back of his legs and his bare bottom, and sometimes, if Papa had too much gin and missed the target, welts ran like red valleys of blood across his back.

Gene rarely remembered later what he had done wrong. What he remembered was the intimidation and the fear. If he had been flogged at school by the Christian Brothers, which was common practice, and if his father learned of it, he was whipped twice as hard at home. There were days when he could barely sit in a chair. There were nights when he cried himself to sleep. It didn't matter that other Irish fathers used a whip, too, because he knew that some fathers never did.

The diversity of Gene's reading and his ability to withdraw into his imagination became essential to his withstanding his father's outbursts. Words became his refuge. At home, there were Bibles, books of poetry, including

"The Rime of the Ancient Mariner" and "The Vision of Sir Launfal," a set of the Encyclopedia Britannica, *Quentin Durward,* and Sidney Lee's *A Life of William Shakespeare.* He borrowed novels from the doctor and from the library and read newspapers and his older sisters' schoolbooks.

Gene saw himself in the romantic adventures of James Fenimore Cooper and in Alexandre Dumas's *Three Musketeers.* The swashbuckling deeds of D'Artagnan in the service of the French king fired his dreams of faraway frontiers and service to his country. He imagined himself a hero — always a hero — fighting duels, engaging in battles in the name of justice, winning the hand of a beautiful princess.

Reading helped him see himself as independent and courageous, and it made him feel he could achieve something great that would make his family proud. As a young fighter, he would journey alone to boxing bouts, fantasizing that he was a Roman gladiator, a mysterious, lonely, defiant Titan out to avenge wrong and save the kingdom, a knight in shining armor, the Ivanhoe of Sir Walter Scott's novel. "Other lads of the neighborhood would go to see me box. They'd want to accompany me to the fight club, but I wouldn't let them. I wanted to go to battle alone, alone with my will...the lone, solitary spirit of self-will."

By the time he was a teenager, Gene was the tallest in his family; at almost 6 feet 2 inches, he hadn't yet filled out his big frame. He was almost four inches taller than his father, a size difference that put an end to Papa's floggings, although his father belittled him further by dubbing him "Skinny." The nickname stung and made Gene only more determined to show that he was tough. He became obsessed with proving his worth, especially to his father.

At age 15, when the family could no longer afford tuition, Gene, like most of his siblings, left school. He found a job for five dollars a week as an office boy at the Ocean Steamship Company near the piers where he lived.

Ring bouts at $5 to $10 became a regular sideline and brought in extra money. At first, he didn't dare tell his parents and so fought defensively, lest black eyes and bruised lips give him away. "Winning was always my only option," Gene said. He spent his days classifying freight loads of cotton moving on ships from Georgia and Alabama to New York and Boston. Hoping to work his way up, he enrolled in correspondence courses in mathematics and English. It was tedious work, and he longed for more stimulation and excitement, an outlet for his nervous energy.

Night was his time. The docks lay in darkness, and the expanse of the Hudson became a shimmering black belt cutting off the empty steamship offices from the rest of the world. After the paperwork was done and the lights turned out, Gene stayed behind, pushed the desks out of the way for space, rolled up his sleeves and laced on his gloves. With the twinkling lights of New Jersey in the distance, he fought imaginary opponents, sparring with the shadows and envisioning himself a champion in a great arena. He liked the seclusion and the quiet, broken only by the occasional piercing whistles and sound of foghorns or buoys in the river. Sometimes other junior clerks stayed with him to practice.

"You can do it," urged his younger brother John, his best friend, supporter and sparring partner. "You will be the greatest champion the Village has ever seen."

At other times, he sat alone behind a shanty on the dock, reading aloud the rousing stories of the early Greeks, words that exercised his lungs and raised his spirits, making him feel that in battling opponents, he was carrying on a noble tradition. He avoided small pleasures, such as ice cream and other desserts, becoming almost monastic, knowing it made him more self-proficient and independent of Papa.

"I felt I could make myself do anything," he said. "I could *will* anything to come true. Anything, everything, was possible. I had fantasies of willpower. I felt nothing, absolutely *nothing*, could ever stop me."

As the oldest son, he could do no wrong in his mother's eyes, and he desperately wanted to please her. He carried his rosary in his pocket, attended Mass regularly and began to take account of his deficiencies: slender arms of ordinary length and average reach, hands that were abnormally small and soft-boned. "But I kept on trying," he said. "I didn't think of the gloves as a career, a profession. It was merely that I loved to box and always tried hard at anything I was doing. I put everything I had into it."

Continuing a practice he had started as a schoolboy, Gene kept a notebook in which he wrote the definitions and correct pronunciations of every new word he read. Words like "expatiate" (to write or speak at length), "prolixity" (needless profusion of words) and "thrasonical" (boastful). He carried a dictionary in his pocket, and he made it a practice to read and reread books until he understood every sentence. He read that mothers in ancient Sparta toughened their infants by having them look into the sun and that Demosthenes put pebbles in his mouth to develop his skill as an orator.

To strengthen his resolve to withstand the tedious repetition he felt would give him focus and self-discipline, Gene would sit in the kitchen in the middle of the night and lay out hundreds of kitchen matches in a row, each match tip facing the opposite direction. Once finished, he reversed the matches. When he returned home at night exhausted, he placed the key in the front door lock, then withdrew it and walked around the block. In his bedroom, he stood on a chair in the dark and counted to 500 or 1000, as his two brothers slept.

"Say, Gene, want to put on the gloves with Willy?"

"Does he want me to?"

"Well, he needs somebody for a workout!"

Gene was flattered. Willy Green, a wisecracking professional who wore

LITHOGRAPHS BY GEORGE WESLEY BELLOWS (1882-1925): *A STAG AT SHARKEY'S*, 1917
(BRIDGEMAN ART LIBRARY/BUTLER INSTITUTE OF AMERICAN ART, YOUNGSTOWN, OHIO),
AND *PRELIMINARIES*, 1916 (BRIDGEMAN ART LIBRARY/SAN DIEGO MUSEUM OF ART).

Broadway's loudest shirts, fancy vests and a heavy gold watch chain, was a veteran lightweight who had fought 168 professional bouts, an impressive number by any standard. He snorted rhythmically while boxing and blew his nose on a glove between flurries of punching, an intimidating practice that carried an air of professional arrogance. After a bout, he would fling off the gloves and turn a row of back flips, the last word in bravado. At age 26, Willy wanted to make a comeback in the ring. He needed sparring partners. It was an honor, thought Gene. He had never taken on a professional fighter. Besides, how bad could it be?

In a corner of a low-ceilinged room called the gymnasium at Public School 41 in the Village, with the neighborhood watching, they had their first bout. Willy hit Gene with a left hook, smashed a right into his mouth and slammed his head against a wall. "I was a human punching bag," Gene remembered. But he didn't give up. He kept fighting Willy. "I look back in wonder that I should have gone on with that sort of thing day after day, week after week. But I did." He felt it was a distinction to be the sparring partner of a neighborhood idol. Once he even boxed Willy in the kitchen of a friend's apartment. "Let's go and see Willy Green make a punching bag of Gene Tunney," became a neighborhood refrain. Gene didn't care. "I wanted to win. I always wanted to win." Through tenacity, in combination with his own galloping physical growth, Gene began to get the best of Willy.

Willy, his first professional, was his crucible. The lessons learned at Willy's hands — how to avoid punches, how to ignore his opponent's braggadocio and focus on tactics — became the blueprint for his ring career.

At 18, he turned professional, and his first fight was a ten-round bout against the experienced pro Bobby Dawson at the Sharkey Athletic Club. He lay awake the night before in near panic, anticipating injuries. But he beat Dawson and won $18, almost as much as his father made in a week. He fought 12 more professional bouts before he was 21, and won them all.

About that same time, his father brought home a distant cousin; he was a bookmaker who made his living waging bets on professional boxers, and he had come "to look me over as if he was a horse trader inspecting a colt." Gene was sitting at the kitchen table reading. The exchange between him and the cousin was brief, but it bothered Gene enough that he remembered vividly being sized up for his small hands, his slender frame and his height as the bookie mentally calculated how much punishment he could withstand before his stamina failed and he collapsed in the ring.

The visitor frowned. "You *reading* that book?" he demanded.

"Yes," replied Gene. "I like to read."

The big guy shook his head, sighed, pursed his lips and shrugged. "Just the same, kid," he said, "I like your looks." But he glared at the book as he left.

Aunt Margaret Lydon, a teacher who lived with the family between jobs, was everyone's favorite confidante. Margaret was small in stature, merry in nature and devoted to her handsome nephew. "Don't worry about your cousin, dear," she told him. "Remember what Shakespeare said," she said brightly: "'Our doubts are traitors, and make us lose the good we oft might win by fearing to attempt.'"

Besides, she said, "Everyone reads books, even prizefighters." Aunt Margaret, for all her knowledge, knew nothing about the ring.

Gene's announcement over dinner that he had enlisted in the Marines for the Great War turned out to be the last straw in the ongoing battle of wills between him and his father. Papa was enraged, claiming that his son's obligations were at home.

"You can't tell *me* what to do," Gene shouted at his father.

As Gene's son John recalled, "Grandfather Tunney and my dad found themselves in a boxing match down in the basement of the apartment house, and grandfather tried to knock him out. Because Dad was so skilled by that time, having become a boxing professional with 12 or 13 fights on record, he was able to stay away from all his father's punches and deliver some punches, not with the idea of hurting him, but just to prove that he was superior."

Gene won a decisive victory over his father, though it would cost them both dearly. The fight caused a break in an emotional fabric already worn down by years of tension and unresolved anger. Without saying good-bye, Gene left the apartment house at dawn the next day wearing a new cream-colored suit and carrying his rosary, his missal and a suitcase. He was determined to create a better life for himself, one better than his parents had had. It was his first trip away from the city, away from family and friends, and for the first time in his life, he would experience moments of excruciating loneliness.

Gene thought that going off to fight in the war would help him prove to Papa that he could be a man; maybe then, Papa would approve of him. But when Gene returned from the war, with the distinction of having won an American Expeditionary Forces boxing championship, nothing had changed in their relationship.

Nothing, that is, except that the altar boy had grown up.

GENE STRIKING A BOXING
POSE AT AGE 17 (MARY
AGNES MCINTYRE ANDERSON
COLLECTION); IN UNIFORM
AS A U.S. MARINE, AUGUST
1918 (TUNNEY COLLECTION).

A WOODCUT BY WILLIAM NICHOLSON (1872-1949) IN *AN ALMANAC OF TWELVE SPORTS*, PUBLISHED IN 1898 BY WILLIAM HEINEMANN, WITH WORDS BY RUDYARD KIPLING (BRIDGEMAN ART LIBRARY).

CHAPTER 2

Ring Rookie

"When he talked about boxing, it seemed like he would jump
up and knock you out himself. G.B.S. loved to talk a big game —
his eyes lit up, and that wit — sort of jabbing here and there."
POLLY LAUDER TUNNEY

The gym had a heavy, pungent smell. The damp stench of sweaty clothes, body odor, liniment, rubbing lotions and lingering tobacco would leak out from the floorboards and cling to the rafters. In dusty corners, there might be benches for hangers-on with shifty eyes and breath reeking of onion, but the presence of men on the outskirts of the racket was common, even in the best gymnasiums. The syncopated rat-a-tat-tat of gloves against leather speed bags, jarring at first, would in time become only background noise. Later, even the smell wouldn't seem to matter so much.

They were an unlikely pair — the short stocky man who jabbered incessantly and the tall, skinny fellow with a red beard and protruding ears. (Ears were a family specialty, according to Shaw, who wrote that when he was a child, "my nurse had to hold me by my waistband to prevent my being blown away when the wind caught them.") Bernard Shaw hadn't wanted to come to the gym, to any gym. It hadn't been his idea in the first place. He had resisted for so long that his best friend, the persistent and excitable Paquito Beatty, had started boxing lessons without him. Beatty was loquacious, even more so than Shaw, and while swinging his fists, he couldn't stop making quips, often in a Cockney dialect that had his tall friend throwing back his head and howling with laughter.

If their snickering and guffawing hadn't already disrupted the men training in the gym, Beatty would make sure it did by lapsing into one of the sing-song rhymes that punctuated his speech, usually at his best friend's expense:

Of all contradictory fellows
In the course of my life whom I saw
None can compare I solemnly swear
For a minute with George Bernard Shaw

Shaw liked to say that the prize ring had a natural attraction for romantic and hysterical people, especially poets like Beatty, who was "crazy" about boxing. There just seemed no way to shut him up. For 2000 years, poets had been the most valued members of Irish society; in the old days, they were the only citizens allowed to move freely around the country. It seemed to have gone to Beatty's head. He was incorrigible, and he continued his chirpy banter while leaping about taking potshots at his tall opponent as if they were entertainers at an Irish country fête:

He'll argue on questions of medicine
And argue on questions of law
He'll argue on boxing and banking
This versatile George Bernard Shaw

Beatty nicknamed his sparring partner "Gully Belcher," combining the names of two famous ring gladiators of the era, Jem Belcher and John Gully. "Gully Belcher Shaw!" Gully, Shaw said later, may have been the first fighter in history who appreciated the value of money. Gully was discovered in a debtor's prison when Hen "The Game Chicken" Pearce visited for a boxing exhibition, fought Gully, and lost. Members of The Fancy, as boxing was called in the 1800s, heard of Gully through this exploit, bailed him out, and he became champion of England. He retired, distanced himself from pugilism, invested in business, became a member of Parliament and died a rich man — a perfect example, said Shaw, of reinventing oneself. Jem Belcher, also a onetime champion, died penniless and friendless at age 30, but not before he discovered a strapping 6 foot 1 inch fighter named Shaw, known as "the Lifeguardsman." The prizefighter Shaw might have made a name in the ring but was killed at Waterloo.

In the beginning, a slender, cautious, intellectual young man like Bernard Shaw would seem among the least likely of men to contemplate getting close to a boxing ring, much less climbing into it. Shaw was a shade over 6 feet, gangly and thin to angularity, with delicate hands, reddish hair and a long, bony face bearing a soft, almost ladylike, transparent complexion. His abrupt and jerky mannerisms in moving his arms and body bore no resemblance whatsoever to the conditioned grace of an athlete, much less a boxer. He hated his first name, George. It was one of the things he tried to unload, along with painful memories of his repressed and socially awkward childhood.

With acquaintances, he could be glib, opinionated, impertinent, argumentative, literate and clever, and not everyone, even close associates or family, liked him. When at age 18, he had made his first appearance in print with a public profession of atheism in an arrogant, satirical letter to Dublin's *Public Opinion*, his churchgoing relatives were scandalized.

Shaw had been a lonely child in an impersonal family with an alcoholic father and a musical mother, neither with time for nor interest in him or his two sisters. Deeply frustrated with life in Ireland, he had arrived in London in 1876, desperate to create a new self and develop the genius that he felt was within him. At age 20, virtually penniless, he became an unwelcome occupant in a cramped London flat that he shared with his mother and elder sister. He brought with him an enormous contempt for snobbery and a comedic wit that masked shyness so deeply embedded that he often covered it with impudence and aggressiveness. He was friendless and anxious to be independent.

For Shaw, meeting the gregarious, intrepid Beatty, a rambunctious, charming Irish renegade who was lavish with his hospitality, had been salve for his soul. Here was a friend who shared his creative imagination and understood his Irish humor, who appreciated wit as an art form and celebrated satire as its most penetrating mode of attack.

Pakenham Thomas Beatty was the unorthodox offspring of a wealthy Irish diplomat; born in Maranhao, Brazil, his nickname fit his crusading spirit and round, boyish face perfectly. Beatty was an impractical idealist who moved through a series of clubs and antimonarchist societies buttressed by a large but fast-dwindling inheritance. He had a flair for the classics and languages, and by the time he and Shaw became friendly in 1878, Beatty was writing poetry in the style of Swinburne.

In the words of Beatty's grandnephew, Claudius Beatty, they were "just two lads together enjoying life, two free spirits longing to be famous for their writing and wanting to be accepted and admired for their ideas." Shaw was 22, and Beatty was 23.

The Victorian England that had drawn Shaw and Beatty, as well as tens of thousands of others, across the Irish Sea had grown dramatically in wealth while Ireland struggled to survive the aftereffects of its largest human disaster in a century: the Great Famine. The scourge of the Black Death began in 1845 with the blighting and failure of the potato crop, the chief means of sustenance for millions of peasant farmers. Deadly black potato rot swept across rural Ireland like a plague, destroying food and life, and dismantling families. By mid-century, two million people had died from starvation and disease or fled to foreign lands, a fate that seared the psyche of a nation and caused the Irish to hate their British landlords and the British government for generations to come.

The Shaw and Beatty families were not among the suffering poor, but in the great waves of emigration to England, the majority of the Irish were forced to live on the fringes of English social life. To be Irish was seen as being a revolutionary, happiest with a grievance against society, especially British society. The Irish were stereotyped as drunks and criminals, accused of breeding without restraint and allowing their own backyard ways to impoverish them. Anti-Irish and anti-Catholic epithets were common. Even by the 1870s, it did not matter that Beatty's father had been well-to-do or that Shaw had been born into an impecunious but refined Protestant family with airs of the privileged and distant ties to the aristocracy.

"Behold me, then, in London in an impossible position," wrote Shaw. "I was a foreigner — an Irishman — the most foreign of all foreigners when he has not gone through the British university mill."

Initially, it was clear that fisticuffs seemed ideally suited to Beatty, someone prone to settling issues by punching first and asking questions later. Once, in an impetuous gesture of heroism, Beatty leaped over the wall of a schoolyard and bashed a schoolmaster in the face for flogging a boy, an action that landed him immediately in Hammersmith Police Court. Shaw bailed him out of jail the next day. On another occasion, a bailiff showed up after Beatty neglected to pay his rent. When Beatty tried to keep him out, the bailiff jammed his foot in the door. "Work and thrift is my motto, young man," chirped an undaunted Beatty, and with that he punched the bailiff in the jaw, sending him sprawling to the ground, and slammed the door. Beatty's coat-of-arms bore the motto *non vi sed arte* (not by strength but by cunning). Artful pugnacity, said the Beattys, ran in the family.

Shaw spent his days under the gigantic glass-and-iron dome of the Reading Room in the British Museum, his working office. As a regular, he had a chair, a folding desk, a small hinged shelf for books, pens and ink, a blotting pad and a peg for his hat. His most cherished possession was his green Reading Room card, a lifetime pass, guaranteeing he would always have a place to ply his trade.

A superintendent who occupied a raised seat in the center of the big, circular room monitored occupants, like Shaw, who sat at tables that radiated from the center of the room like spokes in a wheel. The Reading Room was open from nine in the morning until about eight o'clock at night, and Shaw spent his days poring over books and writing articles and novels that he hoped to publish. He had made it plain to Beatty he had no time for sports and wanted no part of his new passion for combat, not that boxing was a sport in the conventional sense, of course. One did not "play" boxing as you would play football or cricket. There was no team nor were there team rules, no one except oneself to make that inspired judgment call at a crucial moment. Boxing was distinctive in that it was performed between two men in a square called a ring, and the sport itself was often referred to as if none other existed and called "The Game," the most punishing and individual of all sporting contests.

Shaw had been introduced to boxing as a boy, during an era when prizefighting could be either an illegal hole-in-the-wall activity or a sanctioned, staged competition. Modern boxing derived from the English bare-knuckle pugilism of the 18th century; the English champion, Daniel Mendoza, "the fighting Jew," had first visited Ireland in 1791. He popularized the sport with touring exhibitions, fighting in farmers' fields and villages around the country. The Irish took to boxing as if fighting was their birthright, and in later years, fans flocked to fights pitting the sons of St. Patrick against visiting English boxers, if only because the events seemed a symbolic staging of the ongoing Anglo-Irish conflict. One of Shaw's boyhood memories was of a prizefighter who was so terrified of injury or death that he kept a mirror in the ring. Even when winning, the fighter only consented to persevere when he could see his face between every round, to be assured that his features had not been obliterated.

Englishmen persuaded themselves that they, too, could use their fists, and were even naturally gifted at it, a presumption that Shaw considered as preposterous as claiming that every Frenchman could use a foil or every Italian a stiletto. In England, boxing was considered the most dramatically masculine of sports because of its association with the cradle of pugilism, ancient Greece. The poet Lord Byron called it a "noble art," the sport in which competitors fought skillfully, displaying Olympian traits of the mind and spirit as well as of the body. The art of self-defense was considered as necessary for the education of a gentleman as dancing a minuet or speaking French. For the landed gentry, the possibility of being injured as an amateur fighter was actually an opportunity for a public show of raw courage and manliness. In typical upper-class understatement, it was often referred to as "the science of sweet bruising."

One of Shaw's favorite clowning poses was to throw his arms around his shoulders to represent himself as a physical coward. He had no intention of becoming involved with Beatty's passion for gloved combat, but that didn't deter the irrepressible poet from pressing Shaw to join him at the gym.

> If found on a desolate mountain
> A vulture his entrails shall gnaw
> He'd choose just that place to argue the case
> Argumentative George Bernard Shaw

"I am about to take boxing up from the scientific Ned Donnelly, a very amiable, though powerful, person in appearance," Beatty wrote in September 1881. Addressing Shaw as Balzac, then one of Beatty's favorite authors, he continued: "The meek Michelle, whom you would rashly have selected out of a room full to strike, is a phenomenon as an amateur bruiser. So much, O'Balzac, for your discrimination! If you wish, those pointers that I learn from the Donnelly I will teach unto you."

Shaw apparently did not respond. Ten days later, his friend wrote again, "I send for your careful reading a copy of Donnelly's admirable *Self-Defense*, the best book of its kind ever published. It explains very clearly what other writers leave in hopeless confusion. 'I am a great man for the body — hit him here, the pit of my stomach,' were his words of wisdom to me, 'and he won't come again.'" Beatty invited Shaw to dinner. "Articles of agreement as to boxing lessons can be drawn up," he added.

Shaw certainly would have gone to dinner, for in the spirited Beatty household, he had found a home away from home, an affectionate family so unlike his own, among whom he could share laughter, mischief, ideas, conversation and genuine fun. The extended Beatty clan had embraced him, fondly dubbing their fastidious friend "Barbarossa" (red beard) and "old man Shaw." To amuse the children, Barbarossa dug in the garden with them, read stories and sang. Once during a rainstorm, he climbed into bed fully dressed in his Jaeger boilersuit, opened all the windows and held open an umbrella to delight his small audience. He studied French with Beatty's wife, Ida, flirted with her sisters, taught and played piano duets with members of the household, was a frequent guest at meals and met grandparents, cousins, in-laws, uncles and friends, becoming godfather to one child and a supporter of all.

When Beatty's first child, nicknamed "Bertie," was christened, the elderly godfather, the poet Richard Hengist Horne, gave the infant tiny boxing gloves and promised that he "shall be taught to lick anybody of his size, or half a head taller, who tries to bully him at first school or 'fag' him at second school." Shaw wrote a comic poem with references to the father's boxing friends and urged the baby to eat to reach fighting weight, warning the infant: "A boxer thou canst not rely on; His wife can but spoil thee with love."

G.B.S. IN 1880 (SHAW FESTIVAL).

Friendship won out. Shaw finally agreed to visit the London Athletic Club, conveniently located in the Haymarket theatre district near busy Piccadilly Circus, a brisk 20-minute walk from his desk at the British Museum. As home to aristocrats of leisure and fine breeding, the club would not have been a natural habitat for either Shaw or Beatty. But the gym specialized in boxing, and Ned Donnelly, who had written the best-selling *Self-Defense; Or, the Art of Boxing*, was head coach and "professor" of the club's most popular sport.

Many considered Donnelly the best instructor in London. A retired prizefighter with the commanding presence of a panther, Donnelly was often called "the Royal Professor" because when he was summoned to spar before the King, he immediately went out and bought a new top hat and frock coat. Shaw based a character on Donnelly, describing him thusly: "A powerful man with a thick neck that swelled out beneath his broad, flat earlobes. He had small eyes, and large teeth over which his lips were slightly parted in a smile, good-humored but affectedly cunning. His hair was black and close cut, his skin indurated, and the bridge of his nose smashed level with his face." He was a modest and affable fellow when sober and unprovoked, Shaw wrote, and about 50 years old.

In the gym, there would have been other aspiring boxers and gentlemen pugilists in fitted shirts, knitted tights and soft, moccasin-like slippers warming up with pushups and by jumping rope, stretching on the bars, shadow boxing and sparring on mats or in the ring. (Like opera singers, boxers generally train and work out alone except when sparring with a partner.) For strength and balance training, a trapeze, flying rings, weights and dumbbells were traditionally used.

Coach Donnelly had revived a scientific method of fighting in the ring

36

from earlier in the 18th century that could be blended with the new Queensberry rules of 1866. Donnelly's method of scientific boxing made the sport a thinking man's game with a series of stylistic movements for every parry and thrust. It appealed to gentlemen amateurs who could rely on the skills of practiced footwork and training, as opposed to a rough, knock-down-and-drag-out scrimmage that relied mostly on strength. Shaw always referred to unthinking brute force as simply "bashing."

The old regulations allowed as many rounds as the combatants could sustain until one fighter was gravely injured or simply gave up from exhaustion; battles could last for a hundred rounds or more. The Queensberry rules called for padded gloves, three-minute rounds, ten-second knockdowns and a cap on the length of the fight. The new rules were created by the 8th Marquis of Queensberry, later known to Shaw as the father of Lord Alfred "Bosie" Douglas, the young aristocrat who had a scandalous homosexual relationship with fellow playwright Oscar Wilde. Amateur fights were promoted in the army and public (private) schools. It was English violence, the wags said, disguised as English honor.

Shaw, looking for inspiration for his writing and a new connection in life for himself, became intrigued with the unconventionality, the hardihood and the inherent danger of the game, as well as the camaraderie and serious-minded atmosphere among those learning Donnelly's "science." In addition, prizefighting was one of the few sports that offered a way out of poverty to the disenfranchised and underprivileged, a social reality that Shaw, the emerging socialist, appreciated.

Beatty, the one with the funds, paid the club dues for both. Shaw purchased a pair of five-pound dumbbells for himself.

Nothing in Shaw's life had prepared him for the surge in confidence and adrenaline, for the vitality he would experience concentrating on the rudiments of trading punches while feinting, jabbing and becoming agile on his feet. He agreed with Lord Byron, who had boasted that the thrill of sparring lifted his spirits and kept him mentally alert. Even the effort to hold up two arms and continually stare an opponent in the face required tremendous stamina and could make the difference in winning a spar. For perhaps the first time in his life, Shaw got a full measure of what it was like to focus his intellect and his body on a single goal, that of avoiding the sharp and sudden punishment in another man's fist while trying to deliver offensive blows himself. Unlike other sports, a boxer must be concerned not only with what he does, but with what is done to him. Because Shaw was tall, with a long left arm that he could use to jab the other fellow in the face, he was surprised to find that he was often successful, especially against the shorter Beatty.

"I had an easy time with him," a pleased Shaw would later tell his friend Gene Tunney. "He was not tall and I had such long arms that I held him off by keeping my left glove in his face. He was annoyed, very."

For Shaw, the give-and-take rhythm of the game would resemble the tempo in his writing, from the sharp and saucy rat-a-tat-tat of his dialogue to the bold sweep of his convictions, hurled against an unsuspecting audience.

"There are," he wrote later, "no sports which bring out the difference in character more dramatically than boxing, wrestling, and fencing...I soon got an imaginary reputation in my little circle as a boxer; and as I looked credibly like a tall man with a straight left and had in fact picked up some notion of how to defend myself, I was never attacked with bodily violence."

Shaw and Beatty sparred between the flower beds and bushes in the Beattys' garden and in the gym, read the sporting papers and regularly attended boxing competitions, often with friends and other amateurs. The inspiration Shaw was looking for came from an exhibition match featuring one of the cleverest fighters of the day, Jack Burke, "the Irish Lad" who used the scientific style taught by Coach Donnelly. Shaw had written three unsuccessful novels, and in writing his fourth, *Cashel Byron's Profession*, decided to focus on boxing, using Burke's exploits as a metaphor for the fighting spirit that he was to display in his own life through the pen.

His fictional hero was named for the medieval seat of kings in Ireland, the Rock of Cashel, and the popular, romantic poet Byron, who had been a well-known boxing enthusiast. Shaw endowed his protagonist with all the qualities that he thought a winner in and out of the ring should possess. Cashel was a young man of Shaw's age who, in striving to create a better life, wills himself into an iron-nerved and fanatically committed fighter able to throw off the chains of the Irish underdog in English society. As an Irish Horatio Alger, Cashel exudes individualism and moral zeal, and he has the ability to control his life's circumstances. He's a thinking, "scientific" fighter who utilizes learned skills to fight defensively and physical strength to stand up to the most ruthless brawlers in the ring. Shaw learns to respect fighters who try to make a living with their fists, and he especially admires their confidence in the face of the condescension often heaped on them by society.

In casting Cashel as a man who becomes master of his fate, Shaw makes him the kind of man he wants to become himself — a writer and reformer. This new self-image is a dramatic change from the Shaw who departs Ireland as a wary, inexperienced intellectual, a boy of modest means who leaves school at 15. The timid young man who arrives in England unsure of himself, now feels that boxing in the gym like English aristocrats puts him on the same plain — and he'd outthink them and outtalk them as well.

Boxing has become a rite of passage, not for what he will win in the ring but as a bridge to self-reliance and a new, weightier identity.

Personal combat, Shaw said, is interesting, "not only technically as an exhibition of skill, but because it's also an exhibition of character concentrating into minutes differences that years of ordinary intercourse leave hidden."

"In the eyes of a phoenix, even the arena — the ring, as they call it — is a better school of character than the drawing room," writes Shaw in the novel.

The fictional Cashel wins the world championship in an honest and skillful manner, raises the standards of a corrupt boxing world by never submitting to a bribe, retires at the top of his game, marries and raises a family, enters business and runs successfully for a seat in Parliament. Shaw wrote that he gave his Cashel "every advantage a prizefighter can have: health and strength and pugilistic genius. In plain fact, the pugilistic profession is like any other profession. Common sense, good manners and a social turn count for as much in it as they do elsewhere." The novel was finished in 1883, and three years later was published in book form. When the publisher inferred from the book that Shaw was a formidable boxer, he said Shaw laughed and replied, "I know the moves, just as I know the moves in chess."

St. Patrick's Day of 1883, a Saturday, was a day that would confound future scholars who studied the worldly Shaw, a man not seen as one likely to risk himself in a sporting contest. In what may have been a flourish of Irish bravado, Shaw and Beatty entered a national amateur boxing competition. Wrote Beatty, referring to himself:

> Old Plantagenet into training must get
> Drink later, eat steaks that are raw
> The Shaw's nose has kist the tip of his fist
> (And you won't like it, George Bernard Shaw)

They signed up for the annual Queensberry Amateur Boxing Championships far enough ahead of time so that their names could be printed in the large official program. The Queensberry Challenge Cup was not just a local tournament, but a public, advertised competition at the sprawling Lillie Bridge Grounds, the home of London's major sporting events and fairs. The Amateur Boxing Association, the sport's first governing body, had been formed in Britain in 1880, only three years earlier. P. Beatty, London, was listed in the lightweight and middleweight division. G.B. Shaw, London, was entered as a middleweight and a heavyweight. (A heavyweight in those days could be any weight, and boxers often changed weight divisions, depending on their opponents.) "I dont call no man a fighting man what aint been in the ring," says Ned Skene, the coach (based on Donnelly) in Shaw's novel. "You're a sparrer, and a clever, pretty sparrer; but sparring aint the real thing. Some day, please God, we'll make up a little match for you."

The competition would have been about a year and a half after Shaw first joined Donnelly's gym. Shaw had seen other amateurs injured and knocked out and had suffered injury himself. It is not entirely clear, but the record indicates that neither actually got in the ring that day. One version holds that Beatty was so nervous that Donnelly gave him a stiff dose of brandy before

entering the ring, the effect being to paralyze him. The official ruling could have been that they did not have enough fights under their belts, or they may not have fought simply because their names were not drawn. The last tantalizing possibility is that one or both of them fought and lost, then sat in the stands to watch the winning match, as boxers often do. In any event, Shaw wrote the winners' names on his official program, in the neat script that he had perfected as a teenage land agent in Dublin.

The raw drama of the ring in all its color, excitement and controversy had captured Shaw's imagination. "Pugilism," he said, "became one of my subjects."

In 1901, Shaw added a preface to his novel in which he expressed surprise that the book had survived so long. He continued to follow prizefights from afar, but he was generally disgusted with the gamblers and the quality of the people who had taken over the sport and felt that his fictional, highly moral Cashel, his ultimate man of action, would never be equaled. Shaw moved on with his life and began writing plays, many of which were peppered with references to pugilism and boxing. Spirited idioms and commentary on the sport would also appear in his letters, books, prefaces and newspaper articles, and as stage directions and dialogue.

Only with Paquito, his old friend and sparring partner, did Gully Belcher Shaw discuss old times in the ring.

It would be another two decades before boxing became important to him again.

SHAW AT HAMMERSMITH TERRACE, LONDON, 1891, PHOTOGRAPH BY EMERY WALKER (DAN H. LAURENCE COLLECTION, UNIVERSITY OF GUELPH LIBRARY ARCHIVES).

CHAPTER 3

Big Sissy Reads

"There is little to suggest the gladiator in this mild, quiet-spoken, blue-eyed individual as he talks of tennis, golf, books — Wells, Tennyson and Omar Khayam are among his favorite authors."
BRIAN BELL, REPORTER

Brian Bell didn't know he was going to change someone's life when he drove up to the Adirondacks, the most northerly place he'd ever been in New York or any other state. He was just glad to get out of New York City and away from the desk on a sweltering summer day. Bell had covered news stories since he was in knee pants, when, at age ten, he mailed clips to *The State*, the largest newspaper in his native South Carolina. Later, he had covered the Scopes "Monkey" Trial — in fact, had broken so many scoops on that trial that he had become something of a legend in the news business. Today was a new assignment, however, and his first sports assignment for the Associated Press.

On this summer day in 1926, Bell was en route to visit Gene Tunney, "The Fighting Marine" from Greenwich Village who was training to battle Jack Dempsey for the world heavyweight championship, the biggest prize in sports. No one knew much about Tunney, a city boy from a poor Irish family whose background reflected the changing demographics of a country moving toward urbanization. At 29, Tunney had fought 74 professional fights and lost only once, to Harry Greb, "the Pittsburgh Windmill." It was a fight so murderous that viewers at ringside were splattered in red, Greb's gloves were soggy, and the canvas was soaked in Tunney's blood. The fighter-Marine defeated Greb three times in return bouts and fought him once to a draw.

"Just go up to Tunney's training camp and look around for the usual stuff and give it a feature touch, for the most part," said his boss and good friend, Alan Gould, the wire service's sports editor. "Get a little something of the personality." It didn't matter, said Gould, that Bell had never been to a training camp and had never met the boxer; Bell was one of the best feature writers in the business, and he'd know what to do when he got there.

In the summer of 1926, there was no better job for a reporter than covering sports. The appetite of the nation's newspapers for sports news had quadrupled since the Great War. The readers' thirst for the minutest details of every aspect of a celebrity's life was insatiable, and sports fans knew more about their heroes than they knew about members of their own families. Personal magnetism, charisma, youthful vitality and the will to win, also the hallmarks of a growing business culture, became imperative in sports. Millions of spectators were crowding into stadiums and onto golf courses, and sports champions became heroes overnight: Bobby Jones in golf, Bill Tilden in tennis, Babe Ruth in baseball, Red Grange in football, Earle Sande in horse racing. In the era called the Golden Age of Sports, boxing was king, drawing the most in money and spectators. Jack Dempsey made more money in one fight than Babe Ruth earned in a year, and he had twice defended his title as heavyweight champion in million-dollar gates. An estimated 12 million Americans watched boxing matches or fought in neighborhood gyms and athletic contests. Reporters vied for scoops, and major newspapers featured columnists with colorful prose meant to sway and titillate the public, as well as sell newspapers.

In London, even the playwright Bernard Shaw occasionally wrote columns on sports, sometimes taking aim at sportswriters themselves. "The time is evidently very near when journalists will have to obtain certificates of competence, like navigating officers, before they are allowed to navigate the ship of state and hypnotize and psycho-analyze the helpless public by their pens," he wrote. "I hope they will be examined just as strictly in pugilism as in political economy when that time comes." At one point he was so fed up with what he felt was inept coverage of boxing that he suggested, somewhat in jest, that a bill be introduced "making it a punishable offence for a newspaper to order or publish any description of a prizefight until they had sent for a professional boxer and made the writer spar a bye with him, and obtain from a couple of competent judges a certificate that he at least knows his right hand from his left."

Bell found Tunney's training camp alongside a placid, pine-rimmed lake called, appropriately enough, Lake Pleasant, just off a two-lane highway that wove through the mountain resort village of Speculator, New York. The Osborne Inn, a sprawling, three-story white-shingled hotel with a wide verandah facing the lake, was run by one of Tunney's Marine buddies and served as headquarters for the press, with rooms, gossip, a well-stocked bar, a telephone and a menu boasting the "best apple pie north of Manhattan."

Outside, only a few steps from the inn, an elevated platform resembling a large open porch served as the training ring. It was roofed to protect it from sun and rain, and open on the sides so that spectators could sit in the grass, on the newly erected pine bleachers or on the tops of cars to see workouts and match wits with the experts on whether the challenger could beat the champ. Not many thought Tunney had a chance. Dempsey had been heavyweight champion for seven years, and reporters writing daily stories from the opposing training camps had almost unanimously picked Dempsey as invincible.

As Bell later recounted, it seemed a little like going to a farm auction and looking over the stock. He arrived too late in the day to schedule an interview, so with ring workouts completed, he jammed a notebook in his pocket and went off to where he was told he might find the target of his story. He tromped along the shoreline and into the trees until he spotted what he called a "secret cabin."

On receiving no answer to his knock, he opened the door and slipped inside. What he saw surprised him for its almost monastic orderliness. There was a neatly made-up single cot, a camp desk with a portable typewriter, a wood chair, a dresser and shelves neatly lined with row upon row of books. Good grief, he thought. One might think that the occupant was a college student or an author. It was hardly the kind of space one would expect for a boxer, not that Bell knew any boxers, but he could tell from the training paraphernalia that it was undoubtedly Tunney's living quarters. Bell sat down in the chair and picked up a book.

As one of nine living in a cramped New York apartment, Gene had found seclusion on the Hudson River docks. Those early memories and a driving need for personal space had made him insist, against the advice of his manager and trainers, that he have a private sanctuary at Speculator. His rough-hewed clapboard cabin, known as "the shack" to reporters, was off-limits to visitors. Jogging back late in the day from an hour's run, Gene was troubled to see the silhouette of someone inside. He opened the door, ready to unleash his anger at the intruder.

Bell was only a few years older than Tunney, a big, burly, Scotch-Irish American with the ability, said friends, to charm anyone's socks off. The reporter instinctively saw that his presence was unappreciated. Without trying to make excuses, Bell simply apologized, saying that he had hoped to get acquainted and would like an interview. Then, looking toward the stack of books on the night table, Bell smiled and asked, "What are you reading?"

Gene's concern about a visitor vanished. He was enormously pleased that someone was asking about authors instead of his punches, knockdowns, right cross and brittle knuckles. It was a relief to be invited to talk to a reporter about books and ideas, subjects that were infinitely more interesting to him than talking about the upcoming fight. Gene sat down on the bed and gestured for Bell to use the chair.

"Reading now? *The Way of All Flesh*," replied Gene, "an autobiographical novel by Samuel Butler." He went on to say that the book had an excellent preface by George Bernard Shaw who praised it as a neglected masterpiece. In fact, Tunney said he had bought it at a used book store for 50 cents during a trip to Los Angeles, specifically because he noticed the preface was written by Shaw, the world-famous playwright who had won the Nobel Prize for literature and was an author he admired for his wit and wisdom.

As if to cap off the conversation, Tunney said he found the book's lessons on an English cleric's self-righteous use of religion to manipulate his son to be absorbing and the discussions of Charles Darwin's *On the Origin of Species* thought-provoking. In questioning the pretentious social class values of Victorian society, he said, Butler, like Shaw, offered hope for the freedom of the individual against hypocritical conventions.

Bell was nonplussed. He took out a new notebook, resettled himself in the chair and prepared to interview this "man of multiple surprises," a man with wide-ranging interests and a command of language who was so filled with energy that he seemed to gesticulate constantly. Often getting up to pull out a book, he spoke faster than Bell could take notes. Tunney had a quick wit and enjoyed repartee, and Bell found him a willing audience for his own humorous tales about the newspaper business and his southern family.

There had been snickering about Tunney's habit of reading during training and of using multi-syllable words. "Most prizefighters talk in words of one syllable and sharpen their jackknives on the backs of their necks," said a Newspaper Enterprise Association syndicated story about Gene written the year before. When Gene said he liked poetry, the surprised interviewer said he "clung to his chair and took a shot from his pocket flask of aromatic spirits of ammonia to steady himself." The article was published in the *Chicago Post*, with the headline "The Boxing Savant." At the time, Tunney was not yet signed to fight Dempsey and the tale of the heavyweight who read poetry was dismissed as laughable.

In general, the sportswriters didn't really care about Tunney's inner life, about what he read, why he read or what he thought. They didn't care that he walked to church, read the editorial pages of newspapers, including *The New York Times*, that he was a member of the Shakespearean Society or that he had memorized *Hamlet*. If anything, they were irritated that his reading habit made him less accessible because it consumed his time away from the ring. Reading skills weren't why Tunney was in the limelight. Tunney hadn't graduated from high school, and his ability, or inability, to decipher a sentence and expand his vocabulary appeared to have no bearing whatsoever on whether he could withstand the crushing onslaughts of "The Manassa Mauler."

Books on the shelves of Tunney's cabin included a leather-bound set of the complete plays of William Shakespeare, novels by H.G. Wells, Thomas Hardy, Jack London, Victor Hugo, Thornton Wilder's *The Cabala*, the poetry of Percy Shelley and W.B. Yeats, a Bible, Jeffrey Farnol's *The Amateur Gentleman* and *The Broad Highway*, and Bernard Shaw's *Cashel Byron's Profession*, and plays including *Back to Methuselah*, *Saint Joan*, and *Pygmalion*. Gene said he had read them all at least once, sometimes several times. "I am always deliberate and methodical, my normal gait for most things," said Gene. "I could never just skim a book and I always appreciate the message more in the rereading."

Bell knew at once that he was onto a bigger and better story than the usual feature about a heavyweight contender hitting speed bags. The contradiction of a boxer reading literature would capture headlines and grab attention. As an experienced newsman who appreciated literature, Bell was also well-equipped to play the role that every newspaper writer hopes to have: that of being the first to develop and elaborate on a major story — a scoop. The Associated Press was the largest general news agency in the world, which made it uniquely suited to sending stories to a far-flung audience.

Several days later, Bell's story on the fighter who loved to read was distributed to virtually every newspaper in the country and to papers overseas. Bell's boss, Alan Gould, said that other sportswriters, suspecting a clever publicity gimmick drummed up to get coverage, initially ignored the report. When they learned it was true, the regulars were irritated to be scooped by a reporter who wasn't even a regular on the beat. Editors clamored for follow-up details. Almost overnight, the story ballooned and the massive maw of the sports press took over, making the tale of Gene's reading a bigger yarn than Rip Van Winkle.

Initially, Gene was elated with the attention the news created. He was pleased and proud to finally be seen as someone distinct from Dempsey, someone smart and a man with more to offer than a boxer's biceps. It made him feel good to be recognized as a reader of fine literature. As if to emphasize his new status, he stashed books in his gear and started carrying volumes around the training camp. Visitors said that at meals, he often dropped a book or two on the table. Gene, still unknown to those who didn't follow sports and impressed simply to see his name spelled correctly, was unaccustomed to being in the headlines. He lacked any understanding of how to cope with the intense publicity brought to bear on public figures during the prosperous post-war era of the Roaring Twenties. He was totally unprepared for celebrity. In the language of the idiom, he was wet behind the ears.

Indeed, one of Gene's greatest strengths — his ability to focus and block out all surroundings — became his biggest weakness outside the ring. The concentration and willpower that enabled him to drive himself almost beyond endurance to utilize his mental and physical powers in pursuit of the championship also made it easier for him to disregard what seemed irrelevant remarks that reporters and the boxing crowd might be saying about him.

"It never occurred to me," he said, "that a habit of reading could be seen as a stunt or a joke. Wasn't reading something we wanted to champion?" He had no inkling of how absurd the notion of a literate prizefighter might seem to the sportswriters. Nor did he appreciate the day-to-day need for competing columnists to write controversial, provocative, even negative, copy to sell newspapers.

Until Bell's story, sportswriters had considered the man challenging Dempsey for the championship to be a boring, colorless figure who kept to himself. Most sports celebrities were easy to write about because they tended toward extravagances with women, gambling, alcohol, temper tantrums, problems with their managers, with money, or tangles with the law.

"The average pug, when he lets down, gets roaring drunk or takes to sitting up all night pounding night-club tables with little wooden mallets, reaching hungrily for the powdered nakedness of the girls who march by," wrote sportswriter Paul Gallico.

Tunney didn't hang around with writers or other visitors playing card games or drinking beer, common pursuits in a training camp that also allowed reporters to know the sports figure better. Instead he spent the five hours between his morning and afternoon workouts reading, and the evenings listening to classical music.

In contrast, "the old Dempsey camps were magnificent social cross-sections of vulgarity and brutality," wrote Gallico. "Phonographs brayed, spar mates brawled, the champ played pinochle or roughhoused, frowsy blondes got themselves into the pictures at nighttime."

Tunney had been a difficult and enigmatic personality to capture on paper and was, in effect, a nonentity. Bell's scoop and all the incredulous stories that followed were dreams come true for reporters, most of whom considered a heavyweight boxer reading books a spoof, as hilarious as a presidential candidate singing arias. It was a story that eventually moved from sports pages to front pages, catching the attention of the general public and incidentally making boxers more interesting to people, including women, who didn't normally follow the sport.

Columnists and comedians picked up the drumbeat that Tunney, the challenger to the heavyweight boxing title, was training to beat the "man-killer" Dempsey on a diet of classical authors. Sportswriters and broadcasters spouted witty remarks about the "Bard of Biff" and "Genteel Gene," sure that no serious contender would read novels and plays, much less poetry, while training for the most important fight of his career.

"In Gene Tunney, pugilism has found a Galahad far more taxing to credulity than novelist, playwright or scenarist would dare to conceive," wrote Ed Van Every of the *New York Evening World*.

Once he realized he was being made a laughingstock, Gene agonized over it, worrying that he was too sensitive yet unable to put it behind him. In telling the truth, in trying to be himself, he had been held up to ridicule. In trying to fix it, he made it worse, and the perception of Gene as impersonal and arrogant took root. From childhood, he had never backed down from confrontation, and his experience at verbal encounters had been finely honed at the family dinner table. He tried to talk his way out of it, but his explanations often engendered disbelief.

"Some think I am high-hatting the boys when I talk about literature. I am not," Gene said defensively. "It is a hobby with me, just as Jem Mace, a bare-knuckle champion of the 1860s, played the violin, and Jem Ward, another prize-ring title holder, painted pictures." Jem Mace? Playing the violin? Few had ever heard of him.

It also didn't help that he had what some called "an oddly British quality" to his speech, especially in public, making him sound pretentious. Gene did not explain that his father had a bit of a British accent, that Aunt Margaret routinely quoted Shakespeare, and that his brother Tom, now a policeman, couldn't get through a dinner without reciting Edgar Allan Poe and Henry Wadsworth Longfellow.

"The kid from Greenwich talked like a gentleman from Mayfair," said columnist Ed Fitzgerald. He had "a most unpugilistic interest in things like art, science, music and literature, and he never used a short word if he could think of a big one instead."

One author wrote that "Tunney's affected convoluted speech patterns were as foreign to most Americans as an untranslated poem by Baudelaire."

"Actually," said Gene, shifting the blame, "some visitors, seeing me reading in my spare moments, had a little fun in their conversations with me by using big words." There was perhaps nothing more likely to raise Gene's ire than the feeling that others were making a fool of him. Instead of bluntly telling someone off, however, Gene was always more likely to bury his feelings, keep a straight face and resort to wordplay to diminish his adversary. This paradoxical Irish propensity for purposely using big words in conversations was misunderstood by reporters and many readers.

"Taking up the joke, I answered back in polysyllables. I'm afraid," he said, in a supreme understatement, "some of the innocent bystanders took me seriously and thought I was parading my knowledge."

He blamed himself, thinking he should have been less cocky, shown more patience, seen a backlash coming and understood that his popularity with the fans might ultimately be affected. "Along came this new guy, Tunney, who makes it clear he's an intellectual, or pretends to be, and the writers took whacks at him — they HATED him, so we hated him," recalled author Studs Terkel, who was a boy at the time. "Dempsey was never much interested in reading, writing and learning, but he was a scrapper, a mauler! No one on our block liked Tunney, except my older brother, an academic. Everyone wanted Tunney to lose."

For Gene, books became ever more an escape, an Alice in Wonderland tumble into world after world after world, providing lyrical language and peaceful landscapes far removed from the fight game. Words and stories were a form of meditation, allowing him to relieve tension and stress. Reading became central to his ability to concentrate and focus, making books invaluable tools of training.

He had always felt that the art of repose was one of a boxer's major challenges. In quiet desperation in the weeks before an important bout, many prizefighters filled spare time with hangers-on, sycophants, idle talk and the rowdy, barlike atmosphere in training camps to try to calm their jangled nerves. A boxer tended to be nervous and jumpy and could easily wear himself down through anticipation and lack of rest. Even in the ring, fighting itself came in flurries. For a large part of the time a boxer was sparring, not hitting, and the less nervous energy he burned and the more relaxed he kept his body, the better he fought.

Gene said that books helped him understand who he was and where he wanted to go and gave him the discipline to distance himself from his work. In the ring, a rested mind allowed him to strategize. "The truth is, I became addicted to reading not in spite of pugilism, but largely because of it," he recalled. "For me, fisticuffs and literature were allied arts, through the medium of training." The explanation was largely dismissed by the unsympathetic fight crowd. But not by Greb.

Harry Greb, one of Dempsey's toughest sparring partners, the only man who ever beat Tunney in the ring, and a boxer who exemplified the physical and brutal life of a prizefighter, took the story of reading seriously.

"Gene reads books? Did you know that?" Greb asked sportswriter James R. Fair.

"Do you think he gets anything out of them?" asked Fair.

"Why, Jim," Greb asked in amazement, "Do you think he don't? When he reads a book, I'll bet my last dollar he knows as much about it as the man who wrote it does. And I'll tell you why. I gave him a lesson in our first fight and he learned it so well that I was never able to hurt him or cut him up again. I don't know *why* he reads them, but by God he knows what he's reading." Greb was one of the few in boxing circles who predicted Tunney would beat Dempsey, but his opinion was ignored.

Tunney was fighting for a life beyond the ring. He was fighting to be "the respectable gentleman" that his mother idolized. He wanted to put the tedious, repetitive work of the dock clerk behind him, along with the sameness of daily living and a paycheck too big to leave him poor but too small to allow him his dreams. In the doctor's waiting room, he had read about poor boys that had triumphed. As a teenager, he had bought standing-room-only tickets for the Metropolitan Opera to hear the most famous singer of the era, Enrico Caruso. Watching alone from the back of the house, he had been as entranced by the social elite passing down the aisles as he had been by the extraordinary power of Caruso's voice. Outside, he remembered huddling in the cold from across a snowy street as men in top hats and white ties and women in long gowns stepped from carriages and chauffer-driven luxury sedans.

Nor had he forgotten that as a schoolboy he had practiced for marathons by racing buses up Fifth Avenue, past grand mansions, apartment houses with doormen in livery, and stores with opulent window displays of clothing, furs and jewelry.

In time, through wealthy friends and backers, Tunney had been introduced to a society where words commanded respect, households had cooks and butlers, homes were big enough to have libraries and gaming rooms, and manicured lawns and formal dinners were commonplace. "I had a 33-room house, a staff, an elevator to the third floor, a butler, and all the things that go with it. He liked that house," said his close friend Samuel F. Pryor, the son of a wealthy gun manufacturer, whom he had met on a troopship returning home from Europe. "He liked to come and stay."

Tunney had been invited to spar at the private and prestigious New York Athletic Club and the City Athletic Club with millionaires and businessmen who lived not in one house but two or three and who vacationed in Florida and Europe. Gene liked that style of living, and he was not going to give up his pursuit of a better life because the press had a different idea of how a boxer should live. In his striving, he did not realize that in rejecting the expectations of the fight crowd, he was also turning his back on their attitudes and values. Many of them were not educated, could not read, never wanted any other life but to be on the fringes of the sport and interpreted Gene's desire for something more as a personal affront. He was separating himself from those whose support he needed to be popular.

Seize opportunities, Gene always said, quoting Shakespeare: "I have wasted time, and now doth time waste me."

"Seizing opportunities reveals the kind of stuff we are made of. Men do not lack opportunities," he said, "they miss them." Learning and reading, he said, were the stepping-stones to opportunity.

In interviews, Gene irritated sportswriters by talking about boxing dispassionately as a science, as a job, discussing musculature and bone structure. He analyzed fighters as if he were an engineer not as a battle-tested pug.

"You know, I always fight my battles out beforehand," he said. "I mean by that, I plan and live through them by myself, figuring out my opponents and my own attack and defense."

He studied fight films for hours as he studied books, watching them over and over again. He hired boxers who had fought his opponents as sparring partners. He drew detailed diagrams of the body's vital points, and as a spectator at bouts sat in a seat near the ring drawing diagrams with a pencil and feverishly taking notes on the action. He relied on Wilburn Pardon Bower's *Applied Anatomy and Kinesiology* and probably read more medical books than any boxer in history.

"I think of pugilism as a fencing bout of gloved fists, rather than an act of assault and battery," he said. "You've got to cultivate the art of thinking as expressed in action."

It reached the point that whatever Gene said seemed alien to the traditional boxing crowd, and in print, the words tasted hypocritical. "Call me a boxer, a pugilist," he said repeatedly, "not a fighter." Not a fighter? A heavyweight contender training for a championship fight? Who was he kidding? they asked.

"As defined in the dictionary," he said, "the word 'fight' connotes a hostile encounter, and there's no room in a boxing contest for hostility." (He always maintained this distinction; he was pleased to say he had been a professional prizefighter who engaged in boxing, but that he never "fought.")

A year later, he arrived in Chicago and noted there was talk "about some fight to be held." He said he knew nothing about it. "I am here to train for a boxing contest, not a fight. I don't like fighting. Never did. But I'm free to admit that I like boxing."

As for the hangers-on who infested the boxing world of the 1920s, Gene had no time for them either. Having grown up in a neighborhood with gangs, he saw no reason why he should tolerate riffraff, bootleggers, two-timing politicians, second-rate managers, roughnecks and criminals. He saw boxing as a profession, much like being a dentist, except that the career was shorter. The rewards were great if one was good enough. Gene was convinced he had trained himself to be not only good but the best, and he confidently told anyone willing to listen that he was ready for Dempsey.

"I shall be champion," he told the British poet Robert Nichols during an interview. "Yes, it's written in the stars that I shall be champion. When I have won — and I shall win," Gene told Nichols, "I want to become a cultivated person." Nichols was one of many non-sportswriters assigned to interview Tunney, to try to determine if he was a fake and whether he actually knew and could correctly quote literature as he claimed.

"Tunney speaks better English than most Englishmen," noted Nichols. "His sentences do not trail off into sheer vagueness." Nichols said the articulate Tunney told him that by cultivated, he meant "a man who has some acquaintance with what man has seen and felt, and uses this acquaintance to understand the present world around him."

When Maine author and writer Roger Batchelder met Tunney, he wrote that he "inquired rather furtively about the pugilist's familiarity with the works of the Bard." As they sat together at luncheon, "My host recited the advice of Polonius to Laertes in a soft rhythm that seemed strange from one of such massive frame." Tunney's big fingers drummed on the table as though to continue the cadence of Shakespeare's rhythm as he quoted these words:

Neither a borrower nor a lender be,
For loan oft loses both itself and friend,
And borrowing dulleth the edge of husbandry.
This above all, to thine own self be true,
And it must follow as the night the day,
Thou canst not then be false to any man.

Before the luncheon was over, Tunney had discussed Dempsey, boxing, his school days, politics, "some sort of 'ology' which gave him complete knowledge of the muscles of the body, their means of functioning, and the results of an onslaught on the defensive muscles." And he had quoted much more Shakespeare, including the soliloquy of Henry IV on sleep, many passages from *The Merchant of Venice* and others, "all effective, well done."

"He speaks easily in fluent English, unlike many of his comrades in the ring," wrote Batchelder. "His poise is absolute, where Dempsey in previous interviews with the writer has often fidgeted, and grasped for words which might enable him best to express himself."

Tunney told him he did not start the ballyhoo in the press, "for I should hate to have any of my followers think that I'm a pseudo-highbrow. Shakespeare," he said, "offers me infinite relaxation, and since that is essential in my business, I turn to him for assistance, as well as for my own enjoyment."

The interview undoubtedly raised the spirits of English teachers everywhere, but did little to help Tunney with his core constituency.

A Chicago policeman named Mike Trant, a self-appointed bodyguard for Dempsey, investigated the peculiar literary goings-on at the Speculator training camp and eagerly took his findings back to the champion.

"The fight's in the bag, Jack," he gloated. "The so-and-so is up there reading a book. A big sissy!" Dempsey believed it. Dempsey's supporters repeated stories that Tunney had no punch, that he was a synthetic fighter, not a natural one, and that he didn't have the killer instinct that fans considered mandatory to win in the ring. Most importantly, he didn't *look* or *act* like a fighter. Now, there were books to go along with the looks.

President Calvin Coolidge would say that Tunney "looked more like a movie actor than a prizefighter." Cornelius J. Vanderbilt, Jr. called him a "perfect Adonis." One columnist said he could be a "young ascetic priest." No one said he looked or acted like a fighter.

"Dempsey fights with the killer spirit," said *The Baltimore Sun*, characterizing the champion as did Bernard Shaw. "He is entirely reckless. He doesn't care what happens to anybody, himself or the other fellow. It is easy to imagine Dempsey in an earlier age fighting the desperate combats of the caveman." Tunney, on the other hand, had the head of a student. "Tunney might be a scientist, a physician, a lawyer, an engineer, if he had been given a chance to study instead of going to work when he was still a boy."

When Grantland Rice, the kindly dean of the boxing writers, arrived at Gene's training camp in the Adirondacks with syndicated columnist Ring Lardner, an ardent Dempsey backer, they ran into the boxer carrying a fat book under one arm. "He could have passed for a young college athlete studying for his master's in English," said Rice.

"What's the title?" asked Lardner, who looked at Tunney in contempt.

"*The Rubaiyat*," replied a smiling Tunney, holding up a translation by Edward Fitzgerald. Then gesturing toward the mountains, the boxer added that the setting was so beautiful he had hardly been able to take his eyes off the scenery.

Lardner fixed Tunney with steely eyes. "Then why the book?"

Paul Gallico of the New York *Daily News*, an influential skeptic, mirrored, as well as stimulated, the sentiment of the majority:

GENE TUNNEY AND JACK DEMPSEY IN THE OFFICES OF THE NEW YORK STATE
BOXING COMMISSION, AUGUST 1926 (BETTMANN ARCHIVE/CORBIS).

I think Tunney has hurt his own game with his cultural nonsense. It is a fine thing that he has educated himself to the point where he no longer says dese and dem and dose, and where he can alone tell one book from another, but also indicate some familiarity with their contents, but his publicity has built him up as a scholar more than a fighter, and the man who steps into the ring with Dempsey with nothing but his hands as weapons needs to be a fighter and nothing else but. He will have to have a natural viciousness and nastiness well up in him that will transcend rules and reason, that will make him want to fight foul if he thinks he can get away with it, that will make him want to commit murder with his two hands. And I don't think that Master Tunney, who likes first editions and rare paintings and works of art, has it in him.

At night, alone in his cabin, Gene paced and began to imagine his fate might match that of Shakespeare's protagonist in *The Tragedy of Coriolanus*. Coriolanus was the fifth-century Roman military hero who thought that bravery was in one's heart and actions and that a man should be recognized on his own merits. While campaigning for the Roman Senate, he ignored the public, who wanted him to trumpet his military accomplishments and actively seek their support. Coriolanus had too much pride and felt demeaned by the political process, just as Gene was prideful and felt demeaned by the press. Coriolanus was assassinated.

"It was no spiritual gratification to know that I was an unpopular champion," he said. "It made me resentful of the very idea of popularity. I developed a sense of perverse amusement in the game of living precisely as I wanted to and damn anyone else's opinion." He stopped reading the sports news and focused only on training, taking long jogs alone and sometimes issuing statements instead of holding press conferences. He was confident that once he became champion, people would admire him.

In dark hours, he grieved over his younger brother and best friend, John, a thoughtful man destined for the priesthood who had always taken his side in household disputes with their difficult and demanding father.

He remembered as if it were yesterday arriving home from Europe, still proudly wearing his uniform, and striding into the small apartment on a sunny August afternoon laughing and bearing gifts. He was the first in his family to travel in Europe, and he was full of boyish wonder, of stories of Paris and the Champs-Elysées and Eiffel Tower, of sailing up the Rhine, of taking up boxing to avoid guarding empty balloon sheds and his triumph as "The Fighting Marine" who won the A.E.F. championship before an audience of dignitaries from the American, French and Belgian governments, including Prince Albert and General John J. Pershing.

Suddenly, he stopped talking. In the pregnant hush, he looked from face to face, and it took but a moment for him to realize one person was missing.

"John? Where's John?" he asked.

No one moved. No one said anything. No one knew what to say. Agnes, the youngest, hid behind her older sisters so she wouldn't have to watch his face. Tom bowed his head and studied the plain wood floor as if he had never seen it before. The family stood there in the parlor of the small walk-up apartment in tense silence, the only sounds the traffic and bleating from vegetable vendors on the streets below. Their eyes were lowered in a tableau of unspoken meaning

"It was a terrible moment," remembered Agnes. "No one knew how to tell him." No one could find the words to explain the unexplainable. John, always the good Samaritan, the only one who could rally the family's spirits when Papa's abuse had spilled over, had been killed — murdered, the family said — at a local club. Police said he had come to the defense of a girl whose name he never knew against a drunken bully who tossed cigarette ashes on her dress. John was shot in the head and died in a hospital two days later.

Heartsick, Gene dropped the gifts, turned, left the apartment without speaking and walked for hours through the city. He returned to the docks to sit alone through a long night, blaming himself for not being by John's side, chastising himself for celebrating a boxing victory in Paris while his closest friend and soul mate lay dying.

Sometimes, he thought of his father. The sarcastic and unforgiving Red had died in April 1923 of an aneurysm, his prized union card under his pillow. He had never offered encouragement to his eldest son, never acknowledged reading newspaper coverage of his son's ring battles, and he never saw Gene in a professional fight. He died without either of them resolving their lifelong animosity. Gene felt a sadness of lost opportunity that he would never be able to put into words. For the rest of his life, he would rarely speak of his father or his beloved brother John again.

Lying on his bunk in his small wood cabin in the Adirondacks, Gene had time to think. He wished for a trusted mentor in whom he could confide, whom he could talk to about his fears and concerns, his dreams for the future. On the brink of preparing for the biggest fight of his life, surrounded by dozens of supporters and ever more a public figure, he felt increasingly isolated and was sometimes desperately lonely.

Bell's article and those that followed exposed his most private yearnings to public ridicule, and despite the assurance of friends, he struggled to understand why he should be shamed for trying to better himself. Books had made him an outsider in his profession at the very moment he was reaching for the crown jewel of sport, the heavyweight championship. He saw winning as the only way out, the only way to prove himself. He thought that once he had won, the public's failure to understand him would pass, and he would be accepted by the boxing crowd for the man he was. He felt he had to slay the dragon to get ahead, and the dragon was Dempsey. "Think it, practice it, do it" became his mantra.

He also turned to prayer, believing that his faith would give him strength. He had grown up so devout that at age 21, he felt sinful that he hid his rosary in his bunk instead of kneeling beside his bed in front of other Marines to pray. He bent his knees at more altar rails than his friends would have known about, but he harbored questions about original sin for which he was ashamed and thought there were no answers.

"He was troubled, but he was truly a very good person," said his friend Sam Pryor.

On days off in Speculator, and sometimes late into the night, he visited Father John Murnane, a Franciscan priest, to discuss God and man and Gene's favorite saint, Saint Francis of Assisi. Saint Francis was a troubadour who captured for Christianity the joy in nature, the love for the sun and the moon, the trees, the clouds, the flowers and the birds, a saint who felt happiness did not come from comfort or material possessions but from serving others. When Gene sat outside alone under the night sky or walked along pine-covered mountain paths, he felt nature was God's cathedral and that he could speak to God directly. Catholic priests were friends and frequent visitors to his camp, and in talking with them, he struggled inwardly with bridging the gap between rigid church doctrine and his own independent thinking. These were not thoughts that he dared talk about with the clergy or his fervently religious family.

Bernard Shaw had shown him a way out.

Gene had seen Shaw's play *Saint Joan*, which had its world premiere in New York in 1923, and he had been profoundly moved by the story of the warrior saint, an ignorant peasant girl of unparalleled vision and courage who led the French army to victory in battles against the English and then was accused of heresy and burned at the stake by the dominant Roman Catholic Church. Joan's alleged blasphemy was listening to what she felt were God's wishes spoken to her through the voices of her angels rather than through obeying the Church's interpretation of God's will. Gene was touched by Joan's plain-spoken individual conscience.

Shaw had written that Joan's lesson was, "Though He slay me, yet will I trust in Him; but I will maintain my own ways before Him." The playwright, whose philosophy of religion did not mesh with traditional Christian teachings, felt the church should accept the freethinker as well as the faithful if it were to maintain authority with a modern congregation. Shaw felt that men of reason and science must be embraced by the church and that the true Christian Church was both Roman Catholic and Protestant in one. He wrote in his preface to the play that Joan's burning at the stake in 1431 made her the first Protestant martyr.

Gene found the play deeply provocative. After reading it, he changed from a doctrinaire Catholic to one who adhered to faith in God as the Creator of all things but who maintained his own conscience and responsibility for moral decisions, without needing his priest as he had as a child. He found comfort in memorizing much of *Saint Joan*, repeating the words during hours of jogging through the Adirondacks:

> To shut me from the light of the sky and the sight of the fields and flowers; to chain my feet so that I can never again ride with the soldiers nor climb the hills; to make me breathe foul damp darkness, and keep from me everything that brings me back to the love of God when your wickedness and foolishness tempt me to hate Him...if only I could still hear the wind in the trees, the larks in the sunshine, the young lambs crying through the healthy frost, and the blessed blessed church bells that send my angel voices floating to me on the wind. But without these things, I cannot live.

Gene told friends that Shaw's preface to the play was one of the finest pieces of writing he'd ever read and that it "ought to have him canonized in a century or two." Shaw felt that Catholicism was not yet catholic enough and Gene agreed. In later years he would name his only daughter, Joan.

In London, Shaw was following daily news reports of the buildup for the fight between Tunney and Dempsey. For the first time since 1924, when he had seen in the newsreels the battle in which Tunney had defeated the French champion, Georges Carpentier, Shaw was excited about a championship bout. Everything he remembered and read about Tunney interested him, in no small part because the boxer seemed to bear a resemblance to his fictional hero Cashel Byron, and Tunney was fighting against a man who was the personification of Cashel's fictional opponent, the mauler Billy Paradise. Shaw told Lawrence Langner, his exclusive agent in New York, that the invincible Dempsey could be beaten by a scientific fighter.

Wait and see, he told Langner.

Late in the day on September 23, 1926, with his manager, trainers, and friends hovering near, Tunney closed himself in his room, and with only hours to go before doing battle for the championship, finished rereading for the fourth time the book that Shaw held up as a masterpiece, Samuel Butler's *The Way of All Flesh*. The day of the fight, nearly every sportswriter in the country predicted he would lose, and they continued to question whether reading was a suitable preoccupation for someone in his profession. The Chicago *Daily Tribune* was almost kindly:

> Mr. Tunney, the refined prizefighter who will endeavor to smear Mr. Dempsey's paraffin nose all over his (Mr. Dempsey's) features, is reading Samuel Butler's *The Way of All Flesh*. Mr. Dempsey confines his reading to the comic strips, his trainer reading the two-syllable words aloud to him. We applaud Mr. Tunney's love of great literature as greatly as we

deplore Mr. Dempsey's indifference to the words of the master minds. However, and after all, the two gentlemen are to meet in a fistic combat and not in a competitive examination on English literature.

The air was thick with moisture, and the rain, which would soon turn into a torrential downpour, had not yet started when Gene pushed aside the top rope, pulled the blue robe with the U.S. Marine emblem tightly around him, and climbed into the ring at Philadelphia's new Sesquicentennial Stadium. There were tens of thousands of spectators, enough to fill a mid-sized American city, and more than 400 reporters. The cheapest seats were so far away that fans sitting in them had brought binoculars to see the ring.

Bob Edgren, whose drawings and columns had been Gene's introduction to reading and boxing, was at ringside with colleagues from the *New York Evening World*. In the first row, on a pine bench so close to the ring he could touch it, wearing a fedora to shield his eyes from the glare of the powerful arc lights, was the reporter who had first written the story on Gene's reading habits, the affable Brian Bell. He had asked Gene to be godfather to his son, born only the day before. Bell told his colleagues that he predicted Tunney would win. "Ha!" said AP's Charlie Dunkley, also sitting at ringside. "Why, the so-and-so can barely punch holes in a lace curtain!"

Gene caught Bell's eye, and smiled.

WORKMEN ERECT THE BOXING RING IN PHILADELPHIA'S SESQUICENTENNIAL STADIUM FOR THE TUNNEY-DEMPSEY FIGHT (TUNNEY COLLECTION).

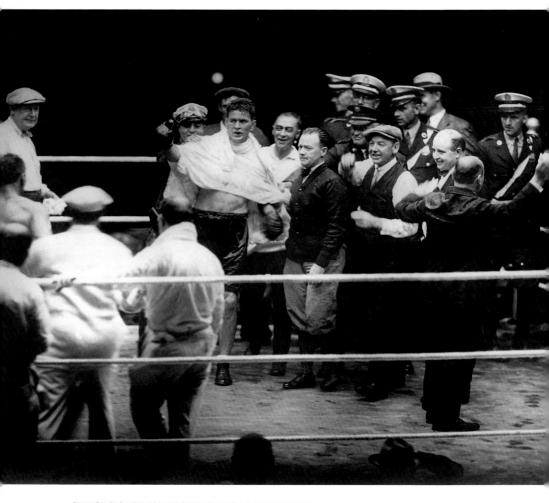

TUNNEY, THE NEW HEAVYWEIGHT CHAMPION OF THE WORLD,
MOMENTS AFTER WINNING THE 1926 DECISION. DEMPSEY IS
VISIBLE AT FAR LEFT, FACING TUNNEY (TUNNEY COLLECTION).

CHAPTER 4

Adelphi Kid

"The prizefighter is no more what the spectators imagine him to be than the lady with the wand and the star in the pantomime is really a fairy queen."
G. BERNARD SHAW

Philadelphia, September 23, 1926.

Gene stood in the puddle, rain dripping down his face, a towel over his shoulders, his shoes and trunks sopping, and allowed his right glove to be raised in the air. The first few seconds in the ring had been the longest of his life, but it was over. A tumultuous ovation like a tsunami's howl cascaded in waves down the canyons of screaming spectators even before the judge's final decision was announced. More than 145,000 fight fans, the largest crowd ever to attend an outdoor spectacle, had seen him upset Jack Dempsey for the heavyweight boxing championship of the world, the climax of seven years of unrelenting work and focus.

He had willed himself to succeed, had demanded of himself that there was no other option, and he had won decisively. It was one of the first heavyweight championships of the modern era to be decided on points for skill, speed and strategy. The beaten Dempsey stumbled laboriously across the ring, blood dripping from a gash under his right eye, his left eye closed completely, his mouth bleeding. Gene moved toward him as the crowd parted. They reached out to embrace, and the torrents of rain didn't stop.

At London's Rialto Theatre, the playwright Shaw would see moving pictures of the fight several times over. "Punches that travel with the velocity of a streak of lightning and footwork that the most flickering shadow would envy cannot be followed intelligently," reported *The Times* of London after its correspondent watched the movie. But it was interesting, the correspondent noted, to have "pictorial proof of Tunney's British style of boxing." Except for the referee, who Shaw thought resembled a churchwarden and ought to get out of the way, Shaw was elated with the outcome of the fight. In fact, so many Britons were enthused that an English boxing promoter made the first offer for a return bout, proposing Wembley Stadium in London, which seated 150,000.

Gene had triumphed in the most important night of his life and had done it his way, discounting naysayers, creating his own training regime and ignoring the sniping and salvos from the press. On the day of the fight, in a joyous jab at being his own man, he had stunned newsmen by climbing into the passenger seat of a blood-red Curtiss Oriole, piloted by stuntman Casey Jones, and lifted off toward a fog bank to fly from his training camp to Philadelphia, 85 miles and an hour and a half away. It was a year before Lindbergh's historic flight across the Atlantic, and air travel was still seen as highly risky. "That son of a bitch!" yelled promoter Tex Rickard, furious that millions of dollars in revenue could be lost.

A reporter asked Gene if he'd been worried.

"If I'd crashed, it wouldn't have mattered," he replied philosophically. "It's Rickard's show, but it's my life, remember." Then, adding a sentiment often heard from his mother, he added, "The longest life is very short."

Fifteen million people, the largest radio audience ever, had heard the broadcast from ringside. News accounts of his victory appeared on front pages, not only in the United States but around the world. In a year when the average annual wage in the United States was $1527, he had won $200,000 for a 30-minute fight. In half an hour, the poor boy from the docks had made more money than most Americans would earn in a lifetime.

The bells of Saint Veronica's Church, his childhood parish, pealed in celebration, and candles were lit throughout the sanctuary for parishioners to give thanks. Gene couldn't walk on the sidewalk without being stopped or visit a shop without a crowd gathering outside to peer in the windows and wave. People surrounded his car if it slowed in traffic and streamed by his

TUNNEY RETURNED TO NEW YORK A HERO AFTER BEATING DEMPSEY IN SEPTEMBER, 1926. HE WALKED WITH MAYOR JIMMIE WALKER AS TENS OF THOUSANDS OF PEOPLE CELEBRATED (TUNNEY COLLECTION).

table if he went to a public restaurant. He planned to take advantage of the moment and of his celebrity.

"Winning a championship and being a champion provide perhaps the most elating experience the modern world regularly affords, a mighty feeling of triumph," he said. Three weeks later, after thousands of hometown fans had greeted his return by train to New York City's Pennsylvania Station, and after Mayor Jimmy Walker had spoken kind words on the crowded City Hall steps, Gene prepared himself for another, more businesslike mission. At this point in his career, almost anyone would willingly grant him an interview.

"Don't you think I am beginning to talk like a businessman?" Gene had jokingly written his friend, Sam Pryor. "The trouble with my business is that I must make hay while the sun shines. Tomorrow," he told Sam, "everyone will have forgotten."

Earlier in the year, Gene had gone to Hollywood as the lead in a silent movie serial called *The Fighting Marine*. He'd played a former Marine who becomes a newspaper reporter (an ironic choice of casting that did not go unnoticed by him). The reporter comes to the aid of a titled young lady forced to reside in a rough mining town or forfeit her inheritance.

Gene had yet to see the film, but he believed studio executives who told him that in playing the starring role of Dick Farrington, he had been an unqualified success and that with his glamorous looks he could be a star. They called it "the greatest serial ever produced" and said it hadn't mattered that he refused to kiss the leading lady, an obstacle rarely encountered in Hollywood, or that he hated the fake blood and rouge. Gene had liked sunny, casual California and felt that if the praise was a reflection of his talent, he might be as successful in acting as he was in the ring.

"I find this new experience surprisingly interesting," he wrote to his friend Sam. "I thought before leaving New York this was going to be the most irksome and boring kind of work imaginable. Much to my astonishment, it has proven itself, so far, to be quite to the contrary. As a matter of fact, I find this somewhat pleasant."

Gene knew that John L. Sullivan had tried acting, touring the country with a tear-jerker called *Honest Hearts and Willing Hands*. Jack Johnson was paid $25 to clank onstage in chains leading prisoners in the triumphal scene in the opera *Aida*. And boxing commissioner William Muldoon was remembered for a scene in Shakespeare's *As You Like It* when, as Charles the wrestler, he was hurled to the floor so realistically he landed with a thud. "Jesus Christ!" roared Muldoon, in an ad lib that became part of boxing lore. Even Dempsey had earned money acting.

"Gene is one of the best actors I've ever worked with," said Spencer Gordon Bennet, the producer later known as the "serial king" for his achievements with *Zorro* and *Superman*. "He is much better right now than some men who have been in the game for eight or ten years. I think Gene would go a long way in the movies."

"Opportunity knocks once, maybe twice," Gene always said. "If you don't answer it, you're not going to hear it again."

Gene's supreme confidence in himself as an actor and his immense pride of accomplishment in winning the heavyweight boxing championship encouraged him three weeks after his triumph in Philadelphia to make a telephone call to the biggest, most important producer on Broadway, Lawrence Langner. Langner was Bernard Shaw's theatrical agent in New York and had co-founded the New York Theatre Guild, which by the mid-1920s had produced the most successful shows on the Great White Way.

An appointment was made for mid-October at the Guild offices.

The boxer whom Langner would meet still retained the earnest, boyish presence, good humor and clear blue eyes that had charmed the nuns, and the honesty and polite manners that had made him John McNamara's best butcher boy. Gene did not have a fighter's face. No sign of the fractured nose received from Greb. No cauliflower ears. The only telltale mark was a raw, hoarse throat, the result of a savage left hook by Dempsey in the fifth round in Philadelphia. The punch had smashed into his Adam's apple and crippled his larynx, preventing him for the rest of his life from ever shouting or talking without a slight rasp in his voice. He moved with the upright, easy gait of an athlete, and his fine, chiseled features and erect carriage would cause people to stop and look, even if they hadn't recognized him. He returned smiles, patted children on the head and was quick to respond if someone needed a door opened, a package carried or help crossing a street. Fastidious about style now that he could afford it, he dressed like a business executive, with the best shoes and blue serge suits, even a gold watch chain on his vest.

Langner was well aware of Shaw's "keen interest in boxing and prize-fighting" and said Shaw "prided himself on his knowledge." The producer had no idea what Tunney wanted to discuss, but he was delighted at the opportunity to meet the new heavyweight champion personally, if only to tell his main client more about him. He also would have been aware that sports celebrities, anxious to take advantage of their fleeting fame, frequently looked toward the theatre, vaudeville or film as a way of expanding their franchise and earning money between sporting events.

They met on a fine autumn day in Langner's private office, its walls hung with dozens of black-and-white theatrical photographs depicting scenes from plays featuring Alfred Lunt, Lynn Fontanne, Helen Hayes and others. There was also a photograph of Winifred Lenihan in the title role of *Saint Joan*, the play that had prompted Shaw's Nobel Prize for literature in 1925.

"Shaw's best," said Gene, referring to *Saint Joan*. "A masterpiece! But how did you resolve the demands to cut it?" The play, as produced, was three and a half hours long and didn't finish until about 11:30 pm. New York commuters complained bitterly that they couldn't make their trains, and Langner said that indeed a considerable amount of pressure had been put on Shaw to trim the dialogue. Langner felt the length of *Back to Methuselah*, another Shaw play, had sabotaged its appeal. But Shaw, he said, wouldn't budge, and rarely did on matters he felt were important. Shaw, he said, was a genius.

At a time when the English stage trafficked in romantic frippery, he said Shaw had awakened audiences to social ills by challenging conventional morality, ossified institutions and bourgeois respectability.

"Before the advent of Shaw, the theatre of ideas was like a church in which a little congregation of so-called intellectual theatregoers took itself so seriously that its influence was confined to a group which regarded itself as the elite custodians of modern thought," Langner would write. Shaw, he said, transported the theatre of ideas into a wider world of the popular theatre.

Gene noted that *Pygmalion*, starring Lynn Fontanne as the flower girl Eliza Doolittle, was sold out for its November opening. Gene had read the play, had seen it produced and was especially struck, he said, by the transforming concept of elocution as a way to help change one's social status. (The idea of perfecting pronunciation was one he had adopted for himself. Gene was inspired by the makeover of the urchin Eliza, who, with lessons in proper speaking and manners, becomes a lady.) Langner invited Gene to be his guest for the new production of *Pygmalion*. Up to this point, the discussion had been so congenial that Langner almost forgot that the bright young man sitting across from his desk had come with an agenda.

Sitting back in the armchair, Langner's visitor crossed his legs, straightened his jacket, cleared his throat and made his pitch: he, Gene Tunney, wanted to take the lead in a stage production based on Bernard Shaw's novel, *Cashel Byron's Profession*, the fourth of five novels Shaw had written before turning to playwriting. The new champion wanted to be an actor.

If he was surprised, Langner, an amateur actor himself, didn't show it. Lawrence Langner was a man who took risks in the theatre. He knew that Shaw had been furious over the theatrical misappropriation of his boxing novel 30 years earlier, but it was also the only one of Shaw's novels still in print. Tunney was a champion with potential box office appeal, and he was offering himself up for what might be a huge commercial success. Women had gone to Tunney's fights in increasing numbers, attracted not by the fighting but by the boxer's sex appeal. Among the 8000 or so women who saw him win the championship were many who had swooned loudly as Tunney arrived.

Women at the fight had repeatedly shouted, "Isn't he handsome!" Ladies saw him as the boxer who read Keats. Newspapers quoted one woman as trilling, "He knows his dictionary." A woman in a black gown embroidered with gold dragons called out, "Has he got a book under his arm?" "Show your Irish, Gene!" women yelled during the fight. "I wish I could hear the sock of the gloves," gushed a female fan. Sex appeal. What better credibility for a stage or movie audience?

Langner showed Tunney around his offices, and Gene noticed on one wall a familiar picture of the English poet John Masefield, who had spent his early days working in a saloon owned by Luke O'Connor, one of Gene's earliest patrons. A stunned Langner wrote Shaw that the boxer "told the entire Theatre Guild, to their amazement, that he had read many of his works and knew Masefield had worked in a saloon down in this part of town when he was a young man. In fact," Langner continued, "though it sounded like a fairy tale, one can almost envisage Tunney as a literary connoisseur who wins world championships to pay for his library."

After cabling the playwright in London, Langner followed up with a letter to Shaw describing the champion as a handsome young man with a charming personality.

"I was impressed with the possibility of his doing a good job of the play," Langner wrote Shaw. "I am extremely favorably impressed with the character of the boy and his ability to play the part. He has none of the characteristics of a prizefighter other than a magnificent physique, which strikes you the moment you see him, but there is nothing brutal or animal about him, like Dempsey. In fact, as everyone who saw the fight testifies, his performance was a fulfillment of your own prophecy, made to me several years ago, that Dempsey would some day be beaten by a boxer."

Leaving Langner's office, Gene almost skipped down Broadway. He was elated at the outcome of the meeting, and at the prospect of being linked up with George Bernard Shaw, a man whose intellect and fame surpassed virtually all other cultural icons of the era. He felt vindicated that he could carry on a two-hour conversation with a man like Langner, discuss Shaw and the theatre, and hold his own. His future, he thought, might be coming together. He was more optimistic about his prospects than he had ever been and felt he had a clearer vision of the life of culture he might pursue beyond the ring.

"Mr. Shaw doesn't usually respond by cable," cautioned Langner. "He feels they cost too much." But Langner said he was in regular contact by mail and would add his endorsement to Gene's proposal. Gene didn't expect to actually meet Shaw but felt that the mere possibility of acting in a film or play with Shaw's blessing would be validation that he had within him talents beyond the boxing arena. Not only that, but the story of Cashel Byron was one he felt destined to play; indeed, it was a story he was actually living.

One of his closest friends, the multimillionaire department store scion Bernard Gimbel, had given him a prized copy of Shaw's novel. "Since our first meeting in 1919," wrote Gimbel, "I've always described you as Shaw's Cashel Byron." Willie Green, the boxing thespian in the Village who by smashing him to smithereens taught him to defend himself, told Gene he was so handsome he *had* to be a movie star. And hadn't Jim Corbett, his childhood hero, played Cashel on stage a generation earlier?

Gene, the confirmed bachelor, also had someone he wanted to impress, someone who didn't know anything about boxing and didn't seem to like boxing. But the girl in question, Mary Josephine Lauder, known to her friends and family as Polly, greatly enjoyed going to the theatre and the cinema. She liked moving pictures so much that she had bought her own projector and rigged up a home theatre to show Charlie Chaplin films and other movies to her family. Gene had written Sam about her from the Hollywood Athletic Club in May while he was working on his film. He had met Polly just before he traveled to Los Angeles.

"Had a most splendid evening with Kay and Ed Dewing and Kay's sister Polly, who is a perfect peach," Gene wrote. "A very interesting girl," he added. "She seems to possess plenty of intellect and character, and is one of the most beautiful girls I have ever seen. She has an odd personality, being terribly shy, but very attractive, sweet and amiable." Sam knew the young woman well, liked her immensely and, knowing she was the daughter of one of the leading families in his hometown of Greenwich, Connecticut, had arranged for Gene to meet her sister, Cot, at various parties given at his father's home, The Pryory.

Gene's warm reception at the Theatre Guild and his eagerness for a possible deal with Shaw had not faded when, a week later, he and Dempsey were to make their first post-fight appearance at Madison Square Garden, the heart and soul of the boxing crowd, and one of the most famous sporting arenas in the world. The Garden was the hometown venue where Gene, the big-city boy, had hoped to fight Dempsey.

As a 16-year-old, Gene had gone to the Garden with his brother John to see their first championship fight. They sat crammed into the cheapest seats, coughing and inhaling the heavy haze of tobacco soot. But he remembered his thrill in watching the swells in suits and hats crowded at ringside, listening to the ear-splitting waves of screams and yells of fans cheering fighters in the ring, and he caught onto the idea that boxing was more than Village smokers for boys. It was an entrée into a high-stakes world of money and uptown society, a ticket away from the docks. Gene wanted nothing more than to be part of this tumultuous new world. As preposterous as it might have been naïve, the brothers made a vow: to make Gene, the older brother, a champion.

In the long, sad, autumn after his return from the Great War, after repeated visits alone to his brother's grave, Gene sat on a bench in Madison Square Park, in the shadow of the Garden. He read books and imagined that the brothers' dream of a Tunney capturing the game's biggest prize could come true. Now his heart swelled with pride at the thought that he would stand in center stage at the Garden as world champion.

As Gene entered the big amphitheatre, he was relaxed, smiling and waving to friends, eagerly anticipating the triumphal moment when he would receive the symbolic wreath of laurels. As honored guests, the former champion and the new champion were both to be introduced and presented with championship belts by the Metropolitan Boxing Writers' Association.

Dempsey was introduced first and climbed into the ring, drawing a thundering ovation with some 2000 spectators cheering lustily, programs and newspapers flying through the air, feet stamping heavily on the floor, fans standing on the bleachers, waving their hats and shouting, "Dempsey! Dempsey!"

Then Gene was introduced. As the new champion began his climb between the ropes, the mood in the big arena suddenly shifted and soured. From the bowels of the Garden, there were boos, hisses and then hooting, a guttural rage that smoldered then swelled in volume so great that it took the announcer long moments to quiet the crowd. Gene realized as he stood to wave that the boos were aimed at him, and he felt sickened.

Silent and uncomplaining, he kept the festering humiliation bottled up inside. He smiled, accepted the prize and left the ring. Though he was an avid student of boxing history, he had neglected to appreciate or understand that to become number one is not necessarily to become an idol to the masses. Even Dempsey called the outburst an outrage. Gene said nothing.

"Practically overnight, I became the most unpopular of all the heavyweight champions," he recalled. After he'd won, he had criticized newspapermen for their doubts about his abilities. Too late, after his words were in print, he realized it had been yet another public relations mistake. "I could have been a more gracious winner. I goaded and goaded. I richly deserved what I got." The humiliation at the Garden did, however, lead to a business decision that helped make Gene wealthy: he never entered a ring again unless he was given 50 percent of the gate receipts. Hecklers, he said, would pay for the privilege: "There would be no free boos."

Increasingly, Gene erected walls around his family and friends, becoming one of the first major celebrities to aggressively try to protect his right to privacy. "I had reached the top. Acclaim, publicity, spotlight, trouble, annoyance — all the fame and fortune the prize ring bestows." He began to realize that his name was bracketed by books and haughtiness. The more he tried to revise his image, the more cynical the press became. Proud of his achievements and certain that the public's understanding of him would come with his preeminence, he tried to ignore that some thought he had become a caricature and that sports reporters felt they knew everything about him they needed to know.

Gene also had private reasons for shielding himself from the press. He was aware that Polly Lauder and her friends in Greenwich were not the kind of people who wanted publicity. Polly's mother was a prominent member of the Social Register, which held headlines and hype in contempt. One's name in the newspaper should appear, if at all, at one's birth and death. The wealthy, white Anglo-Saxon Protestant families constituted the old-money elite who primarily represented descendants of early English or Dutch settlers, the merchant class that had built Manhattan. Polly was related to 17th-century immigrants, including Richard Varick, an aide to General George Washington and one of the first mayors of New York City.

In this world of privilege, persons were shunned as outsiders for their scandals or peccadilloes, even for simply pursuing "undesirable careers." Gene had been reminded of this when the Sunday after he'd won the championship in Philadelphia, he and Pryor were invited to the sprawling Lauder estate for lunch and great effort had been made to keep the visit out of the newspapers. The Lauders did not want to be associated publicly with a boxer — or an Irish Catholic.

And then there was Gene's mother. Nana was so terrified of seeing her name or picture in the newspaper that she refused to speak to reporters and well-wishers who called to congratulate her on her son's achievement. She left instructions to tell them all she had gone to bed. When Gene went to visit his mother's home, he had to plead with reporters to stay away.

Whatever the future held, Gene knew that to get ahead, he had to continue boxing until *he* decided it was time to quit, and he wanted to do it on his own terms, earning as much money as he could, while leaving his honor and reputation intact. As champion, he decided he could handle the public by himself, the way he did most things: by being cordial and by bulldogging through it, like a good Marine. He would simply say what was on his mind, regardless of the consequences.

Shortly after becoming champion, Gene spoke in an interview about Shaw's novel. "Because of my pugilistic viewpoint," he said, "I like particularly Shaw's prize-ring story of *Cashel Byron's Profession*." Gene was fully aware that his first influences from Shaw came from that novel, and it comforted him by strengthening his resolve. With Cashel as a role model, Gene had permitted himself to envision a gentlemanly life beyond the ring as a realistic alternative, not a pipe dream. Even more significantly, Shaw's Cashel allowed Gene to consider marriage beyond his own class, to a woman far removed from his world.

The book also helped him appreciate the role of pugilism in 19th-century literature, a subject Gene began to include in speeches. "Every popular English novel becomes a gospel of pugilism," Shaw wrote in the preface. Shaw's examples of pugilism ranged from Shakespeare and Sir Walter Scott to Charles Dickens and Lord Byron.

Gene kept the full extent of this new knowledge to himself, but the novel as a primer became part of his traveling baggage. When interviewed, he said his recommended book list also included Victor Hugo's *Les Miserables*; *My Unknown Chum* (about a year's trip to Europe), as well as Shakespeare and the poets Shelley, Keats and Tennyson, "especially Shelley." He had a long list and said that he could go on forever naming books. No one but teachers and publishers wanted him to go on naming books.

Langner had not heard back from Shaw about doing a theatrical production based on the book, so he had suggested the idea of starring Gene as the fictional Cashel Byron to Hollywood movie producer Jesse Lasky. Lasky contacted the playwright in England and offered him $75,000 for rights to a movie to be adapted by Shaw and starring Gene as Cashel. The offer was met with silence.

Gene was used to being in control, and as the weeks went by, he couldn't figure out what the delays meant. Even worse, he had seen the first installments of *The Fighting Marine*, the series that was destined to make him a movie star. "A timely subject — it's a knockout!" said a handout from Pathe Films. "*The Fighting Marine* with Gene Tunney did a gross business about 200 percent higher than the usual Monday night!" boasted the Colonial Theatre in Depew, Iowa.

Gene had chosen the old Provincetown Cinema, a theatre he used to frequent in the Village, and he was pleased to be by himself on familiar streets. He ducked his head while buying his ticket so he wouldn't be recognized by the teller, then slipped inside. It was midday, with only a handful of people in the theatre. He chose a seat in the back, probably mulling over his impending stardom and the chance to appear on the big screen like Garbo and his friend Valentino, whom he had often visited on the studio lot in Hollywood. The marquee headlined *The Fighting Marine*. A lobby poster showed Gene on horseback looking like Robert E. Lee. In another picture, he was standing at the top of a broken stairwell scowling darkly at the pile of bad guys he had whipped conclusively in a fight.

Some minutes into the film, Gene was startled out of his reverie, jarred by what he saw on the screen: jerky black-and-white images of himself with a monocle and mascara running off his lashes. His pulse quickening, he watched the Gene-actor lose his monocle as he slugged it out with stuntmen who didn't know a right cross from a left, couldn't hit a post in front of them and would have fainted on facing even a flyweight in the ring. In play-

TUNNEY, IN COSTUME, DURING A BREAK IN SHOOTIN *THE FIGHTING MARINE* (TUNNEY COLLECTION).

ing the part of reporter Dick Farrington, he thought he looked like a blithering idiot. In a sweat, he left hurriedly, before the film ended.

No amount of subsequent fan mail would change his mind: it had been a total flop. He silently blamed the director he had trusted, and he blamed himself for getting talked into doing it. He made certain that no one in his family ever saw it. Meanwhile, in order to keep his name before the public, his manager, Billy Gibson, had already convinced him to sign a contract to do a 14-week stint in vaudeville, which he could not cancel. He was frustrated and anxious to get back to boxing, where he felt he could control his surroundings.

Four weeks after his initial visit to Langner's Theatre Guild, word came from London, not by letter, but reported in *The New York Times*. Shaw had received Lasky's offer and wanted time to think the matter over. He reportedly thought the novel might be worth a quarter-million dollars, but admitted — in what seemed to Gene a snide aside — that he might change his mind. Later, Shaw asked for $100,000, coupled with the suggestion that Dempsey appear as the novel's ring mauler who loses to the skillful Cashel. Lasky, who felt he was being toyed with, refused and countered with his original offer of $75,000. Again, there was silence from London.

Gene felt uneasy, and he worried that the deal he had proposed to Langner was going to make him look foolish. He was concerned that with his popularity slipping, if his aspirations beyond the ring came up short, he could fall into a life defined only by pugilism, surrounded by criminals and racketeers. Mobsters in the underbelly of the fight world routinely raked in tens, sometimes hundreds of thousands of dollars in illegal betting payoffs by bribing boxers to fix fights or take falls. Gene had spoken out so often about dishonesty in the sport that he was derisively called "Clean Gene."

Not everyone accepted that he couldn't be bribed. "Gene was approached by henchmen from the mob used to making big bets to fix fights," recalled Jimmy Hourihan. Jimmy's grandfather, Dan Hourihan, one of Gene's sparring partners, also lived in the Tunneys' apartment building. Dan and Gene's policeman brother Tom were both over 6 feet tall. They were pugnacious, muscular, fearless Irishmen who knew the streets, and both relished a good brawl. "Tom and Dan ordered the hoodlums to back off, but they returned — only more aggressively, directly threatening Gene and the family," said Jimmy. Nana was frantic. Tom Tunney moved back home into the apartment building, first sitting on the steps with two loaded revolvers for several weeks, then sleeping in front of the door, guns at the ready. "There's no doubt that Tom would have shot them," said Tom's daughter, Rosemary. The mob finally backed off, but Gene moved his family out of the city to suburban Riverdale, New York, and took up residence at a premier hotel with more security.

The Breslin was a luxurious, old-world-style hotel at the corner of Broadway and 29th Street, within walking distance of theatres, trolleys, restaurants, office, and clubs. It had a carpeted marble lobby with columns and vaulted ceilings, which gave it a feeling of grandeur, and a staff who treated Gene like visiting royalty, bowing slightly as he passed by.

"Hello, Mr. Tunney." "Visitor for you, Mr. Tunney." "How was your day, Mr. Tunney?" Gene loved it.

An interview with the *New York Sun* was scheduled in mid-November, and Gene had asked the reporter to meet him in his hotel suite rather than in the noisier atmosphere of a newspaper office or a restaurant. The interviewer was new to him, and Gene said later that if he had known what was coming, he would have hidden Shaw's novel, which was in plain sight on his dressing table. The reporter saw the book and turned the questions from boxing to Gene's proposed acting career.

By this time, more than a month after he had met with the producer Langner, Tunney was beginning to feel like a slab of beef for sale, a feeling made all the worse because details were being reported in the press before he heard about them from either Langner or Lasky. Gene had spent a lifetime being told by his father that he was trying to overreach, and he was highly sensitive to being made to feel the chump. He was going to put a stop to it. To save face, he had to get the upper hand on the deal and say something, because Langner and Lasky had not.

"The character of Cashel Byron is badly drawn, and the story is silly," he was quoted as saying. "Frankly, I had not read the book until there was some talk of my making the picture, and I was very much disappointed in it." This was not correct, but once he began uttering opinions, the interviewer was silent. The reporter, as reporters are wont to do, saved the spiciest comments for the story. "When Shaw conceived the idea of writing a novel around a boxer, he had a splendid opportunity, but he missed it. In the beginning of the book, there is a promise of fine things to come, but the promise is not fulfilled. Shaw understands neither the temperament nor the psychology of the professional boxer, with the result that Byron is made to appear as no more than a blundering vulgarian. There are no gentlemanly traits about him, save a dash of chivalry."

The Irish say pride means not admitting you're wrong, even when you know you are. One might have thought Gene would stop his critique, realizing that Bernard Shaw was a writer he much admired and it had been his own idea to play the role of Cashel Byron in the first place.

But once cornered, Gene was never one to hold back a punch or an opinion, even if it was misguided, and he was angered that the playwright had not responded directly to Langner privately. He then blasted the fictional Cashel, saying he was "scarcely a character to excite the admiration of anyone." And he even had an opinion on Cashel's love interest: "That the girl in the book, reared in an atmosphere of culture and refinement, should fall in love with a man whose only appeal was a magnificent body, is absurd."

Gene went on to say that he regarded Shaw as "one of the greatest minds among living men — possibly the greatest — and *Cashel Byron's Profession* must be viewed only as a product of his immature years. He would be incapable of writing such a book today." (He did not mention that in the book's preface Shaw said that he regarded himself as an "immature poet" when he wrote the novel.)

"I certainly would not lend myself to the filming of the book as it is written," said Gene, reflecting comments he had heard from the movie producer. "I would insist that the scenario merely be based on the story, as is done in many film versions of famous works." With changes, he said the fictional Cashel would be a stronger, finer character, and the story "would proceed along more rational lines."

Once again, Gene's literary comments were news — and not just on the sports pages. "Tunney Takes a Swing at Shaw" read the bold headline on the *Sun* story. As if to reinforce Gene's gaffe, there was a story on the same page about Shaw's plan to forfeit the money he had won earlier in the year for a Nobel Prize in Literature. (Shaw accepted the honor and gave the prize money to the Anglo-Swedish Literary Foundation's trust fund.)

Gene realized belatedly that he had said too much about a book that he had himself promoted, thus jeopardizing any chance of a stage or movie deal with Shaw. As soon as he read the interview, side by side with the Shaw story, he rebuked himself for running off at the mouth, and he knew there would be some sort of reaction. He just didn't anticipate that it would come from Shaw himself and would once again be in the newspapers.

"If the book were modernized for a film," Shaw told the London *Daily Mail*, "it would upset its character a good deal. I think it would be rather amusing to bring the book up to date and make the fight in it that between Dempsey and Tunney. I haven't time to do it now," he said, "but I might do it sometime." Shaw told London reporters that he also considered the book immature, but said he was not sure "whether Tunney knows what 19th-century boxers were like." He pointed out that "Cashel would be glad to get a guinea for a fight, while Tunney might want a hundred thousand dollars."

"If Tunney thinks he can rewrite the book, and improve it, he'd better do so," said Shaw. "He ought to know more about it than I."

Reading Shaw's remarks had been embarrassing for Gene, and the headlines had been worse. "G.B. Shaw Answers Tunney's Criticism," said *The New York Times*. "He suggests that the champion rewrite novel which fighter called immature." A *United News* story was headlined: "Bernard Shaw Bows to Gene."

When Gene arrived in Youngstown, Ohio, for an appearance two days later, he did what politicians and countless other celebrities have done: he alibied. He said he did not mean to tell Shaw, whom he had never met, how to write a book, that he was misunderstood when his remarks were interpreted as a literary criticism.

"I never criticized the book's literary merit, for I feel I am unqualified," he said. "But I did say that the story would have to be changed somewhat for modern screen adaptation. I think Shaw one of the greatest literary minds of the day. I would not attempt to advise him now how to finish a work of literature any more than I would expect him to advise me how to box an opponent."

"Tunney takes poke at George Bernard Shaw," said a headline in the *Modesto News Herald*. "Tunney spurns movie offers," said the *Ogden Standard Examiner*. The back-and-forth had brought to the forefront Gene's habit of speaking about books instead of boxing, and it reinforced the fight crowd's growing perception that they had a heavyweight champion who would rather be in a library than in a prize ring.

"In the matter of Gene versus Bernard," said *The New York Times*, "Mr. Tunney must have thought he was being placatory when he hastened to assure Bernard Shaw that in commenting on *Cashel Byron's Profession*, the champion was speaking from the technical and not the artistic standpoint. This only makes things a little worse than before. It is not a friendly act to suggest that Bernard is unqualified to offer advice to anybody about anything. He always does. He specializes in the human race and concentrates on the Cosmos.

"For the American people, the incident offers reason for a fine glow of pride," continued the *Times*. "It is something to have produced a heavyweight champion capable of putting up a good pair of fists to Bernard Shaw. Who among the enterprising publishers will seize the opportunity to expand the exchange of cable dispatches into a full-sized octavo debate between Champion Gene and the 'Adelphi Kid?'" (Shaw lived at Adelphi Terrace in London.)

A few days later, roughly two weeks after Gene's first newspaper comments on the book and a month and a half after Langner's cable to the playwright, front-page stories in newspapers from London quoted Shaw as saying he was flattered to hear that Tunney was to pay him a visit to discuss the controversy. A British promoter said he would put up $25,000 for Gene to visit Shaw in London. It was the last straw.

Gene had never said he wanted to visit Shaw to discuss "the controversy." He had no intention of rewriting anything Shaw wrote, and he had never meant to get into a dialogue with a world-famous author about a book written before he was born. Shaw, well accustomed to tabloid-style newspaper coverage and known for the severity of his responses in the press, had been courtly in his reply, surprising reporters who assumed that the playwright would take Gene to task over his comments. No backlash was forthcoming. Instead, the playwright seemed intrigued.

"Did Tunney actually say those things?" Shaw asked reporters. "If he did, the young man must have some literary taste. I'd like to meet him."

With the flap over the book, the talk of a movie deal died. Jesse Lasky refused to pay more money for the screen rights and said Shaw's idea of putting Dempsey in the film was ridiculous. Gene was now so disillusioned by his own performance in *The Fighting Marine* that he wanted no part of the celluloid world. He vowed never to discuss Bernard Shaw in public again. Dead authors, he reasoned, were safer.

Within weeks, he was fulfilling his contractual obligations in vaudeville, first on the East Coast. The New York and Boston newspapers generally left coverage to the entertainment writers, who treated him like a curiosity brought in to drum up business. Spectators paid from five cents to 50 cents and saw a show, which typically included a reluctant Gene sparring with another boxer he was extremely careful not to hurt and a movie or another song-and-dance act.

At year's end, he headed west. He carried his little black book of words in his pocket, his dictionary and a stack of books. It was a tour that he found boring, wasteful, tiring and frustrating, and he tried unsuccessfully to break his contract several times. But on the West Coast, he was in for a surprise: the reporters and the audiences loved him. Away from the big-city sportswriters, he found a solid fan base and writers who understood him better. This period temporarily soothed the brittle edges of his public experience.

"Today I spent over two hours chatting with the pugilistic champion of the world, who socked me syllabically, charmed me with his clear diction, and then knocked me groggy with a word," wrote Andy Lytle of the *Vancouver Sun* in British Columbia. Andy interviewed him while the champion stood at the bathroom sink smearing shaving lather on his face.

"Lytle?" Gene asked Andy, while he continued with his shave. "Wasn't there a famous English writer — ? Let me see, Lyddon or something like that?"

"Lytton, perhaps," Andy hazarded.

"Yes, yes, of course," grinned Gene. "Lord Bulwer Lytton wrote *The Last Days of Pompeii*, among other things," Gene replied. He said he had read the book.

Andy was stunned.

Talk turned to the fight in Philadelphia. How did Gene do it? He was to describe his victory over Dempsey at almost every stop in roughly the same language, using the same obscure word that inevitably baffled his listeners.

"There is a somewhat indefinable thing, a sort of reserve force," said Gene, "that if you happen to possess, may mean the margin between success and failure in the ring or anywhere else. Psychologists like to describe it as 'autonomic,'" he said.

Spell it, said Andy.

"A-u-t-o-n-o-m-i-c," said Gene. He reached into his traveling case and brought out his little dictionary.

Andy wrote that Webster defines the word as meaning automatic, occurring involuntarily and spontaneously. "That word is Gene Tunney's answer to how he beat Jack Dempsey. The ability to think fast and clearly and to follow the thought with a straight dynamic punch with the speed of thought itself."

In these remarks, Gene unwittingly echoed the writer he so admired. Bernard Shaw had written that "there are men to whom the right answer" in boxing "is instantly obvious without any consciousness of calculation on their part…There are pugilists to whom the process of aiming and estimating distance in hitting, of considering the evidence as to what their opponent is going to do, arriving at a conclusion and devising and carrying out effective countermeasures, is as instantaneous and unconscious as the calculation of the born mathematician or the verbal expression of the born writer…A man with this gift, and with no physical infirmities to disable him, is a born prize-fighter."

When Gene used the word "autonomic" in Los Angeles, Saddie Mossler of the *Los Angeles Record* wrote that none of the reporters knew what he was talking about until he explained. "After many years of interviewing high-brows, including some leading college professors and writers," Saddie wrote, "I can say I have never heard clearer diction nor noted closer adherence to grammatical rules than when Tunney talks." She was impressed but warned girls who might "fall for him" or his "Irish blue eyes" that he isn't interested in anything but fighting, "and not at all in feminine wiles."

In Portland, Oregon, Bob Swaze of the *Daily Journal* wrote that Tunney "is none of the things which Eastern reports have made him out to be. Many who came to sneer at the supposed high-hatter went away to admire a rather modest young man who is making his way through this world as a fighting machine. Tunney has none of the earmarks of the braggart."

In his dressing room backstage, Gene had a stack of books on a shelf. "He thinks George Eliot was one of the world's great women and loves her writings," wrote Swaze. "How is that for a heavyweight pugilist?"

Reporters who interviewed him found him unusually honest and forth-right for a celebrity. At one breakfast with reporters, he discussed the Chinese revolution. He made an unannounced visit to a hospital for crippled children, visited schools, dedicated buildings and attended luncheons and dinners. Elliott Metcalf of the Tacoma, Washington, *News Tribune* said, "Tunney is the type of young man who has praise for all, malice toward none. The champion, free from any self-esteem, which so many of us have been led to believe predominated in his makeup, as reports from the East have been wont to infer, did not act bored. Don't jump at conclusions or let unfavorable reports sway you against him, like so many of us, yours truly among them, have done in the past."

"He wears the bauble lightly," wrote Edgar T. Gleeson, a San Francisco columnist. "Even when he was training in the Stroudsburg camp in the Pocono Mountains, Tunney made you feel there were a lot of things more important than boxing.

"The impression has been created by some writers that Tunney has affect-ed a pose. I don't think Tunney is the least conscious he is acting differently than a heavyweight champion should. He is a fine, frank person, interested in the world in which he lives. He is more like what you would expect to find among architects or visiting diplomats."

Despite the local interviews and positive press that held him up as a model for young men and drew the attention of well-meaning mayors and civic leaders, Gene was tired of being an actor in vaudeville and a boxing curiosity in what he called a "dog and pony show." He hungered for another prizefight, a chance to defend his championship and seal his place in sports history. His goal had been to win, to make enough money to set up a life for himself, and he wasn't finished. Underneath the big words and the easy smile, he worried that the real prize, a life beyond the noisy, dirty streets where he had grown up, might elude him. He felt like a warrior on a crusade and knew that in order to get on with his life, he had to get back in the ring and beat the next man up. He hoped that man would again be Dempsey.

With a month to go before the end of his vaudeville stunt, he told a group of reporters in Portland, Oregon, that he was sick of the tour. He said the $12,000 a week he was paid had to cover so many expenses for himself and others that it was not worth the annoyance of putting up with all that he had to do.

"Tunney may never reach the peak of popularity that some of his predecessors held, but he will have the respect and admiration of all who believe that honesty, sobriety, sincerity, clean-mindedness, intelligence and unusual modesty are attributes that outlast those for which former world champions were notorious," wrote a reporter on the *Oregonian*.

Before he left the West Coast, Gene put his news clippings in a big envelope and shipped them home to his mother, who he knew would be pleased to see her boy being heralded in positive terms for a change. A prized oil portrait hanging in her new home in Riverdale showed Gene, not in boxing togs but in suit and tie, looking exactly like a local bank president. Gene saved the rest of the news clippings for himself.

He wasn't the only one who saved clippings. Bernard Shaw, who now felt he had a personal connection to Tunney, kept up with the champion's adventures through the press. Nor had Shaw's old friend Paquito Beatty, suffering both financial and physical ruin, lost his sense of gaiety or humor. When Beatty's grandnephew was born on Boxing Day, the day after Christmas in England, Beatty merrily suggested the baby be named "Dempsey."

As plans moved forward for another match between Tunney and Dempsey, between the scientific boxer and the brawler, Shaw was more interested in boxing than at any time since he had worn gloves himself.

120,000 FANS WATCH "THE LONG COUNT" FIGHT AT SOLDIER FIELD, CHICAGO.
BOTTOM: TUNNEY, BEFORE THE FIGHT (BOTH CHICAGO HISTORY MUSEUM).

CHAPTER 5

The Long Count

"I never saw anything so wonderful as Tunney's dance round the ring when he got up...with Dempsey rushing after him and slogging wildly until Gene suddenly stopped and countered with a biff that made poor Jack believe he was going to die."

G. BERNARD SHAW

The fight was scheduled to start at 4 am, London time, and fight fans crowded in anticipation around every news ticker in Fleet Street.

In Rio de Janeiro, thousands of persons thronged into Carioca Square to read bulletins posted outside the newspaper offices.

In Shanghai, clubs and bars were jammed with people elbowing one another to get close to radios. Shortwave newscasts were beamed across Europe, South America, Australia, New Zealand and South Africa. Hundreds of persons aboard the *Berengaria*, in mid-Atlantic, huddled around a deluxe "Radiola" receiver capable of picking up long-range transmissions. In Guayaquil, Equador, 6000 men and women crowded in front of *El Telegrafo* to wait for an AP news flash on the winner.

At the New Jersey State Prison in Trenton, all but four of the 500 inmates got permission to listen by radio. At Sing Sing in New York, all the convicts listened, including the nation's most notorious murderer, party girl Ruth Snyder, who was awaiting execution for the strangulation of her husband.

And in the upstairs bedroom of a house in downtown Chicago, the heavyweight champion lay stretched out on the bed for an hour and a half, slowly reading the last two chapters of Somerset Maugham's *Of Human Bondage*, a novel that explores the intellectual and emotional development of an orphan raised by a pious uncle.

Gene's friend Bernard Gimbel, chosen to escort him to the fight, and Father Francis P. Duffy, chaplain of the Fighting 69th Regiment, paced in the living room.

"Do you think he realizes what time it is?" asked a worried Father Duffy.

"Maybe not," said Gimbel. "He's alone up there, probably with his head in a book. We're late! We've got to get him down here right away." With that, Gimbel headed for the stairs, only to meet Gene casually walking down.

"Sorry," said the apologetic champion. "I lost track of time. Didn't mean to worry you. Had to finish Maugham, you know, the last few pages. It's his best." You would have thought, muttered an agitated Gimbel, that they were simply taking Gene out for ice cream and a spin in the park. They were late enough that Jack Dempsey would have to wait several minutes alone in the ring. Gimbel said Gene was so relaxed he nearly dozed off in the limousine hired to take him to the stadium.

"I'll knock that big bookworm out inside of eight rounds," Dempsey sneered the day of the fight. This was Chicago, and the Chicago crowd was a Dempsey crowd. The fight crowd gravitated to Dempsey's image as an easygoing, good-natured fellow, while characterizing Gene as a reader rather than a fighter. "The Americans do not exactly object to overconfidence," wrote *The Times* of London, "but a 'highbrow' boxing champion did rather go against the grain." Gene was 30 years old, and Dempsey was 32.

The bell for the seventh round of the world heavyweight boxing championship clanged in Chicago's Soldier Field, where more than 120,000 fans had thronged into the stadium the night of September 22, 1927, for what was billed as the second "Battle of the Century." It was the fifth and last million-dollar gate in boxing history.

During the week, trains pulling private and Pullman cars had converged on Chicago carrying Hollywood entertainers, European royalty, bankers, industrialists and politicians from Hollywood, Tulsa, Pittsburgh, Florida, New Orleans and St. Louis. Great and near-great, governors, movie stars, old-time fight kings, industrial giants, financiers, and plain sports fans arrived from all over the country. The son of the Duke of Marlborough came by private rail coach with Harold Vanderbilt, and Princess Xenia of Greece flew in with 12 friends from New York. Kings of the money market, czars of the underworld, governors and porters sat side by side, said the *Chicago Herald and Examiner,* "an open air op'ra of slug." Hotel rooms were sold out.

Crowds moved toward the stadium starting at 4 pm, six hours before the fight, as tens of thousands of people swarmed across Michigan Avenue, making it almost impossible to walk along the sidewalks in the Loop. Grant Park, adjoining the stadium along Lake Michigan, had been cleared of people, and 6000 police set up a cordon four blocks from the arena with orders to allow only ticket holders further access.

The ringside area for premier ticket holders was so vast that some of the seats were 137 rows, or several city blocks, away from the action. Spectators in the top bleachers were advised to bring opera glasses, telescopes and radios to follow what was happening far below. More than 1200 journalists from around the world gathered to capture the spectacle in print, pictures, audio and film reels. "Typewriters snarled their keys endeavoring to outdo the next machine with bombastic descriptives and double superlatives." There were enough fans to fill two Yankee Stadiums. "A sight for the ages," said James Harrison of *The New York Times.*

"The crowd stretched away so far that sitting in the heat and glare of the cone lights just under the ring, you couldn't see the last row of customers. You could only sense that they were there from the combers of sound that came

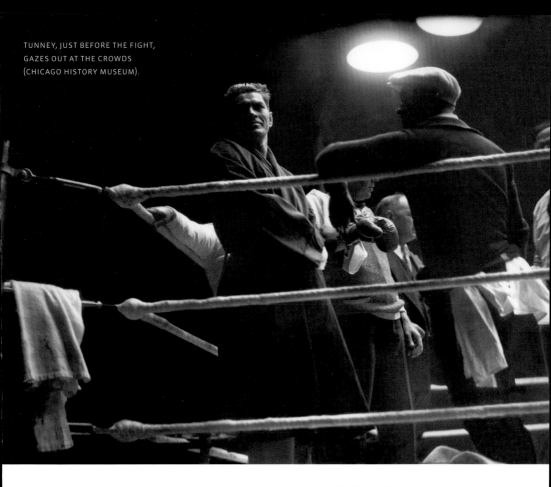

booming down the slope of the stadium out of the darkness," wrote columnist Westbrook Pegler. "The greatest boxing spectacle of all time…the mightiest throng in fight or sporting history," wrote AP's Alan Gould.

A light rain had fallen earlier, and the night was cool enough for overcoats, stadium blankets and windbreakers. British sportswriter Trevor Wignall said he was glad a chambermaid in his hotel suggested he bring the blanket off his bed. To heighten the drama and set the stage, boxing promoter Tex Rickard issued armbands to ushers that read, "Tunney-Dempsey Boxing Exhibition." Red, white and blue American flags waved in a soft, westerly wind above lighted Doric columns lining the upper battlements of the classic horseshoe-shaped coliseum. Ring posts had been gilded gold, and battered corner water buckets had been replaced with gold-painted containers that glittered like bullion under the spotlights. Even the gloves had been brought to ringside with ceremony, in boxes tied with blue ribbons.

"Never again will I witness the mass of seething humanity that jammed Soldier Field," wrote columnist Grantland Rice. To those looking out across the big stadium from ringside, it was like being surrounded by dark, moving mountains, groaning with the low murmur of thousands of voices and lit only by the occasional exit sign and flickers of cigarettes, which seemed like fireflies in the night. Fifty million people, the largest broadcast audience ever, tuned in to their home radios and crystal sets to hear announcer Graham McNamee speak to more people at one time than any man in history ever had before.

"All is darkness in the muttering mass of crowd beyond the light," said the excitable McNamee.

In Paola, Kansas, few people had radios. Ringer's Photo Studio, located on the east side of the town square, rigged a radio up to a loudspeaker in a second-floor window, and 12-year-old Laurence Smith stood with his father and older brother, Paul, in the biggest farming crowd he had ever seen or would ever see again. The Smiths, and millions like them, gathered together in town squares, outside newspaper offices and at home, holding their breath, listening to McNamee describe the awesome din: "It's like the Roman Coliseum!"

Round seven was underway.

Dempsey moved across the ring like a lion after a gazelle; such was the speed necessary to catch Tunney. In the first six rounds, Tunney deftly circled his opponent, peppering him with cool, deliberate, two-fisted fire: one-two, one-two, left jabs, straight right crosses, left hooks, right hooks. The fight was turning out to be a replay of their first match, a year earlier in Philadelphia, when Tunney took all ten rounds and the heavyweight championship. Six rounds into the rematch, Tunney had yet to lose a round.

Even for a slugger, there's more to professional boxing than hitting and bashing: there's instinct, the art of reacting to what's being thrown before it happens, anticipating the other fellow's thoughts and moving in quicksilver flashes faster than the eye can see by counter-punching, ducking or blocking. There are weeks, months, years of training muscles to respond and keep responding, even when the mind may have been slugged into oblivion. Moreover, there's the skill honed through hard-won experience of understanding an adversary's vulnerable body points and concentrating on these. Heavyweight boxing pits the most dangerous of big athletes, trained fighters throwing powerful punches that can impact the head or the stomach at 40 to 50 miles an hour or more, wielding a paralyzing force with the ever-present possibility of a fatal blow.

Most fans didn't know anatomy; moreover, many weren't close enough to see the punches landing home. They came for the knockout, the thrill of anticipation and assault as one body slammed another. Boxing in the century's most exciting sports era was very little removed from the gladiator contests of 2000 years ago, with one revealing exception: modern fans couldn't stomach death, but they still craved blood. Customers paid to see courage. Good boxers knew that if they weren't game, if they showed any yellow, they wouldn't get bouts and wouldn't get money. It was no accident that Dempsey was "The Manassa Mauler" or that Tunney was "The Fighting Marine." For fights, Dempsey wore a three-day growth of beard and bronzed his body in the sun, which gave him a rough, caveman appearance meant to intimidate opponents and excite the imagination of the fans.

Fifty seconds into the seventh round, Tunney and Dempsey moved around each other, shuffling in and out, jabbing, clinching and feinting, never taking their eyes off one another, oblivious to sounds or motion beyond the pool of light around them. Tunney was one of the ring's masters at feinting, a tactic that exasperated Dempsey fans regarded as a delaying action. The contenders broke and circled again, wary and careful. For each man, there was a career at stake as well as a world championship.

Dempsey, always the aggressor, took the fight to Tunney, and Tunney waited for it so he could do what no other boxer did as well: counterattack. He threw a straight left jab into Dempsey's face. Tunney then readied to unload his overhand right, his strongest punch, a magnificent arc of power straight from the shoulder.

Dempsey crossed over and countered with a sharp right into the left side of Tunney's face. It hit high, startling Tunney, who moved back a few steps and suddenly felt the raw burn of the ropes at his back, unable to retreat further.

Seeing an advantage, Dempsey moved forward swiftly and uncorked his favorite punch, a vicious, long, swinging left hook. It plowed into the right side of Tunney's jaw with a force that shook Tunney to his toes. His legs buckled for one of the few times in his career. Another glancing right followed as Tunney began to fall to the canvas. Dempsey let go with a second left hook that slipped through Tunney's guard and again smashed full flush into his jaw. An explosion erupted inside Tunney's brain, followed by bright lights and then darkness. He was barely conscious as Dempsey's final blows drove him to the canvas. It was the first knockdown in his professional career.

The masses at Soldier Field rose to their feet as one — shouting, screaming, waving their arms and hats, standing on the seats and jumping up and down. A knockdown is the single most dramatic moment in boxing, and a gigantic howl of pure adrenaline careened across the darkened stadium, sounding like freight trains in the night. Blocks away, listeners in restaurants and apartment buildings heard the echoes bouncing off the buildings down Michigan Avenue.

Tunney, proud of his eyesight and his ability to see what others often could not, would say later that he was stunned when Dempsey's blow found a blind spot. The suddenness and force of the hit took his breath away. A week before, a sparring partner had jabbed a glove into his right eye, leaving it red and swollen, a consequence of his refusal to wear headgear in training as did other boxers. The eye, so vital to a boxer's ability to move with lightning speed and precision, was slow by a blink.

Tunney lay there with his left glove-hand instinctively grasping at the rope, feeling "a silly sensation." Aware of hot white lights in his eyes, he smelled the familiar chalky scent of resin on the canvas, and he heard the thunderous, cannon-like roar of the crowd. He felt a painful wrenching in his right leg, as if it were snapping off at the knee. Photographs would show later that he had fallen on his side, his right leg jutting out awkwardly at an angle.

The ring spun around, stopped for a moment, then spun the other way as full consciousness returned and his head cleared. He pulled himself to a sitting position, straightened out his leg, and felt the canvas floor. It was comfortable, but the ground seemed too close. Good Lord, he thought, I must be sitting on the canvas. "I never experienced it before. I've got to get up."

Referee Dave Barry, a veteran of some 600 fights, was dressed like a bank clerk in a long-sleeved white shirt and bow tie, and sweat rolled down his face and beneath his collar from the intense heat of the arc lights over the ring. Barry was experienced and well-versed in the rules of the Illinois Athletic Commission, and he knew he was not to begin counting until Dempsey moved to a neutral corner. The referee was not the kind of man to lose his head.

Before Barry started the count, he noticed out of the corner of his eye that Dempsey had not gone to a neutral corner as instructed; he'd retreated to his own corner, just a few feet from the fallen Tunney, making it easier to get a better shot at him when he got up. Two corners of the 20-by-20-square-foot ring had been assigned to the fighters and their retinues for the one-minute break between rounds. The two remaining corners were neutral territory, to be used in the event of a knockdown.

Barry yelled at Dempsey, prodding him to move. At the same time, bedlam in the stadium made it almost impossible for even those at ringside to follow what was taking place. Reporters in the press seats were shouting at one another. Those with stopwatches couldn't follow the action. Photographers were jockeying for pictures. The judges, who were to score the bout, were yelling at people to sit down. The voice of the broadcaster, McNamee, was lost in the titanic waves of sound sweeping across the blackness. Fans listening on the radio heard only screaming, shouting and bewildering, unidentifiable confusion.

At ringside, Mrs. Vincent Astor was shouting. A stunned Mrs. Samuel Insull, who had had water from Tunney's towel splashed across her ermine, kept her handkerchief to her mouth. "I don't think Mrs. Insull could have stood much more," wrote a *Chicago Herald and Examiner* columnist.

"I can't hear! Please, tell me what's happening!" Polly Lauder remembered saying. She was listening at home with her family in Greenwich, Connecticut. "My brother George was hopping up and down, screaming, 'Get up! Get up!' All we could hear on the radio was panic and noise. It was frightening and it seemed to go on and on and on. No one came on the radio to say whether Gene was all right, whether he had been hurt. We only knew he was down."

At the start of the fight, Barry had called the boxers, their trainers and seconds to the center of the ring. "Both you boys have received a book of rules of this boxing commission," he said. "They are the rules under which you are going to fight." He went on to remind them that the rules had been discussed with their representatives at the commission for several days.

THE CONTROVERSY: IN ROUND SEVEN, DEMPSEY FLOORED TUNNEY, BUT FAILED
TO MOVE TO A NEUTRAL CORNER — DELAYING THE START OF THE COUNT, AND GIVING
TUNNEY EXTRA TIME TO RECOVER FROM THE FIRST AND ONLY KNOCKDOWN OF HIS
CAREER (BOTH CHICAGO HISTORY MUSEUM).

Barry reminded the fighters that the rabbit punch, aimed at the back of the skull, and the kidney punch, dangerous and sometimes fatal, were outlawed. Then he continued: "Now I want to get this one point clear. In the event of a knockdown, the man scoring the knockdown will go to the farthest neutral corner. Is that clear, Jack? Is that clear, Champ?"

Both fighters nodded yes. Tunney remembered that it was the first time he had been called "Champ" in the ring before a fight. Champ had always been Dempsey. Barry continued, repeating that in the event of a knockdown, he would not begin the count unless the fighter scoring went to the farthest neutral corner. Again, he asked if they understood. Again, Tunney and Dempsey had nodded yes.

Now, the seething humanity that was Soldier Field roared like a hurricane thundering down from the distant bleachers, shaking the big stadium to its foundations. Police on security at the far perimeters of the stadium tensed, even as most could not avert their eyes from the small, lighted square at the center of the black vortex.

"It was a picture that should have been seen from the air, from the cockpit of an airplane, where the lights and shadows and the blacks and whites of the panorama could have been viewed in their proper perspective," wrote Harrison of the *Times*.

For approximately five seconds before he started counting, Barry continued to yell at Dempsey, pushing at him to move away. But Dempsey ignored the referee and angrily grunted, "I stay here." Then, as if it suddenly dawned on him that he was being penalized or heard his trainer screaming from outside the ring, Dempsey abruptly headed to the neutral corner as was required. Only then did Barry begin to count. ONE. TWO.

Tunney heard the count of "Two," looked up at the referee at "Three," and glanced over to his corner where his chief second, Jimmy Bronson, and his manager, Billy Gibson, were outside the ropes. Their eyes nervous, they yelled at him to stay down until nine, the final second, before springing up at the ten count.

Jimmy Bronson was someone Tunney trusted, a referee from his Marine days in Europe and a man of character in a sport that attracted many unsavory people. As chief second, he acted as Tunney's eyes and ears. The blue-and-scarlet bathrobe Tunney wore into the ring was emblazoned on the back with the emblem of the Marine Corps, and disabled Marines sat at ringside as his guests. In the dressing room before the first fight against Dempsey, "Bow-tie Jimmy" had put his face next to Tunney's and roared into his ear, "You were molded by fate for the task that faces you. Out of two million men who responded to our country's call, you have been delegated to wrest the title from Dempsey. You *can't* fail. You must not fail!" And for Jimmy and the Marines, he hadn't, then. And he didn't intend to now.

Tunney waited in the sitting position, ready to spring, rehearsing in his head the months of training and roadwork, the jogging backwards five grueling miles, day after day, all preparing for just this possibility. "I had often thought that I might be knocked down some time," he said. "I had considered ways to offset that moment, when and if it came." He would remember that he felt his mind focus with an energy that he always believed gave him immense, even superhuman, powers to concentrate and think and utilize untapped reserves of strength and fortitude.

A knockdown is a fighter's ultimate crisis, the instant in battle when he has to prove he's a general in the ring. Whether a boxer can physically and mentally handle those seconds on the canvas determines not only who wins the fight but often marks the rest of his career. Through clearing eyes, Tunney saw Bronson in the bright lights on the other side of the ropes and nodded.

"The boxer who knows his business after he has been knocked down, remains down until the count of nine," said Tunney later. "Those nine seconds belong to him, not to his opponent. They are his and his alone. Only a foolish person, with perhaps some false pride, comes bounding to his feet before he has his nine seconds' rest." Strategy and the intelligence to use it were his strengths, and Gene knew it.

As he waited for the count of nine, Tunney became momentarily aware of the pandemonium around him. "The prize ring is a terrifying place. You're on a platform glaring with bright light. All around, you see the dim expanse of the crowd. Faces nearby are clearly lighted by the glare. You see expressions of frantic excitement, emotions produced by sympathetic reaction, fear, the lust for battle, rage, gloating, savagery, mouths open and yelling. You hear the roar, individual voices screaming through — cheers, jubilation, anger, menace. It is the howl of the mob for blood."

At ringside, his face white against the lights, was his friend Brian Bell, the wire-service reporter. He saw Father Duffy behind him, his eyes closed, praying. One row back was Sam Pryor, who had spent the night before the fight in Tunney's hotel room to be sure, Sam said, that no one broke in. Sam had refused to let him eat food without tasting it first and he had thrown out a half-full water bottle because he didn't know who opened it. "Bad people want to slow you down," said the careful Sam.

In a thunderous chorus, the crowd was shouting savagely for Tunney's scalp. "Kill him!! Kill him!!" screamed 10,000 voices. "Come on, Jack — finish it!" The referee, Barry, later wrote that he had felt a physical force that "swept down on the three of us from the far reaches of Soldier Field. Maybe it was vibrations. I know not just what to call it. But someday if a great torrent of water should suddenly strike me, I think the effect of that torrent might approximate the force of that mysterious blow."

At the crest of that tidal yell, Barry's right arm started to drop. Tunney focused and suddenly jerked himself to his feet. He was up.

"TEN!" bellowed Barry.

The crowd was suddenly, uncommonly hushed, as if air had been sucked from the gigantic stadium. The two fighters began to circle again. The pro-Dempsey throng waited grudgingly for the next opportunity to have their hero demolish this interloper and become the first champion to win back the crown. Tunney's mind instinctively concentrated and closed out all noise, all movement, all sense of place except for the big man facing him, and he registered instant relief that his legs seemed in working order. He had by now boxed 16 rounds with Dempsey, and he'd never lost a round. Gene instinctively followed his training. He hoofed it backwards, zigzagging across the ring away from Dempsey, feeling stronger and more confident with each step. You see, but you don't hear, he said of such moments. The brain registers only what it needs to tap the inner power for survival.

TUNNEY PUMMELS DEMPSEY IN ROUND EIGHT (CHICAGO HISTORY MUSEUM).

The snarling Dempsey rushed forward, eyes smoldering and head bowed, jaw tucked down behind his shoulder and body bent forward. By crouching, Dempsey made himself shorter, more elusive, harder to hit. His strong left-glove hand was cocked, waiting. This time, however, Tunney deflected Dempsey's left hook by quickly sidestepping. Dempsey tried to follow Tunney in his backward retreat, swinging futilely into the air, and Tunney realized that if he could stay out of range from the plodding Dempsey, he might still win.

Tunney took his time, skating sideways around the ring like a dancer, staying just out of reach. As Dempsey drove in with his plunging, desperate attack, Tunney lunged forward with a straight right cross that landed squarely on Dempsey's temple. Stunned, Dempsey tried to keep up, but Tunney kept changing direction and was now circling to his right. Tunney lunged forward with an overhand right and hit Dempsey hard on the cheekbone. Dempsey's knees sagged into the clinch. The referee separated them.

Tunney renewed circling to his left, and now Dempsey seemed to be thinking, Why am I chasing this guy? He stopped in the middle of the ring, pawed the air with his gloves and despairingly motioned to Tunney, yelling, "Come on and fight." The crowd resumed its cheers for Dempsey, but Tunney kept his distance. Gene would later call Dempsey's taunt, beckoning him to come in dangerously close, a grandstand gesture and an invitation that only an inexperienced prizefighter would accept. At the same time, Tunney sensed the truth in Dempsey's eyes: he's discouraged, he's going to lose, and he knows it.

With another opening, Tunney threw what might have been his hardest blow: a straight, six-inch right that hit directly under Dempsey's heart. Dempsey grunted and bent forward, his arms close to his body, weaving until the bell rang, ending the round — a round that would live in people's minds for as long as they talk about boxing. The fight went three more rounds, and Tunney retained the championship. Dempsey never fought again.

As Gene had waited for the count of nine to get up, ten fight fans listening to the radio in six different states had died of heart attacks. Two more died immediately after the Long Count. Many more fainted from it, including Gene's older sister, Maude, a nun, listening at home with the family. Nana was so overcome, she couldn't bear to listen to the rest of the fight. She went to her bedroom to say her prayers. The millions listening on the radio couldn't visualize the approximately five seconds it took for the referee to get Dempsey to move to the neutral corner and many felt Tunney spent several minutes on the canvas.

The following day, the fight was the top story on the front page of virtually every newspaper in America, if not the world. Word of the outcome reached London, and "within a few minutes papers giving a description of the fight and the result were selling on the streets."

"He was a consummate boxer in the best classical tradition; his physique was magnificent, his boxing unsurpassed," said Lord Knebworth in London of the winner. The Marquis of Douglas and Clydesdale, an amateur boxer whose ancestors had served Charles II, pushed into the champion's dressing room and found Gene sitting calmly, while around him, "attendants and friends were breathless in their joy."

The chairman of the Shakespeare Memorial Theatre at Stratford-on-Avon, Archibald B. Flower, revealed that during the vaudeville tour, Tunney had spent two hours alone looking over a fine Shakespearean collection in Victoria, British Columbia. "One might by a little stretch of the imagination in a psychological position claim that Shakespeare helped Tunney beat Dempsey," he said.

Bernard Shaw sent out for copies of every daily and sporting newspaper in London and read the accounts round by round, mesmerized by reports of Tunney's dramatic recovery. When, two weeks later, Shaw attended a private showing of the fight film, he dismissed contemptuously a screen caption which implied that Tunney should have lost because he took full advantage of the count.

"Stuff and nonsense," said Shaw. "Tunney is quite able to get up. He is watching the referee closely. He has got his wits about him."

"You see — his eyes have cleared!" an excited Shaw was quoted as saying as he peered at the prone Tunney on screen.

Shaw saw Tunney's craft and ring shrewdness as a measure of intelligence. "He does not need to be a brilliant boxer like Carpentier or a terror like Dempsey; he wins by mental and moral superiority combined with plenty of strength, an inaccessible head, and that very disheartening biff that sickened Dempsey when he rushed for an apparently certain victory after the count in the seventh round."

For Shaw, the championship had been drama of the highest caliber, a contest with an outcome he could not have imagined and no one would have believed if he had written it. The scientific fighter, the Cashel Byron, had defeated the mauler Billy Paradise in a fight that would go down as one of the most dramatic in boxing history. It was nothing short of a storybook fantasy come to life. Who could have imagined such a thing?

Later, when told ringside tickets were sold for $40 apiece, the highest price ever charged for a sporting event, Shaw guffawed and snapped, "What mugs!" Soon, said Shaw, not realizing how right he was, these things will be broadcast all over the world and everyone will be listening to them. He suggested that the next championship be held in a studio with nobody present but the seconds, the referee and the showmen.

The gated receipts totaled $2,658,660. In 2010 currency, fans paid $31 million to attend the fight, a record for on-site attendance that is still unmatched. Tunney's purse for the night was $990,445.54 ($11.5 million in

2010 dollars), the highest amount that had ever been paid to an athlete, and because he wanted to hold a check for one million dollars in his hand, he wrote a personal check for the difference so the promoter could give him the one million he had dreamed of. (For years, a photocopy of the million-dollar check hung in Gene's garage, next to his car.) Dempsey received $425,000.

Dempsey would later admit that he had forgotten the rules and that the Long Count was entirely his fault, adding that one blow he received after Tunney got up almost killed him. "The right-hand punch under the heart that Tunney hit me with in the seventh round was the hardest blow I've ever received. It was not a question in my mind of being knocked out — I thought I was going to die. I could not get my breath."

History refers to the Chicago fight as the "Long Count," the most controversial three minutes in boxing history, because Tunney had those approximately five extra seconds to recover from his knockdown, setting off one of the longest debates in sports. Dempsey fans thought their man was robbed — that when Tunney went down, the count should have started immediately and not stopped, no matter the rules. They believed that Tunney could not have gotten back up in time, or, if he had, that his legs would not have carried him through the rest of the fight. Tunney fans said their guy used his head, his training and his skills as a thinking man's fighter to defeat a brawler fair and square.

In Connecticut, at the big house on Lake Avenue owned by the Lauders, there was celebration. Polly and her family listened to the radio reports of the fight, well aware that Polly and Gene had taken what her mother called "a fancy" to one another. They were pouring champagne when, in a post-fight interview, Gene said the words from ringside that went straight to Polly's heart, words that 80 years later, she could still remember with a shiver of girlish delight:

"Good evening," he said, "especially to all my friends in Greenwich."

Especially. *Especially!* He had told her he would think of her, and if he won the fight, she must listen and he would send her a secret message that she, and only she, would understand. And with millions of listeners, while still standing in the ring with his towel around his shoulders, he had reached out to her "especially."

It was a melody, she said, the most beautiful she had ever heard.

THE NEWLY-WED TUNNEYS, 1930, IN PALM BEACH, FLORIDA (AP IMAGES/ASSOCIATED PRESS).

CHAPTER 6

Love Story

"Thinking in a prizefight is as solitary
an exercise of mind as writing poetry."
GENE TUNNEY

In what deep pocket of the heart does love begin to stir, especially when distance seems so great? She said she never could have imagined meeting a boxer, an Irish Catholic at that, a city man with humble roots. "It would have been like looking from the carriage of a train and perhaps seeing a worker toiling in the fields far, far off. In the normal way of things, our paths simply would never have crossed," she said. "Our lives, you see, were in completely different circles. In those days, Greenwich Village and Greenwich, Connecticut, might have been continents away from each other."

"Love! I fall into the claws of time," wrote Francis Thompson, one of Gene's favorite poets.

Polly remembered sitting at her ivory, hand-painted dressing table fumbling with pearls, trying to decide if the necklace suited her outfit and worried, mostly, that it didn't. She didn't think she was very good with jewelry, not like her mother and her older sister, Katherine, whom she called "Cotton" or "Cot," and who always dressed impeccably. She heard the doorbell, the footsteps of dear old "Dowie" McDonald shuffling across the polished wood floor, heard Dowie open the door, and panicked. Why, oh why, she wondered, had she promised Cot that she was free to have dinner with Gene Tunney, the boxer? She had homework for Helen Ufford's English class, and she was working desperately to finish her last year at the prestigious Lenox School with honors.

Cot, who was four years older, had met the boxer at parties she'd attended with her husband, Edward Dewing. In comparison with her gregarious older sister, Polly considered herself painfully shy. She would rather read Keats and Shelley than spend time meeting socialites and college men flirting over idle chatter among the "flapper set." She was frustrated that between Cot and their friend, Sam Pryor, she was constantly being egged on and pushed to engage in social functions. She was comfortable with her girl chums, and she dismissed Cot's insistence that in approaching her 19th birthday, she ought to meet some boys. Was this a date?

"Think of it as dinner," Cot had said. "Definitely *not* a date." So she had reluctantly agreed.

"I heard his voice first. I was sitting at my dressing table in the bedroom when Dowie let him in the door. I was dreadfully nervous, wringing my hands, ready to feign sickness on the spot!" Dowie, a longtime retainer of the Lauders, had moved into the family apartment on Fifth Avenue as chaperone when Polly chose to attend school in New York City. "Dowie knitted all day while I was at school. Then I came home, we ate, I did homework, and we both went to bed. That was pretty much it."

Polly opened the bedroom door just enough to peek out. She saw the broad back of a tall man in a dark suit with thick hair so wavy that even the close crop couldn't stop waves from floating like brown crescents around his head. The overhead light of the sitting room picked up flecks of red in his hair. which seemed to dance like a burnished halo.

"They were laughing and telling stories! You would think Dowie was an old washerwoman reunited with a lost son. I just couldn't believe it." Dowie's reaction was as reassuring as it was surprising. "Dowie was strictly formal with mother's friends."

Polly took several deep breaths, mustered her courage and went out to meet her escort feeling like a terrified Bambi meeting the king of the forest. Hearing her, he turned around. "His eyes! His luminous, brilliant, beautiful blue eyes. That's what I remember," she said, "I was speechless. I can't remember for the life of me whether I uttered a single word the whole night. I just remember those piercing blue eyes."

The Gene that Polly met was, at nearly 29, a decade older than she was, but he had no more experience than she with the opposite sex. Like Shaw's Cashel Byron, he had never dated or even taken a girl out to dinner. He had agreed to the evening only because he especially liked Kay Lauder Dewing, whom he saw frequently at gatherings in Greenwich.

Like Polly, Gene had a modest, shy nature, and as the oldest son of a highly protective Irish Catholic mother, he was almost fanatical in his caution toward women who sought to become friends. External passions embarrassed him, and he felt that few things were more unpleasant than being marked as a ladies' man, a label that to him suggested a male weakness and a propensity to seduce women with unwarranted compliments, instead of living a life of physical and spiritual discipline. There was no room in his life for sexuality. When asked, he always said that he was too busy training to consider courtship.

At dinner, Gene had been surprised that the pretty Miss Lauder, unlike her enthusiastic sister Kay and most women he met, showed no interest at all in his ring career, even as polite conversation. Miss Lauder never even asked him a question about boxing. He wondered if it were perhaps because she thought he was uninteresting, even boring. He wasn't sure, but for the first time in his life, he felt a little like a boy meeting a beautiful princess, and he wished his social skills were more polished. She was shy, with the patina acquired naturally in a girl growing up with cultural advantages. She was most animated when he mentioned he had heard Caruso sing at the Metropolitan

Opera, and she smiled broadly when he referred to Robert Herrick: "Gather ye rosebuds while ye may / Old time is still a-flying; / And this same flower that smiles today / Tomorrow will be dying."

Over the next 18 months, when Gene was a guest at the Pryors' mansion in Greenwich, Gene and Polly saw one another casually at parties, lunches and concerts, but always in the company of other friends, as part of a group. The quiet Polly, by now a student at the fashionable Finch finishing school for young women in New York City, considered their relationship platonic. She said she had "never dreamed that such a handsome, intelligent man could be really interested in me." Her heart sometimes wished it could be so, she said, but her mind told her that this articulate man who was frequently the center of attention, who so easily quoted Shakespeare in conversation and kept poems in his pocket, a man whom nearly all other women, both married and single, found fascinating and romantic, could never focus on her alone. They never dated. He never asked.

At the same time, Tunney, as champion, was ever more the center of speculation about his love life.

"They would bring girls to him, thinking he'd like to have a little sex, and he would have no part of it," said his friend Pryor. "I knew the girls who tried to get him and how he treated them. He was what you might call a prude. He was a handsome, tough, rough guy — a good object for a girl to want to have sex with. But Gene was very strict. He didn't go out with girls." He thought actions toward women spoke louder than words. (Years later in Manila, he marched out of a hotel ballroom after the hosts surprised him at the speaker's table with scantily clad dancing girls.)

Pryor began to notice that his friend Gene, who had never much liked large social gatherings, and the demure Polly Lauder, who didn't like them either, usually turned up at his parties and were sometimes seen chatting with one another. "I thought, Ah-ha!" said Pryor. "I pushed him, but Gene didn't talk about girls, as the usual fellow might."

It wasn't until the summer of 1927, only weeks before the second fight with Dempsey in Chicago, that Gene and Polly overcame their hesitation toward each other: "[Cashel] took the hand timidly, and gave it a little shake, not daring to meet her eyes." Polly was to depart by ship for France at the end of September to attend a Finch program in Versailles, and she would be abroad and out of touch until early the following year.

Sam Pryor, an unusually personable fellow who collected people as eagerly as deacons collect souls, was hosting an evening dinner dance to celebrate the end of summer. The Pryors' sprawling family estate facing Long Island Sound was decked in masses of round, pastel-colored tables and summer flowers. Candlelight lit the great drawing room with its antique English furniture, paintings and old china, and paper lanterns were hung on the terrace and around the tennis court. The setting was picture perfect, a scene from a novel. There were Rockefellers, Wall Street brokers, men from Yale and visitors from Philadelphia and Washington. Young women in chiffon danced cheek-to-cheek with tanned young men in tuxedos as a popular band played music under a large white tent. Gene, in training for his rematch with Dempsey, was a surprise guest. He and Polly found themselves seated at the same table, side by side.

After dinner, the boxer and the girl strolled alone down the sloping lawn of the Pryors' home toward the pier for the family boats, leaving the sounds of the piano and saxophone and the revelry behind them. Across the channel, sailboats bobbed at anchor at the exclusive Indian Harbor Yacht Club, where Polly's father had been one of the club's most distinguished commodores.

Beyond were the distant lights of waterside communities on Long Island. Polly had grown up near the sea and cherished the sense of space and security the water gave her, much as Gene had been drawn to the docks near his home in Greenwich Village. They watched white clouds drift aimlessly around the moon and talked about Percy Bysshe Shelley, a romantic who died tragically at age 29 when his sailboat overturned during a storm. Gene mentioned that Shelley's lyric drama *Prometheus Unbound* was one of his favorites:

> All love is sweet
> Given or returned,
> Common as light is love,
> And its familiar voice wearies not ever...
> They who inspire it most are fortunate,
> As I am now; but those who felt it most
> Are happier still.

There, on the shores of the Sound, in the moonlight, they held tight to one another, oblivious of his engagement in Chicago or her date to sail overseas. It was the first time Gene had kissed a girl, she said ("One knows"), and she hoped with all her heart that their moment could last.

> And the moonbeams kiss the sea;
> What are all these kissings worth
> If thou kiss not me?

By month's end — and after she had heard Gene's memorable words of greeting at the end of the Chicago fight — Polly departed for Europe with her classmates as scheduled, taking her books, her poetry and the breathless wonder that she was falling in love. Gene had promised he would stay in touch.

"Wreaths!" she said. "He kept sending funeral wreaths to France! The other girls with me couldn't believe it, and neither could I. We didn't even know where to put them. Have you tried to water a wreath? I'm sure he just ordered the biggest, most expensive thing he could find, and maybe the French misunderstood what he wanted. But week after week of funeral wreaths got to be quite hilarious. I couldn't help but pay attention to him."

She told her school chums that her admirer was "an old friend of my sister Kay" and was not someone she would ever be seriously interested in, an easy subterfuge because Polly was known for favoring poetry over boys. Only her friend and teacher Helen Ufford knew better.

In early 1928, after Polly's return from Europe (and "enough wreaths to fill a cemetery"), they saw each other more frequently, though always among other people. Both found it awkward to try to carry on a courtship in public, and they had only snippets of time alone. Each glance, each smile, became important, each gesture shared but unspoken. One of Polly's favorite photographs, taken at a reception, shows two tanned young people smiling in a crowd, intimate yet distant. Other people can be seen in the background totally unaware that the boxing champion's eyes are on a beautiful young woman too far away from him to reach out and touch.

Gene didn't want to lose Polly. She had come to embody everything he wanted in life. She was poetic, caring and thoughtful — an angel in human form, he said — and she represented the best of the world he envisioned for himself. In his wildest dreams, he hadn't thought he would follow in the footsteps of Shaw's boxing hero Cashel Byron, and be able to meet a beautiful, cultivated woman and fall in love with her, and she with him. He began to consider how he could wrap up his professional life and win Polly's heart for good.

Gene had contracted to defend his championship later in the year. He hoped it would be a third title bout against Dempsey so that he could prove once and for all that he deserved the title, but his old adversary declined the fight. To keep himself busy, Gene focused on meeting a wider range of people and exploring business contacts. He corresponded with the British novelist Hugh Walpole, whom he had met while both were visiting Portland, Oregon, in 1927. Walpole sent him an autographed copy of his book *Fortitude*, and a bound set of his complete works. "The most valuable Christmas present I have ever received," gushed an appreciative Gene.

In New York, Gene attended a party in his honor and the guest list included F. Scott Fitzgerald, author of *The Great Gatsby*, and his wife, Zelda. "Fitzgerald stuck close to Tunney all evening and did not want to leave," wrote author Matthew J. Bruccoli. Afterwards, Fitzgerald sent Gene a copy of the English translation of Oswald Spengler's *The Decline of the West*. "Dear Mr. Tunney," wrote Fitzgerald on the front endpaper. "I couldn't find either Boyd's book or Brown's book. This is an extraordinary thing you've perhaps heard of — the idea that civilizations have as definite mortality as people."

While visiting Miami Beach over the holidays, Gene received a letter at his hotel from another author, Thornton Wilder, introducing himself. Always eager to discuss books, Gene responded enthusiastically by inviting the bouncy, ebullient Wilder to breakfast. Then, learning that his guest liked music as he did, Gene secretly arranged that the waiter be an opera singer. Midway through their scrambled eggs, they were serenaded by a rendition of the toreador song.

But Gene was unable to find a way to spend time with the one person he most desired to be with, Polly Lauder. By this point in his career, Gene was recognized virtually everywhere he went. One author wrote that the only other Americans who were as well known — though slightly less accessible — were President Calvin Coolidge and Charles Lindbergh. The couple felt they could not meet at Polly's home and certainly not at his hotel suite, they did not want friends to be aware they were courting for fear the secret would leak out to newspapers. They needed a safe place where they could become better acquainted while divesting themselves of the stereotypes of rich girl meeting pug that hung over their romance.

"I have an idea!" said Helen Ufford, the high school and college teacher who had become a close friend of both. Helen was a spirited, optimistic woman with *joie de vivre* who sympathized with their plight. Aside from Polly's married sister, she was the only one in whom Polly confided.

"I have a small apartment we could use, but only if I were chaperone. It *must* be our secret," warned Helen, who also knew Polly's mother and did not wish to be regarded as a traitor. Helen's apartment on West 58th Street in Manhattan, had a Victrola, stacks of phonograph records and shelves of books. "Marmalade and toast. A teacher's lodging on a teacher's salary," she said. In the afternoons, sun streamed through the window of Helen's small sitting room, brightening the chintz and worn Persian rug, accentuating the closeness and intimacy of the couple's hours together in a way that paneled drawing rooms and formal social gatherings never allowed.

"It was there, in that tiny little apartment, where we really got to know one another, where we fell deeply in love," remembered Polly. They took turns reading aloud poems such as John Keats's epic, *Endymion*, the name given her father's 136-foot schooner. The words of the poem were so deeply touching to her that she had made a pilgrimage to Keats's grave in Rome during a visit to Italy in 1924, taking a picture of the poet's tombstone for her personal scrapbook. She gave Gene a copy of the picture and he kept it in his traveling bag, as much a reminder of Keats as of where Polly once stood on the grass in Rome.

"A thing of beauty is a joy forever," the poem's opening, is Keats's most famous line. *Endymion* tells the story of a Greek myth about a mortal, a handsome shepherd who, while asleep guarding his flock, is visited by the moon goddess Selene, who falls in love with him. The love is mutual, and tormented by his longing for Selene, Endymion shares his love story with his sister, Peona. Eventually, Endymion and Selene are joined. The sister, Peona, is left behind in the wonder of it all: [Endymion] "...knelt down / Before his goddess, in a blissful swoon. / She gave her fair hands to him, and behold, /

Before three swiftest kisses he had told, / They vanished far away!"

For the love-struck Gene and Polly, *Endymion* became a metaphor for their secret romance. Gene, represented by the young shepherd boy, was hopelessly in love with his goddess, Polly. They envisioned their life together on a magic carpet, spirited away from the sweat of the docks, from the dullness and suffocation of a rich, sheltered childhood and from the ungrateful boxing public and chiding publicity. Gene was no longer poor and felt he could afford a lifestyle that included culture, and one day, a wife. Polly relished travel and adventure, and in Gene, she saw a strong but tender, romantic man who shared her intellectual interests and deep yearning for independence and autonomy and who wanted desperately to keep learning, as she did.

They talked about Shakespeare, William Wordsworth, Lord Byron and other romantic poets, with Gene often quoting passages by heart. Gene told Polly about his embarrassing public tête-à-tête with Shaw over *Cashel Byron*. They read aloud from *Saint Joan*, which both thought one of Shaw's finest works, and they listened for hours to music and opera. He liked Wagner, Chopin and Richard Strauss, and she chose Handel, Gluck, Gounod and Puccini. Gene showed her the poems he carried in his pocket, such as Stephen Philipps's *Marpessa*, based on a tragic story from the *Iliad*. They had so much to talk about, there was never enough time. The boxer from the docks and the shy rich girl who buried herself in 19th-century classics had found their bond through poetry, music and literature.

As they got to know each other, Gene began to absorb nuances that would help him use his colossal energies to cross the cultural divide between prizefighting and life on the manicured lawns of Connecticut. They found meaning in values they shared — for compassion, honesty, tolerance, loyalty and generosity — but above all, they shared romance. He learned to waltz and two-step, with Helen as the teacher. Polly convinced Gene to dispense with a large diamond ring that he wore on the third finger of his left hand as a symbol of his achievements ("Not the kind of jewelry that would be appreciated in Greenwich"). She admired his devotion to his family, whom he was supporting on his boxing earnings, and he was amazed that such a wealthy girl needed so little to be happy. Her quest for a life of more than material possessions and social conventions mirrored Gene's own aspirations.

"Those were wonderful times," said Polly, "and always *very* proper, of course, because Helen was always there with us. She protected our secret." Gene brought fresh flowers; Polly's donations were cucumber, chicken and grape jelly sandwiches, egg custards, Dowie's chocolate cookies and tea cakes; and Helen brewed tea. They laughed that they would have to take up Gene's training regime or get fat from all that eating. "She was one of our dear and most beloved friends," Gene wrote of their chaperone. Without Helen's help and support, the courtship would almost certainly have foundered.

Only once were they nearly discovered.

"A woman in Helen's apartment building ran into her one morning and said, 'Dear me — didn't I see Gene Tunney on the elevator yesterday going to your apartment?' Helen, quick on the uptake, simply replied, 'You *must* be mistaken. I don't know a Gene Tunney. Who is he?'"

Careful not to risk a publicity lapse that would expose his secret, Gene tiptoed around questions regarding marriage. "Maybe I shall marry after 1932," he told the *New York Evening World*. "I have decided I shall then be too old to fight." He told one interviewer that his secretary looked after the 60 to 80 mash notes he received weekly from women fans.

The Hearst Hollywood columnist, Louella Parsons, said Gene might enter the priesthood. "Women don't interest Gene in the slightest. Ask any feminine reporter who has tried to interview him."

He treated women reporters on an equal basis with men, and women were comfortable in his presence. Once, during training, he discovered a sparring partner making unwanted passes at a woman working at the camp. "Didn't I tell all you to keep away from girls while you're training here?" scolded Gene. "You're fired."

He had by this time fought and won two championship bouts, yet was still hounded by stories that he was "high-toning his profession." In the *New York World*, Hype Igore wrote, "This battle, twice fought between Gene and Jack, has divided everybody. You are either a downright Tunney man or you are a shouting Dempseyite. Perhaps Dempsey dotes on Puccini, and Tunney idolizes Brahms. Jack may rave over Monet, and Gene may cheer for Manet. Who cares?"

Winning the championship and the million dollars that came with it gave Gene tremendous confidence, but as he grew closer to Polly and away from his own roots in the Village, he was acutely aware that unlike many of her social group, he lacked a university degree, making him an outsider once again, this time in a world of Ivy League graduates. He felt he was sometimes made to look disadvantaged; if asked where he had received his schooling, he hid any embarrassment behind a quick mind and knowledge of literature. With his new friends, he wanted to be known as more than a champion prizefighter, but he was wary of repeating the missteps he had made with the boxing crowd.

Over the winter, Gene had been introduced to William Lyon Phelps, known as Professor Billy to his students, an English professor at Yale University in New Haven, Connecticut, a friend to many authors and aspiring authors, and a teacher with a reputation for bringing literature to life in unorthodox ways.

"Why do you read Shakespeare?" Professor Phelps wanted to know.

"He has taught me about life," replied Gene, "and all that's beautiful in it." As an eighth-grader, he had played a small part in *Hamlet* and had been given the part of Antonio in *The Merchant of Venice*, until a prank caused the nuns to yank him from the final performance. He startled Phelps by saying that until he joined the Marines, he had never appreciated Shakespeare, that is, he had never read the Bard as one might read a book or a poem and never thought of a play as more than action on a stage.

On the way to Europe with the 11th Marine Regiment, Gene's education changed dramatically over a minor incident: a seasick company clerk grabbed the young Marine's dress shirt to use as a towel, and when Gene needed that same shirt clean for inspection and couldn't produce it, he was punished with 24 hours of kitchen duty. In order to apologize, the clerk, a bookish man, offered Gene a copy of Shakespeare's *The Winter's Tale*. Gene reported that he read the play ten times with the clerk as his tutor to thoroughly understand it.

Later, he went on to read all of Shakespeare's plays, memorizing many passages. Gene's story of his introduction to Shakespeare was, at heart, the story of how he mastered much of literature, reading his way through his self-devised college courses. Never too proud to say he didn't know something, he was also never too proud to ask for help. Gene was openly eager to learn. He invited learned men to his training camp to tutor him. He listened well, and he kept notes of questions and answers that troubled him.

"I was impressed with him," said Phelps. "He is a reader of good books, and has taste and intelligence." Phelps invited Tunney to speak at Yale.

When Gene told Polly, she worried that a school like Yale, a bastion of social aristocrats, might not take kindly to a boxer. Polly's father and uncles had attended the university, and she had visited the imposing walls, court-yards and English-style quads and seen Harkness Tower's granite masks of Homer, Virgil, Dante and Shakespeare. Yale's roots dated to the 1640s, when colonial clergymen first led the effort to establish a college in New Haven, and it was one of the oldest universities in the country. Its arched doorways, pav-ing-stone walkways, lawns and wrought-iron grillwork reminded her of old monasteries she had visited in Europe.

"He doesn't know what he's getting into. How can you let him do it?" she pleaded to Sam Pryor, a Yale graduate.

"I told her that no one tells Gene anything," said Pryor. "He's his own man, but she was worried he would be eaten alive."

On the day of Gene's appearance, the three-story-high Cathedral Room in Harkness Hall was jammed with 400 students and members of the press. More stood in the hallways, craning their heads to peer inside or waiting outside on the lawn. Special police had to be called to force Gene through the crowd. "The scene was like a pitched battle, a crowd storming the place, jam-ming, pushing and shouting," he remembered. These were college students and erudite people who cared about books and knowledge and who com-manded respect with words, not fists.

Sunlight drifted in shadows through the long, mullioned, leaded-glass windows. Above Gene was a vaulted ceiling and stone plates carved with the names of Yale presidents dating from 1701. He felt as if he were in West-minster Abbey. Gene knew that nothing in the world of boxing reflected his hopes for the future as closely as this moment. As he stepped to the podium, he shoved his fists in his jacket pockets to cover his nervousness, smiled and took a deep breath. He had seen the lecture as a resplendent moment for him, much like stepping into the ring on that rainy Philadelphia night to win the championship. Here, at one of the most prestigious universities in the world, he felt he was finally putting the life of the streets squarely behind him and walking through a looking glass toward a new beginning.

"Why have I been invited to speak at Yale?" he asked, his voice quaver-ing. "I have been invited because I am the champion boxer of the world. But how long do you suppose that will last?" He had their attention. He relaxed, talked louder and quicker, and, as always, chose his words carefully so that there would be no mistaking his meaning.

"Ten years from now, nobody will care what I do or what I say. It is important for me therefore to make the most of the present moment, for the present moment is all I have."

"Tunney used no notes," wrote Phelps. "He spoke informally for three-quarters of an hour. He told the students they had had every educational

TUNNEY, WITH WILLIAM LYON PHELPS (LEFT), AT YALE UNIVERSITY IN 1928 (TUNNEY COLLECTION).

advantage and he had had none. But when you are graduated and out in the world, he said, then your case will be like mine. You will have to do it all for yourself. If you succeed, it will be because you have had the necessary will-power and perseverance."

Gene told the students that one of the Shakespeare plays most intriguing to him was the little-known *Troilus and Cressida*. Though he didn't say so, he was undoubtedly aware that it was also a play of particular interest to Bernard Shaw. In 1884, Shaw had prepared a provocative paper on the play for the New Shakespeare Society in London, drawing attention to the dramatist's treatment of the professional swordsmen in the story, and to Cressida, a character Shaw considered Shakespeare's first thoughtful and liberated woman. The play is a medieval story set during the Trojan War.

Drawing parallels from the play, Gene discussed his own world of boxing. He described a passage in *Troilus and Cressida* in which the Trojan hero, Hector, challenges the Greek army to send him their best fighter, saying combat between the two will decide the outcome of the Trojan War. The Greek champion, Achilles, who could save the day, has angrily withdrawn to his tent to sulk because of a bad turn done to him by the leader of the Greek forces. Ulysses, the crafty Greek general, puts Ajax into the limelight to make Achilles feel passed over, hoping to provoke him into fighting the Trojan.

"Ajax was just a great big ambitious fellow like Jack Sharkey, given to extended mouthing. He didn't have the stuff, and the Greek generals knew it," said Tunney. Sharkey was a heavyweight contender in the 1920s and 1930s, known for his frequent public bellyaching and claims of unfair treatment.

Gene recited the words of Ulysses, as he advises Achilles that the world gravitates toward the new and flashy, throwing out the stale and tested:

> Time hath, my lord, a wallet at his back,
> Wherein he puts alms for oblivion...
> Love, friendship, charity, are subject all
> To envious and calumniating time.
> One touch of nature makes the whole world kin —
> That all, with one consent, praise new-born gawds,
> Though they are made and molded of things past...
> The present eye praises the present object.

The lecture made the front page of *The New York Times*. Though the *Times* reporter was generally impressed, most other newspapermen were harder to win over and continued to question why a champion boxer aspired to anything beyond the ring. As the *Philadelphia Public Ledger* succinctly put it: "Gene's lecture at New Haven won't make him any more popular with the boxing fans."

The *Washington Evening Star* took the issue further, pondering the motives behind the champion's performance. "It is of no value to him to be known as one whose heart is really not in his chosen profession of pugilism, but in the higher realm of intellectual pursuit. The world that supports pugilism as a sport prefers to regard the boxing champion as an exemplar of brawn, not of brains. Its ideal of superiority is of a powerful, tenacious, durable fighting machine, not a student."

Heywood Broun, a writer for the *New York World*, claimed that he could remember the days when one wouldn't find "prizefighters, trained seals or motion-picture stars in the classroom." He said, "Harvard, I trust, will counter by asking Babe Ruth to tell the boys in Cambridge just what Milton has meant to him."

Will Rogers seemed to speak for all when he said, "Let's have prizefighters with harder wallops and less Shakespeare." In his column, Rogers wrote:

> Gene Tunney just lectured before Yale's class on Shakespeare. He said he read Shakespeare ten times before he could get what he meant. Now that brings up the question: Is there something wrong with Shakespeare or with Gene? If everybody has to read his stuff ten times, why, Shakespeare is not the author he is cracked up to be. But if somebody else can read

him and get him the first time, why, Tunney is not the high-brow that *he* is cracked up to be.

The students were enthusiastic, and hundreds of them pursued Gene for autographs and to shake his hand. In *Gene Tunney Shows the Way*, published soon after the lecture, Professor Phelps wrote: "Here is a man who emerged from the ruck in a field of activity generally despised; where even those who are successful are not taken seriously in fashionable, commercial, or intellectual society; indeed, where their opinions or views on any subject outside of fisticuffs are laughed at. When I invited him to lecture on Shakespeare at Yale, I knew he would tell us not what somebody else thought of Shakespeare, but what, in daily life, Shakespeare meant to him. Tunney has an interesting mind."

In London, Shaw read news reports of Gene's talk. He could not fail to be reminded of a scene he had written for his novel, when the hero Cashel Byron startles English aristocrats by showing up at a soirée and glibly speaking up about the gospel of "executive power" and the need to look at life as a contest in which one needs courage, fighting instincts, training, character and knowledge to attain victory:

> "You have to know how to fight, you can't hire someone else to do it for you, nor can you sit back and pretend you're an example that others can learn from, in order to get your way. You have to go in and take the prize by fighting for it."

Gene stayed overnight with Phelps, and the next day, caught the same New York-bound train that he knew Polly was on to return home. She had visited her sister in West Hartford, an hour's train ride from New Haven, along with her classmate Helen Sligo, a close friend.

"He was ecstatic," remembered Helen. "He was on top of the world, and so pleased with himself. We were thrilled for him, and I think Polly felt a big hurdle had somehow been cleared." The three moved to a vacant car and Polly and Gene sat alone in the back. Helen, who was reading a book, occasionally peeked back at them. "They had their heads together and were laughing and talking and very secretive and close. You could see they were in love with each other."

By the time the train arrived in Greenwich, the boxer and the heiress were secretly engaged to marry. It was April 24, Polly's 21st birthday, and almost exactly two years since Dowie let him in the door for the blind date at which they first met.

CLOCKWISE FROM
TOP LEFT: POLLY WITH
HER GRANDFATHER
GEORGE LAUDER; AT
AGE THREE ON HER
MOTHER KATHERINE
ROWLAND LAUDER'S
LAP, WITH HER SISTER
"COT"; AT AGE FOUR
ABOARD *ENDYMION*,
HER FATHER'S OCEAN
RACING SCHOONER.
(TUNNEY COLLECTION).

CHAPTER 7

Fishing South of Quebec

"He is a good man all through, and entirely presentable in any society."
G. BERNARD SHAW ON TUNNEY

Polly's family home was called *Tighnabruaich* (Tawn-ah-bru-ick), a Gaelic word that means "house on a hill," that is, if one could call the Lauders' sprawling, Tudor-style mansion a house. "It was a big, brooding sort of place," said Robert Taylor, who used to deliver groceries. "Kind of scary for a kid from the other side of town."

The estate was set far off Lake Avenue on 55 acres of rolling countryside, including the rambling four-story mansion, a horse stable and barn, a garage for six cars, a house for the chauffeur and his wife, greenhouses, chicken coops, dog kennels, a gardener's tool house, underground storage for fruit and cider and a large, elegant Victorian guest house. There was even a colorfully painted miniature house outfitted as a playhouse, where the children had tea with their nanny.

One of the finest compounds in Greenwich, it was the only household Polly had ever known, and it was populated by maids, butlers, cooks, gardeners, chauffeurs and governesses. Growing up, her best friends had been the children of Percy Rockefeller on the estate next door. Weekends were spent on her father's Boston-built, two-masted schooner, which for years held the record for the fastest transatlantic yacht passage ever made. In 1905, with a crew of 28, the *Endymion* had placed fourth in the legendary Kaiser's Cup Transatlantic Race, the final privileged tournament of a gilded age and the last great race of yachting princes.

"Wigglesmuch," her father called her, and Polly adored him, often curling up beside him as he read, peeking into the darkroom he had built to develop photographs and tagging along with him to the stables. She couldn't sit still for longer than a moment. On board the *Endymion*, her father played a game, giving her nickels if she could sit or stand on one of the round medicine balls for five minutes. Polly enjoyed the game, but she made few nickels and inevitably bounced off the ball to race along the wood decks, her governess or a crewman in pursuit to protect her from falls.

When George Lauder, Jr., the father who doted on her, died, Polly was 8 years old. She was utterly devastated. Her grieving mother secluded herself in her room, and Polly, feeling abandoned and lonely, withdrew into books. Cot was 12 and their younger brother, George, was 6. Her grandfather, multimillionaire George Lauder, a first cousin and retired business partner of the steel magnate Andrew Carnegie, sometimes visited, sitting in the porch swing with his crisp bow tie and vest to read stories and share lemonade, but for an

8-year-old, the visits were too few and too formal. She lived in a household of women, with a timid younger brother and no father figure. Books became her refuge and her strength.

From the beginning, Gene's courtship of Polly had also been a courtship of her mother, whose approval would be needed if Polly were ever to marry. Katherine Rowland Lauder had grown up in a moderately well-to-do, creative, well educated and slightly bohemian household in Greenwich, one of five children, descendants of a Rowland who settled in Connecticut in 1640. Her great-uncle Edwin D. Morgan had been a Union Army general during the Civil War, a United States senator and governor of New York State. One brother was a doctor and novelist who had moved to France. Another sailed the Arctic Sea. Several cousins lived in England. Her father, a railroad man, had traveled by horseback to seek out guerilla leader Pancho Villa in Mexico.

Even her grandmother was independent-minded. When her father and brothers returned from hunting to find the house on fire, they rushed inside to find their indignant grandmother angrily demanding why men were stomping on the roof. Told they were firemen and she had to evacuate, she briskly replied, "Tell the fools to put it out!"

Katherine was a champion golfer, a horseback rider and a skilled sailor, and her children reflected those tastes. Polly was tall at 5 feet 8 inches, an exceptionally pretty young woman with a natural radiance who had inherited her mother's dignified, ladylike grace. Katherine Lauder was someone who liked travel and admired a sense of humor. She had little taste for social platitudes, and Gene would find her an ally.

The large paneled library in *Tighnabruaich*, with floor-to-ceiling bookshelves on all sides, was Polly's favorite room, and the first one she showed Gene. Finely bound sets of prominent British and American poets and authors, including all of Shakespeare's and Shaw's works, lined the walls. Even the wood-paneled billiard room was walled with bookshelves, as well as display cases for trophies and portraits of family members.

"Mother used to complain that all I did day after day was hide in the barn or a corner of the library by myself and read poetry," said Polly. "She was right."

Mary Jane Lydon Tunney, a woman who had grown up in poverty and scrubbed floors, could have been intimidated as she was driven up the curving drive and under the great arched portico of *Tighnabruaich*. But Gene's devotedly Roman Catholic mother was rarely intimidated; instead, it was Polly who felt uneasy. She was concerned whether, as a Protestant, she would be accepted by a woman who had prayed her oldest son would become a priest and who had a Dominican nun for a daughter.

They lunched in the Chinese-papered dining room used by the family (not the paneled formal dining room) and, as Polly remembered, got on beautifully. Gene did most of the talking.

"I liked Gene's mother very much, and she obviously cared for him terribly," Polly said later.

Mary Jane enjoyed the gardens, laughed about the chicken coop (it was better than the ones her family had in Ireland, she said) and left, apparently satisfied. About the house, she said only that she wouldn't want to have to clean it.

Mary Jane Lydon Tunney and Katherine Lauder were both widows, both publicity-shy and both hated cameras so much that they didn't even like family members to take pictures of them. It was understood that any future plans by the couple should remain totally secret. As an afterthought, one of them pointed out that no one would be the least bit interested anyway, once Gene quit boxing.

Gene returned to Speculator in the summer of 1928 to train for what he had decided would be his final professional bout. Polly had never seen a boxing match.

"Come visit," said Gene.

"Oh, but I couldn't possibly," said Polly. "Someone would see us."

Nonsense, said Gene, convinced that people see only what they expect to see. Gene had become a master of disguise, and several times had used his trademark red sweater as subterfuge. When John Garfield, a Cleveland millionaire and grandson of President Garfield, visited for several days, Gene traded sweaters with him to get some privacy. Garfield, a full head taller than Gene, walked around town signing autographs and saying hello to tourists as "the Champ" while Gene was left alone.

"It always works," Gene promised. "You'll see."

Thus inspired, Polly and her friend Helen Ufford planned a clandestine overnight trip. They disguised themselves in a way that they felt no one except Gene could recognize them, wearing dated clothes and old but stylish cloche hats pulled low to cover their faces. Helen borrowed a car and they drove themselves, almost dizzy with the mystery and excitement of their adventure.

"I was a cub reporter," said Polly. Helen, who had written magazine stories, used her credentials as a reporter. They carried notebooks and pens. Gene arranged for them to stay at the hotel using false names.

Blending into the Speculator camp turned out to be surprisingly easy, and the boxing crowd took little notice of them. Women reporters already had interviewed Tunney and editors had discovered that women readers were keenly interested in the champion's taste in literature and his view of marriage. In addition, there were many women around the training site — hangers-on, schoolgirls and interested local citizens.

TUNNEY IN TRAINING AT SPECULATOR, NEW YORK, 1928 (CORBIS).
OPPOSITE: POLLY DISGUISED HERSELF IN ORDER TO BLEND INTO THE
CROWDS SURROUNDING GENE'S TRAINING RING (TUNNEY COLLECTION).

"I was so sure I might give myself away," said Polly. She and Helen sat on a wood bleacher among other reporters and Polly tucked her feet tightly underneath her to try to calm her nerves as she opened her reporter's notebook. Her hands were trembling so much that she couldn't write, so she listened. "Of course, I heard plenty of remarks about the fact that my husband-to-be, being a very extraordinarily good boxer, was making a good show of his practice sessions. He knew that art of backing up without losing his balance and falling on the floor. He did it very professionally and beautifully. I could hear remarks constantly around me from the other reporters and especially comments about a recent picture taken of him reading a book outside the ring, under a tree, obviously very relaxed and enjoying himself. They were all saying what a total phony the picture was — that he was making a show, acting a part. I was furious!"

Gene's appearance in the elevated training ring quieted the audience. He climbed over the ropes, took off the towel that hung loosely around his neck, moved his arms to and fro in his warm-up, laced on his gloves and, before starting, bent down to touch the outstretched hands of several excited schoolboys.

"I kept my face down so I wouldn't look at him much," said Polly.

The workout session, and the hard-punching exchange between Gene and his sparring partners, revealed a new, tough, driven side of her intended that startled her. She enjoyed tennis matches and football games, but those players wore clothes and followed straightforward rules. She was stunned to see Gene lashing out at his opponent and unprepared for the pounding of leather on skin and the powerful speed with which a heavyweight boxer turns, twists, jabs and punches in a small space, almost too fast to see. (In Shaw's boxing novel, Cashel's lady friend says, "I was shocked by the severity with which he treated his opponent.")

One of Gene's sparring partners was knocked off his feet with a bloodied lip and blood flowing from his nose, and the consequences of what could happen in a real bout frightened Polly. She said she was not cut out to be a boxing fan. "I said I was *never* going back to another training camp, even if I could be a cub reporter. It was very lucky that we got away with it, because if the newspaper people found out, that would have been awful. They never knew who I was, of course."

Helen and Polly joined Gene and a visiting naturalist, Orrie Nobles, for supper. Orrie had met Gene by chance in Seattle when he "found the heavyweight champion huddled alone in the shadow of a pile of lumber on Pier 7, reading." Polly said they spent a perfectly wonderful evening talking about Henry Thoreau and *Walden Pond*. Nobles explained that the pond represented the natural soul of humankind, reflecting the heaven we can discover within ourselves, by experiencing the Divine through nature. Thoreau's "luminous wisdom on man and nature" had become Gene's primary reading in preparation for what would be his last title fight, on July 26, 1928, against Tom Heeney from New Zealand.

Leaving the Adirondacks the day of the fight was a sweet-sad departure from a place Gene had liked so much that he had established residence with an eye toward making it his permanent home. The entire village turned out for his sendoff. Leaning out of the windows to wave as the pontoon plane lifted off, he pointed out landmarks to sportswriters accompanying him, then surprised them all by going to sleep.

At Yankee Stadium, he fought a near-perfect fight, pleasing the crowd, if not promoter Rickard, who lost money on it. Gene's reputation as an astute businessman had already caught the attention of Bernard Shaw, and newspapers reported Tunney had demanded and received a guaranteed $500,000. In the eighth round, Tunney drove a right to the challenger's left eye that rendered him temporarily blind. Instead of following up his advantage, Tunney moved away, deliberately withholding another blow, waiting until Heeney was in a position to protect himself before letting loose a right.

"The act of a gentleman, a sportsman," noted Nat Fleischer, editor of *The Ring* magazine.

In the 10th round, Tunney had Heeney stretched flat on his back. With the crowd cheering, the announcer rushed to hold up Tunney's hand as victor. But Gene, the calmest one in the stadium, told the announcer that the closing bell had sounded two seconds *after* the knockdown. The count could not be completed and the fight still wasn't over. By the 11th round, with Heeney's face a bloody mask, the fight was halted with Tunney the winner.

In his last fight, he worked his way into the hearts of the fans, said Fleischer. "He possessed everything — speed, accuracy, splendid blocking, fine countering and perfect calculation in every movement. In addition, he carried that day a harder punch than he had ever before placed on view." He demonstrated that he could not only avoid an opponent with speed, but that he was a fighter of the cutting, bruising style, a style that reduced the stamina of an opponent and made him helpless. Tunney received the biggest ovation of his career, and sportswriters universally agreed that he was the best he had ever been.

In the dressing room afterward, as John Kieran of *The New York Times* wrote, the champion didn't seem to want to leave. "The mob of hand shakers who never fail to throng around a winner had come and gone. Lights were going out all over the huge structure. The show was over. It was time to go home." The door opened and in came Tom Heeney, a beaten and badly battered man. "I just came in here to tell you that you're a square fighter and great fighter. Here's my hand. The best of luck go with you wherever you go." And for once, Kieran said, the imperturbable champion choked up with emotion. No one else took much notice, and no one but Gene knew he would never box professionally again.

It had taken ten years to fight his way to the top. Now, in less than a week, Gene wanted to get out, to leave the trappings and the bad press and the glory and exhaustion behind him. Celebrity was something that he still thought he could turn on and off like a light switch. He wanted to get married, and he didn't want anyone else to know about it. "I had lost interest in boxing. I had fallen in love. I never did think that professional boxing and marriage went together. Marriage, to my mind, meant retirement and a new beginning." In this, too, he was like Cashel Byron. "Boxing [to Cashel] was too serious a pursuit…to be either an amusement or a mere exercise. Besides, he had a prejudice that it did not become a married man. His career as a pugilist was closed by his marriage."

Kent Cooper presided over the world's largest news-gathering agency, the Associated Press, and among his friends was Bernard Gimbel. Two days after the Heeney fight, Tunney and Gimbel arrived at Cooper's office on Madison Avenue with what Cooper saw as an impossible request: keep Gene *out* of the newspapers. "To do that would be harder than fighting again with one arm tied behind him," said Cooper, laughing.

"My future life will have no connection whatever with the fight game," insisted Gene. "I am entering on a new life that has no relation whatever with my ring career."

"Some other kind of ring?" asked Cooper.

"You guessed it," said Gimbel. "The lady didn't fall in love with Gene because of his ring prowess, but actually in spite of it," pointing out it was Tunney's idea "to drop out of public notice before the engagement is announced." Cooper smiled, warning that an engagement would increase interest in Gene, not decrease it.

"Despite anything you can do, you are going to be linked romantically in the newspapers, and the more you try to prevent it, the more you are going to be talked about. It is a first-page news story," said Cooper, and to be married secretly makes the wedding an even bigger story.

On August 1, six days after the Heeney fight, Gene stunned the sports world at a lunch for writers and boxing supporters in Manhattan by announcing that he was retiring as the world's heavyweight boxing champion. He would be the first champion — with the exception of the fictional Cashel Byron — to retire undefeated at the top of his game.

Gene said that it was with a certain amount of regret that he was stepping down from a game that had treated him well and given him fame, fortune and friendships. But he said ten years was long enough to pursue a violent sport. Privately, he felt he had been lucky to be unscarred, and he wanted to retire before he suffered dementia or received a more permanent injury than the rasp in his voice. It would be several years before he publicly admitted to a three-day concussion so severe that he temporarily lost his memory.

"Queer street," the old boxers called it. "Fight too long and you start hearing bells."

"There is no finer physical exercise or more engrossing science," he said in a talk remembered by many as eloquent. "One of my chief desires has been to leave the game better than I found it. I have tried to be not only a champion, but a sportsman." He said there were no surprises left for him, no new punches that had not been used, and no strong contenders on the horizon. "I am going to miss it. I'll miss the smell of resin, the glare of lights, and the roar of the crowd."

As if he were speaking directly to Bernard Shaw, he said boxing was the most democratic sport of all: "There is something in it that appeals to all. It is the one form of amusement that has real, actual drama. A melodrama on the stage is, after all, only a play, but a fight in the ring is real. The primitive in us comes to the surface when men fight for physical superiority. It appeals to all classes and types — the truck man, the intellectual, and the aesthete. The truck man sees the 'sock' on the jaw, the intellectual enjoys the duel of fighting brains, and the aesthetic appreciates the rhythm of the action. They all rub elbows at ringside."

As a postscript, he told reporters he might take a short trip, "south of Quebec for some fishing." He also said he would begin preparations for his first trip abroad since visiting Ireland in 1923 and that he would take a walking trip in Europe with his close friend, the Pulitzer Prize–winning author Thornton Wilder.

The New York Times said Gene's decision reflected "his temperament and tastes, the most unusual in the recorded history of the prize ring. He has done all that he asked of himself and all that the public demanded of him save the one thing he would not do, and that was to look and act and talk like the traditional prizefighter. He has given to the ring, for an interval, the presence of a gentleman who has left it to be also a scholar."

"One of the indictments against Mr. Tunney," wrote Joe Williams of the *New York Telegram*, "was that on a certain unfortunate occasion he had been caught red-handed with a book of verse, an offense that he has never been able to live down. Mr. Tunney had another obnoxious failing — he picked his companions, and he used rather passable English." It may be, said Williams, "that neither the fight game nor the fight customer was designed to absorb any great amount of uplift or refinement."

On August 8, two weeks after Gene's last fight and a week after his retirement, the Associated Press received a telegram from Mrs. George Lauder, Jr., formally announcing the engagement of her daughter, Miss Mary Josephine Rowland Lauder, to Mr. Gene Tunney of New York. No date was set for the wedding. The telegram came from South Bristol, Maine, where Mrs. Lauder had a summer home on the family's private John's Island, named after Captain John Smith, who explored the area in 1614. It didn't take long for the press to figure out that instead of fishing, Gene was in Maine with his betrothed. An armada of reporters followed.

"We hid," said Polly. "Actually, we hid in plain sight." An old log lean-to outfitted with pillows and blankets, nestled against the rocks and concealed beneath a broad cover of pines facing the open sea, became their hideaway. The green belly of the sweeping Atlantic Ocean swayed gently in the sparkling August sunshine in front of them, illuminating every lobster boat and press launch circling the island. Sitting inside the big lean-to, shaded by green boughs and the darkness of the log interior, Polly and Gene were invisible to passing boats, yet like guests in the royal box at the opera, they had a full view of the stage itself: they could see other islands and the rocky coast of the mainland curving onward on either side. Just out of sight were the distant cliffs of Monhegan Island. With binoculars, Gene and Polly were close enough to practically read newspapers carried by the reporters, and they were jubilant about surreptitiously foiling their pursuers.

"No one *ever* saw us!" remembered Polly. "We spent the week watching osprey, reading books to each other, talking, making plans." They ate boned chicken and egg salad sandwiches, wild raspberries and blueberry tarts, and peered at the press boats searching for them "like we were quail on the fly." Exasperated photographers with powerful lenses took shots of anyone in the main house that appeared at a window, crossed the lawn or walked to the dock. The New York *Daily News* sent a plane for aerial photographs of the house, the grounds and the rocky coastal outcroppings to try to locate the couple, but the island's pine cover proved too dense to penetrate. No one managed to snag pictures of Polly and Gene. One photograph that showed a shadow of a woman behind a second-floor curtain was revealed to be a picture of a maid.

The pressure of the media increased daily, and deprived of the main characters, the press drama was soon unrelenting. Newspaper and magazine reporters contacted their friends, their families, Gene's boxing associates, their grocers and their gardeners and staked out the Lauder house in Greenwich

A 1928 AERIAL PHOTOGRAPH OF THE LAUDER RESIDENCE ON JOHN'S ISLAND, MAINE, WHERE THE ENGAGED COUPLE HID FROM THE PRESS (TUNNEY COLLECTION).

to question every delivery boy and even the postman. Photographers hid in bushes, and reporters bribed people the couple barely knew or had never met to get interviews. Police, private security guards and guard dogs had to be posted to provide protection on the island and on the docks in Maine, in Connecticut and even at Nana's house in Riverdale.

News organizations fought with one another over the story, and tensions were made worse at having Polly and Gene inaccessible and on an island that one report said "might have been a rendezvous for pirates before the early settlers of Maine." Alone and unprotected, "the wooded acres, wave-lashed, are practically impregnable," complained the Cincinnati *Times-Star*. When a reporter for the International News Service wrote a story insinuating that

the champion had greeted his bride-to-be with a kiss, other news organizations screamed foul.

"The question is not when did the I.N.S. reporter arrive on the scene, but as I see it, whether Gene or Jo kissed each other," wrote Moses Strauss, managing editor of the *Times-Star* to the Associated Press. Did they kiss? Other reporters claimed there had been no kiss at all, but a simple, "Hello, Gene," as the two walked arm-in-arm from the island dock to the house. Even this information came from an island worker.

Gene felt victimized and defenseless, and by week's end, he was furious to find his bride-to-be at the epicenter of a new onslaught of attention. "Nothing," he said, "ever made me madder than the invasion of my privacy." He had once again miscalculated his own celebrity. "I had not changed. I was the same man as before, and I was not going to allow myself, or the family, to be prisoners of the press." He wanted to vanish from the landscape silently, swiftly and completely.

Gene returned alone to New York wearing smoked dark glasses, his coat collar turned up and a Panama hat with the brim turned down, only to find photographers at every station stop. "Poor Tunney!" wrote the Winsted, Connecticut, *Citizen*. "It did him little good to renounce the fighting crown, become engaged like an ordinary young man and go to an isolated island to visit his fiancée."

Gene made plans to sail to Europe.

Meanwhile, in London, Bernard Shaw had dinner with the professor from Yale.

CHAPTER 8

In Pursuit of the Groom

"I have been asked how it is that I, critic and playwright whose interests, taste and practice are ultra-classical, should concern myself with anything so barbarous as boxing. I have even had to ask myself this question."
G. BERNARD SHAW

For years, Shaw's flat in Adelphi Terrace had been one floor apart from that of James M. Barrie, the novelist and dramatist best known for his enduring *Peter Pan*. Barrie liked to say that when he wished to chat with Shaw, even in the middle of the night, he merely threw up his window, and when he saw lights in Shaw's apartment, he gave a shout and both men leaned over their windowsills to talk. Once, Barrie said, he threw pieces of bread to grab Shaw's attention. In late July 1928, Barrie's American friend, the Yale University professor William Lyon Phelps, visited London, and Barrie hosted a dinner for him, inviting the Shaws. It was two days after Shaw's 72nd birthday and, coincidentally, also two days after the Heeney fight.

By this time, the jovial, white-haired Billy Phelps had become a minor international celebrity, a rarity for an academic, and Gene Tunney's lecture on Shakespeare several months earlier was the sole reason for it. Phelps had the makings of a showman, and he enjoyed the attention of the media. As Barrie expected, the professor and the playwright had an immediate interest in one another. The professor said the charming, energetic Shaw was interested in every subject but most especially in talking about the heavyweight boxing champion.

Phelps told them he had received hundreds of newspaper pictures and press clippings on Gene's speech at Yale from all over the world, from the British Isles, India, New Zealand, Japan, Germany and even South America. "Tunney found himself more famous for having lectured at Yale than for having defeated Dempsey," he said. "And I found myself more famous for having invited him than for any book I had written or any professional work I had done."

Shaw reported that there had been special interest in Tunney's most recent defense of the championship because of his opponent. "Many years have passed since an accredited British heavyweight boxer figured in an actual fight for the world's championship," noted *The Times* of London. "Tunney won a good deal of respect, if not popularity, by reason of the fact that his upstanding style and use of the left to pave the way for the right vindicated to some extent the old British idea of fisticuffs against the raging, tearing methods associated...with the American ring."

The playwright had read all the news accounts the morning after the fight, especially the round-by-round coverage, a dry but crisp blow-by-blow account favored by boxing aficionados. The round-by-round gave him a ringside sense of the action and he could visualize every punch and counterpunch. Shaw didn't yet know, of course, any more than did anyone else who followed boxing, that it was Tunney's last fight.

The professor was asked by his dinner companions what the American boxer was really like. Professor Phelps said that since he had become identified as a friend of Tunney the matter of Gene's "real personality" was the most common question people asked him. "He's genuine," Phelps said. "He is always himself. He never expresses an opinion about a book unless he himself has read that book and thought about it. His ideas and his language are his own, neither crude nor elaborate." Tunney was not at all like a prizefighter, he said, and talking to him, one forgot that he was famous or an athlete. He seemed, said Phelps, like a college student.

Phelps told his companions that Tunney spoke a good deal about Mr. Shaw's work and quoted passages from Shakespeare and the poets. In fact, the professor said he had another younger friend who was about to embark on a tour of Europe with the boxer. He was Thornton Wilder, author of *The Bridge of San Luis Rey*, a novel that Phelps had called "a star of the first magnitude." Earlier in the year, the book had won the first of Wilder's three Pulitzer Prizes; nearly 50,000 copies were sold in Great Britain alone. Phelps noted that Barrie was deeply impressed with Wilder's novel, and Charlotte Shaw raved about it, saying that she had already read it three times.

How curious, said Charlotte, that men from such divergent fields, a boxer and an author, would be traveling mates. Were they actually *friends?* Phelps told her that Tunney especially enjoyed meeting literary men, as he had discovered himself when he invited Tunney to lunch and dinner.

Phelps then told a story about Tunney and the novelist Somerset Maugham.

"Last spring, before he addressed my class, I gave a luncheon for him at my own home," said Phelps. "Among the guests was a well-known novelist [Maugham], who told Tunney that he should read *As You Like It*. 'Why?' asked the boxer. 'Because,' replied the novelist, 'it has a great prizefight scene.' 'You probably mean the wrestling match,' Tunney said, 'for there is no prizefight in *As You Like It*.' He did not say this boastfully but with amusement, and it happened he was right."

Maugham laughed uproariously, said Phelps. The novelist also said how surprised and pleased he had been by the worldwide publicity he received when word leaked out that Gene was reading *Of Human Bondage* before the Chicago fight. Sales of the book skyrocketed. "My dear fellow," the novelist told Tunney, "I want to thank you for the most free advertising I ever had!"

To Bernard Shaw, the idea of a prizefighter hobnobbing with literary figures probably seemed more artifice than reality, though he was already intrigued. The professor was an academic of impeccable credentials, and though a new acquaintance, his favorable report of the fighter coincided with the earlier assessment by his agent, Lawrence Langner. Shaw told Phelps that he hoped to meet the boxer.

Shortly afterward, Thornton Wilder was interviewed in Paris by André Maurois, the distinguished French novelist and biographer. Told that Wilder would soon meet up with the world heavyweight boxing champion for a tour of Europe, Maurois was also perplexed by an author's friendship with a boxer.

"A strange companion," he told Wilder.

"Don't think that," Thornton replied. "I'm very fond of him." About the same time, Wilder wrote Ernest Hemingway, saying Tunney was "as fine a person as you'd want to meet. Not much humor, but I've always had a taste for the doggedly earnest ones."

In mid-August, Gene fought through crowds of curiosity seekers to board a ship for Europe, to join Wilder and to secure a place to get married. He and Polly had decided to wed where there was more distance from the American press and less chance of being hounded by reporters. "It was the most advertised marriage in the world," said Sis Jenkins Wastcoat, who remembered her family being mesmerized by the romance. "Here was this incredibly handsome man, a celebrity, sailing to Europe to marry an heiress and it was all supposed to be secret. People who never cared about boxing were caught up in it."

Reporters and photographers dogged every step. "It was unbelievable, really unbelievable!" said Sam Pryor. "A beautiful society girl from one of the country's most prominent families — and she was marrying a *prizefighter*! No one could fathom it. Every newspaper had stories. People in Greenwich were flabbergasted." The romantic marriage was "one of the idylls of the news," wrote *Vanity Fair*.

Gene's first stop was Ireland, to spend a week at Moore Abbey outside Dublin with the renowned tenor John McCormack, whom he had known in New York. Shaw sent a cable to Gene in Ireland inviting him to visit, but the cable missed him. Meanwhile, the press in rural County Kildare turned out to be as brutally intrusive as in New York. "We had quite a time getting Gene around during his stay because he was practically mobbed everywhere we went," said Lily McCormack. Gene was so exasperated that when he visited the birthplace of his parents in County Mayo, he drove in the middle of the night and stopped only to get out on a dirt road, wander through the sleeping village of Kiltimagh and depart, having seen no one.

"Rocks and fields," he reported later. "Nothing else to see."

Arriving in England, Gene slipped away for a day trip to the southern coast to see where his father had shipped out as a cabin boy for the Merchant Marine. Privately, he had wanted to square his father's tales of the sea with his personal memories of the often sullen, dour and cold man who believed dreams never came true. He had hoped to find on the docks of Portsmouth something that would give him clues to understanding the man he felt he had never known. "Like an Irish jig," someone once said of Papa. It was a dance in which only the feet moved, while the body was rigid, as if purposefully repressed. Clouds of hungry gulls and fishing vessels crowded the harbor, and Gene found nothing to satisfy him.

When he returned to London, near-hysterical crowds of hero worshippers followed him, demanding autographs. "Good old Gene!" they shouted. Women pulled at his suit jacket, threw flowers and waved at him wherever he went. Hundreds of fans sent letters to his hotel. While fleeing from a crowd by taxi with a newspaper reporter, he asked to swing by Adelphi Terrace because he wanted to see where Bernard Shaw lived.

"Shaw used to live there," the reporter said, pointing as the taxi passed the Adelphi, a row of narrow Georgian buildings stretching about 500 feet above the embankment of the Thames.

"What? In there?" asked Gene, disbelieving. His idea of a writer's solitude was a woody glen such as his cabin in the Adirondacks, not a soot-covered row house with a front door on the sidewalk. "Say, how could he write in that place?"

Gene found he couldn't take the underground or walk through a hotel lobby without attracting attention. "I want to sink as far into obscurity as possible," he said. But it wasn't to happen. Everyone loved a lover. "The English like to write letters and the Irish want souvenirs of one's clothes," Gene wrote. "Between the two, I was partially blind and nearly naked."

At the end of August, on an unseasonably warm evening, dozens of reporters and photographers, as well as a sizeable crowd of onlookers, gathered outside a fashionable London residence while well-known men of literature, the theatre, law, finance, sports and the nobility passed by them in evening dress on their way to dinner. The dinner host was sportsman Harry Preston, a popular hotelier and one of England's major boxing supporters. George Bernard Shaw, vacationing in France, had to decline the invitation.

The lure, the much-heralded boxing champion, was the last to arrive. A reporter, who waited in the crowd outside, noted with surprise that in evening dress Tunney did not look or talk in the least like a "bruiser." "He seems just a serious-minded gentleman with cultured rather than solar-plexus-finding instincts." Another reporter noted that his dinner jacket failed to hide his shoulder muscles. "The first impression was that of a mountain guide, of a man you would trust your sons with on a camping holiday or a man you would trust your daughter with anywhere."

A columnist for the *London Evening Standard* wrote that, "It appears to be accepted as extraordinarily incongruous, and even rather humorous, that a world-famous boxer should be interested in literature." Why, he asked Gene, did he care about books?

"Why," Gene asked the stupefied reporter, "should it be taken for granted that a boxer must be a bone-head, and that any boxer who is not must be a freak?"

When asked to speak at dinner, Gene rose from the table and gave a spontaneous 30 minute talk on the psychology of boxing and the arts. He seemed shy, the guests said, but paradoxically at ease and sincere in his surprise that his fame was so great in Europe. "I don't know why you make this fuss over me," he said. "What is boxing? The ability to coordinate mind and muscle at a critical moment — that is all. If I had been a great painter, I would have been met by a couple of long-haired men and short-haired women. Had I been a famous litterateur, my welcome would have been left to posterity."

He said that he had intentionally refrained from being a man-killer in the ring and on the point of victory had more than once pulled back to spare a final punishing blow when he knew he was the victor. A man-killer is a menace to boxing, he said. "The only joy in a fight was while the other man was your physical and intellectual equal." Boxing is an art, he said, allied with all arts. Knowledge of boxing and its history provided the springboard that allowed him to tunnel through masterpieces of literature, offering insight into the character of authors as well as the fictional fighters in plays and novels, giving him a syllabus to understand all arts more broadly. He discussed boxing in literature, from Shakespeare to contemporary works. In *Tom Jones*, for instance, novelist Henry Fielding described a pugilistic encounter at length, according to Gene, "and so incorrectly, that I could state my belief that Fielding had never seen a prizefight."

The speech was a triumph, news reports said. Comedian George Graves called the speech an "oratorical knockout. Mark my words, that man would have scored in any walk of life." Lord Decies thought the speech was "the most remarkable I had ever heard. It would have made an income-tax official forget his demand note." The novelist Arnold Bennett said Gene was not simple-minded after all. Theatrical manager C.B. Cochran said Tunney "showed himself to be the type of world champion such as we have thought could only exist in the mind of the idealistic writer. We are so suspicious of propaganda in this sphere of sport that I confess I went to the dinner somewhat skeptical about the ecstatic language in which some of the eulogies had been couched."

The Prince of Wales, a boxing fan whose namesake supported the sport in the 18th century, had sent his equerry to the dinner and the next day invited Gene to St. James's Palace. Originally erected by King Henry VIII in the 1500s, the palace had been partly destroyed by fire and rebuilt, and though it was no longer the chief residence of English sovereigns, the British court was officially still known as the Court of St. James. Gene was honored but couldn't help but see the irony. As a teenager, he had joined the anti-English fervor of the Irish immigrant community in the period before America became allied with Britain in the Great War. He and several friends had barely escaped arrest after hurling raw eggs and tomatoes at U.S. Secretary of State William Jennings Bryan during a New York speech to raise money to support England.

"As we walked through the courtyard, we could see people peeping out of most of the palace windows," said William B. Powell, a friend charged with keeping the press at a distance. "They had heard Gene was coming." They were ushered into a stately room filled with portraits and other artworks and treated graciously, as if they were visiting a family home instead of a palace built for the heir to the British throne.

Never one to be intimidated, Gene enjoyed himself. Throughout his life, he treated presidents and princes the same as if they were barbers or taxi drivers. "It was one of his most stunning traits," said an ambassador. "He was modest without show of embarrassment and had that cherished possession with which one is or is not born — personality." The London papers noted that Gene wore not the formal court dress usually required for such meetings but a blue suit, "so that he could be taken as a simple American citizen."

Prince Edward often attended prizefights. On the day of the 1926 fight in Philadelphia, Tunney's manager, Billy Gibson, had fired off a cablegram to the palace, offering to make "a sporting wager" that Tunney would win against Dempsey. "The prince has an astonishing grip on the technical side of boxing," Gene said after the visit. They discussed Tunney's walking trip with Wilder and preparations for a royal visit to the colonies in Africa. Prince Edward lamented they had no time for golf, saying, "It might have been a good one-round battle."

Bernard Shaw, foiled in his hope to be among those meeting Tunney in London, told a newspaper correspondent to tell Gene he wished to meet him and then wrote a letter to the boxer from Cap d'Antibes on the French Riviera. It was dated August 31, 1928, but Shaw would find that getting hold of Gene was like trying to communicate with a moving target.

Dear Mr. Tunney,
On Tuesday next I leave this address and change to Hotel La Residence, Geneva, Switzerland. I shall stay there until the middle of the month. I must return home about the 15th.

If you are still on this side of the Atlantic then, give me a hail, and I will fix up a meeting if you are not by that time tired of literary people.

Not a word of this to any living soul or we shall be dogged by cameras, microphones and journalists. I take it that we are both desirous of complete privacy.

You might drop me a line to Geneva as to your movements. I do not know where you are, so am addressing this to the American Express Co., which is usually a sure fire for visitors from America.

Faithfully,
G. Bernard Shaw

The bride-to-be was having her own challenges trying to get to Europe. At the end of September, after weeks of preparations, Polly and the wedding party arrived at New York City's Pier No.83, on 44th Street, in five seven-passenger limousines. The *Daily Mirror* said there had been a "game of hide-and-seek with newspapermen that extended halfway across the city" before they arrived at the port to board the luxury liner *M.V. Saturnia*. Final arrangements for the departure had been made in secret, and the party's suitcases and trunks had been loaded onto the ship in advance. Polly hoped they would be able to avoid the reporters who had harassed her constantly since the engagement was announced. At Gene's urging, she had steeled herself for the possibility that members of the press might stake out the dock, but no one in the wedding party was prepared for the reception that awaited them.

Hundreds of newspaper reporters, photographers and throngs of celebrity watchers were lingering on the pier as the limousines arrived, followed by more reporters in cars. There were "blinding bursts" of camera flash bulbs, said news reports. The excited crowds rushed toward the cars, trying to encircle them even before they glided to a stop. As the limousines jerked to a standstill, shades were quickly drawn, making each vehicle an enclosed island in a crashing sea of squealing, shouting spectators who surged forward to touch the cars, peek behind the shaded windows, bang on the hood and call out greetings and questions.

The ship's captain called the police and sent his officers to try to restore order. Polly's teenaged brother George exited one car and furtively carried messages between occupants in other vehicles, nervously ducking his head to avoid hoots and shouts aimed in his direction. For half an hour, the limousine's occupants frantically tried to figure out a way to get aboard the ship safely. When finally the limousines were surrounded by police on horseback, they were driven one by one onto the lower deck loading dock, ordinarily used by trucks. Reporters and photographers bounded past barriers to board the ship. The wedding party of 13 included the bride, her mother, sister and brother, as well as friends, Rowland cousins, Polly's classmates Faith Rockefeller, Virginia Storm and Helen Sligo, and Helen Ufford, her teacher.

"It was a mob," said Helen Sligo, "but we finally realized we had to get out of the cars. We tried to run up the gangway to the stateroom. Polly had to get on the boat via a freight passage for safety, but she still ran into photographers yelling 'Shoot! Shoot!' It was terrifying. All of our names and pictures had already been in the newspapers, so the reporters knew who they were looking for. We ran up and down passageways, looking for our rooms, but there were so many people and so many flashbulbs that we couldn't see." Helen stumbled and lost a shoe.

"It seemed so unreal," Helen later wrote her mother. "It was the most exciting thing that has ever happened in my life. Even the wild dash before boarding."

The exhausted bride helped calm the pandemonium. Newsmen and photographers had been allowed to remain on the ship until the pilot boat picked them off a few miles out to sea, and the wedding party sent word that Miss Lauder would grant a conversation with one pool reporter and would pose for a photograph, only one, if they would leave the rest of her party in peace.

"Happy? I'm the happiest girl in the world," she said, smiling in an interview in the sitting room of her mother's suite. She clasped her hands tightly, burying them — unobtrusively, she hoped, as she tried to hide her nervousness — in a brown cashmere dress. "Even with those awfully complicated Italian marriage laws to face, I would not change places with any girl in the world today. Yes, I do feel romantic about it. I've never been so thrilled in my life, because, whatever happens, I'm sure I'm going to be married." News reports said she was sweet, charming, girlishly radiant — and surrounded by silver vases of pink and white tea roses.

When asked why she was going to Italy, she replied thoughtfully, "Have you ever been to Italy? No? Oh, then, you can't understand. Maybe it's romance. I suppose it is the land everyone would choose to be married in, if everyone could."

Since her visit as a student in 1924, long before she met Gene, Polly had considered Italy the most romantic place in the world, and she had dreamed of returning to the hilltop villages, the medieval monasteries, the rolling fawn-colored hills and the Adriatic Sea, the land where poetry spoke to her.

News reports said she took with her a trousseau worthy of a queen and valued at $40,000, including a $10,000 mink coat, the lining of which was embroidered with 16-inch script letters forming her new monogram, "PLT." Her luggage reportedly included 48 dinner and evening dresses, four ensemble costumes, a beaver coat and gloves worth $600, lingerie costing $800 and shoes by Frank, the theatrical boot maker, to match every costume. Later she would say this was greatly exaggerated, as was the oft-repeated claim that she was heiress to $50 million. "I got very *very* tired of all those zeros after my name."

At midnight, as the *Saturnia* pulled into open sea, the wedding party gathered in Mrs. Lauder's five-room $6000 *Appartamento Miramare* Imperial suite, surrounded by dozens of bouquets of roses and red and yellow gladioli from friends, and celebrated with tiny tea sandwiches, caviar, and tall flutes of sparkling champagne. Polly gathered her books and with her sister Cot as her roommate, fell into bed "thrilled to be eloping into the journey of a lifetime."

Polly's mother sat at the desk in her cabin and in a black pen wrote in unhurried script on gray personal stationery these lines: "She was so small so short a time ago / She lay against my heart a baby-thing / And now I watch the lovely flush and glow /...that only love can bring."

Gene's plan to do a walking tour with Thornton Wilder — or "Thornt," as Gene called him — hit one snag after another. Gene and Wilder had been born within one month of one another in 1897, "under the same moon," they always said. They enjoyed long, solitary walks together, often gesticulating in nonstop conversation, and said it helped them be more productive. Wilder composed dialogue, and Gene quoted works from classical English authors that they both knew. Neither took part in the type of locker-room banter about girls common to many of their friends, and Gene felt they had a close relationship based on an appreciation of literature, classical music and philosophy, their discussions often taking up the search for pattern and meaning of God and the universe.

"I should like to think that some day I might know you *better*, for long talks, and so well that we could even just hang around in silence," wrote Wilder in January 1928. In March, Gene wrote back to Wilder, "Gosh, I wish I could see you in the privacy of my room here or in New York and talk without interruption."

"I think of you often with the most affectionate laughter," Wilder wrote years later. "The fun we had at the training camp in the Adirondacks; or with delighted surprise, as I was trotting beside you and you turned to me (after stepping on a caterpillar) and quoted solemnly a passage from Act III, Scene I, of *Measure for Measure*: "And the poor beetle, that we tread upon, in corporal sufferance finds a pang as great / As when a giant dies."

Wilder was frequently pestered by friends who wondered whether the champion was all pose and even knew *how* to open a book, much less read. When a reporter from the *Bulletin* in Glasgow, New Hampshire, questioned whether Tunney was a phony, the amused Wilder replied that it was "quite true that Gene is a great student of literature, and even when training for a fight, he spends a lot of time reading.

"Not long ago, I was in a canoe with him on a lake in the Adirondacks and our craft overturned," said Wilder. "Tunney had a copy of Hazlitt's essays. It went down with him, but when he came up again, that book was between his teeth!" He assured the reporter they were close friends: "When we go on our walking tour, we shall make for unfrequented places unknown to the tourist, where there will be opportunities for quiet conversation and literary walks."

"We'd do the Rhein and Munich, Vienna and then Venice," Wilder wrote Gene. "Then the islands of Greece. I'd make a wonderful travel book about it with a vivid and humorous and tremendously admiring picture of you moving in and out. There would be no formal stupid descriptions of places in the book but stray glimpses of a church or an island, full of our conversations real and imaginary, all kinds of essays and 'thoughts' thrown in, unexpected and fresh reviews of the classics we would be reading in obscure German inns and so on. And the whole thing conservative and gracious and almost noble — a sort of rebuke to the gin-and-Scotch age. Anyway, think it over, oh Prince, and at least like the idea, even if it isn't practical."

Much to their mutual disappointment, the trip didn't work out the way they had hoped. It had been planned months before Tunney's engagement, and before the publication of Wilder's best-selling novel, and neither had adequately considered the problems compounded by their celebrity. One writer said the trip "had the same kind of impact that President Coolidge might have achieved if he had announced that after *his* retirement he was joining Helen Keller to open a gift shop in Albuquerque." They were cartooned and caricatured; the newspapers devoted yards of front-page coverage to the journey.

They took short hikes in the Swiss Alps and had day-long walks in France and Italy, enough to have to buy rubbing alcohol, cotton and adhesive tape for blisters. Gene said Wilder could out-walk him, out-climb him and out-eat him. But Tunney frequently needed to be near a cable office or a telephone to try to finalize wedding plans, and it was increasingly obvious that he couldn't do it hiking in the mountains. Gene and Thornt spent more time at cafés and bistros waiting for word from Italy than they did pursuing the wonders of nature and reading to one another.

"We do everything in an auto!" Wilder wrote his sister, Isabel. "I long for walking and resting and staying somewhere. But at least we saw some of the splendid mountain roads."

In Paris, Wilder introduced Gene to Ernest Hemingway at Brasserie Lipp, and they renewed acquaintances with F. Scott Fitzgerald at the Ritz Bar. "Gene and I called by to meet Zelda and chew the rag with you," Wilder wrote on a card left at Fitzgerald's flat. "See you Tuesday at the Racquet." Reporters dogged their footsteps and after leaving town, Wilder wrote a friend: "All the racket and the literary introductions leave a bad taste in my mouth. And I wish the noble Gene weren't so famous. I'm gnawing a curious discontent."

Following one unsuccessful day of trying to contact the bride by ship's radio, Tunney's nerves were on edge, and he and Wilder were at loggerheads. "I am sorry — damn sorry," Gene wrote Wilder. "It is far from my wish to ever say a mean or hurtful thing to you. I was quite peeved for a moment yesterday after you had for the third time during the day refused to do something or other that I suggested. I may have said something mean after the third refusal, for I was mad enough to. If I did, please forgive me. I am genuinely sorry." Wilder headed for the seashore alone, and Gene told his friend that he hoped he had a good rest, "for you certainly must need it after spending two weeks with a love-impregnated person."

TUNNEY AND THORNTON
WILDER HIKING IN THE SWISS
ALPS IN 1928. TUNNEY WROTE
ON THE BACK OF THE PRINT
"JUST A COUPLE OF REGULAR
TOURISTS DOING THE USUAL
THING ON THE *MER DE GLACE*.
KEEP THIS OUT OF THE HAND
OF PRESSMEN" (TUNNEY
COLLECTION).

SITTING FOR A RARE POSED
PORTRAIT IN PARIS WERE
THORNTON WILDER AND
TUNNEY (FRONT), WITH
F. SCOTT FITZGERALD
(MIDDLE, BACK) BETWEEN
TWO UNIDENTIFIED FRIENDS
(TUNNEY COLLECTION).

The impending marriage had drawn so much press attention that to have any privacy, Gene decided the wedding had to be held as soon as Polly arrived, two weeks earlier than anticipated, in effect cutting short the long-planned tour with Wilder. "I shall never cease regretting that we did not leave Paris...weeks earlier," he wrote Wilder.

Tunney drove to Rome and contacted Salvatore Cortesi, the influential head of the Associated Press bureau, a recommendation from the news agency's chief executive. (When Cortesi joined the AP in 1902, he gave two references: Giuseppe Sarto, the Pope of the Roman Catholic Church, and Victor Emmanuel, the King of Italy.) Cortesi would become Gene's wedding planner and the key to unraveling the Byzantine labyrinth of the Italian civil and religious laws for an American Catholic who wished to marry a Protestant. Cortesi's wife was a Bostonian named Isabella Lauder Cochrane, and though not known to be related to Polly, the Cortesi family embraced Gene, helping him to keep the details secret and advising him on matters of style and etiquette.

"I did not know until three days before our marriage when or where it would take place," Gene wrote Adelaide Marquand, wife of author John Marquand. "It was not until the ship docked at midnight, in Naples, that I could risk making plans."

The New York Times said the couple was "besieged by almost all the journalists and press photographers in Europe." New York's *Daily Mirror*, claiming it had scooped all other papers with titillating updates of the world's most sensational romance, assigned a former war correspondent to dog the couple's every step.

The marriage had become the biggest love story of the year.

While waiting in Naples for Polly's ship, Gene had to barricade himself in a hotel room to escape reporters. Minstrels with guitars and mandolins, paid off by newsmen, sang love songs under his closed windows for two days and nights. When Gene telephoned the desk clerk to check if he could get through the lobby, he was told it was full of members of the press biding their time. Finally, after hours of being captive in his room, he arranged for a diversion with the hotel manager and bolted out the back door through the kitchen with photographers racing in close pursuit.

When Polly disembarked late in the day on October 2 to be met by the groom, the couple was mobbed by reporters demanding details of the upcoming nuptials. Aided by port police and security guards, they pushed their way through jostling crowds of cameramen and sightseers to climb into the limousines waiting for the wedding party.

"The story is one as beautiful as any ever written by a romanticist or a poet," wrote columnist Walter Trumbull. "It is the story of the princess in the ivory car and the boy who stood, wide-eyed and bare-headed, by the roadside to watch her pass. She was a lady in a high tower. She couldn't come down to him. He had to climb up to her." That explains many things about Gene Tunney, wrote Trumbull. "The heavyweight championship of the world was not his ultimate goal. He worked and he studied, and he developed physically, mentally and spiritually. He finally gathered such wealth and knowledge that the champion's crown was of no further value, but only a detriment, and he tossed it aside."

The marriage, wrote many columnists, was an American fairy tale. The public was mesmerized, and its appetite for intimate details far exceeded the couple's willingness to cooperate with the press.

"If the object of all Tunney's secretive tactics is to keep the details of his wedding projects secret, it must be conceded that he has succeeded," wrote *The New York Times*. "The mystery is almost as deep now as it was before his arrival in Rome." While word was purposely leaked that they might marry in Naples or Trieste or even Scotland, the wedding party raced through the night directly to Rome and the elegant Grand Hotel de Russie with its terraced gardens, sumptuous rooms and flowering orange, palm and cypress trees, the favorite hostelry of the last Tsar of Russia. On the way, Polly learned she had only a day to prepare.

Before noon on October 3, hotel staff were gathered in antechambers and sworn to secrecy, and dozens of uniformed bellmen and waiters were dis-

WEDDING DAY IN ROM
(TUNNEY COLLECTION

tributed at intervals along all corridors leading to the Royal Apartments, normally reserved for visiting sovereigns, where the wedding was to take place. The only additional guests, besides those who had arrived by ship, were Wilder, the tenor John McCormack with his wife and daughter, and the officials needed to conduct and witness the ceremony.

Massive gilt chandeliers hung from the ceiling in the suite's main salon, and a simple altar was set up surrounded by a dozen tall vases of white roses in front of a large reproduction of Michelangelo's *Madonna della Scala*. Dark inlaid marble tables lined the walls with porcelains and bronzes, and screens defining the majestic room were painted with rococo scrollwork, animals and butterflies and figures of the goddess Ariadne reclining while Pan played his pipes and Bacchus danced with grapes in his hair.

The Vatican had given a special dispensation for the religious ceremony to be performed in a hotel and not in the sacristy of a church. But despite intervention by the American ambassador and pleadings from the Italian ministry on behalf of the press, Tunney refused to allow news coverage or even confirm the day and time of the wedding. The only outsider permitted was Cortesi's son, who, posing as a waiter, gave AP exclusive coverage.

As Gene had been warned, the wedding was front-page news. It was reported "as exhaustively as though [it] involved a wedding between crowned heads of state," wrote one author. Dozens of newspaper and magazine reporters and photographers representing every major news outlet in Europe and the United States had been alerted that the nuptials were imminent. Barred from the hotel, members of the press took up positions outside. Taxis, bicycles, cars and carts jammed the narrow sidewalks and streets adjacent to the hotel, snarling traffic and backing up vehicles in the center of the city. Hundreds of tourists and curious Italians, drawn by the cameras and tripods, pushed into the crowds around the press to try to see what was happening. *Carabinieri*, some on horseback, were called in to help police control the increasingly restless throng of onlookers.

"Tunney is Married to Mary J. Lauder in Hotel in Rome," blared a page-one *New York Times* headline. "Photographers, banned from rites, charge in body as pair go — cameras smashed, man arrested," said another headline.

A civil ceremony in Italian was held first, with the bride and groom replying "*Si*," at appropriate passages. The religious ceremony was conducted by Monsignor Joseph A. Breslin, formerly of New York, rector of the American College and an old friend of the groom. A string quartet concealed behind screens in an adjoining room played Mendelssohn's *Wedding March*, and kisses, champagne and a gala luncheon followed the ceremony. "*Grazie tante*," said Gene repeatedly, in accepting congratulations. Thank you so much. The bridegroom was half-shy and half-jovial, and the radiant bride had sweet smiles, noted the waiter Cortesi. Polly, who had nothing to do with the arrangements, was thrilled to have the secrecy behind her but became alarmed once she learned of the crowds milling outside the hotel.

When the newlyweds arrived at the entrance of the hotel to depart for their honeymoon, the mob of reporters and photographers, their tempers worn thin by hours of fruitless waiting, charged at Polly and Gene, their cameras high and flashbulbs popping. "It was a perfect nightmare," she wrote. "All those bright lights and the dim sea of faces and ogling eyes. Every time I tried to smile and look pleasant my lips would tremble as though I were going to cry — sheer nerves!"

As a large chauffeur-driven touring car moved into the crowd, Gene put his arm around his terrified bride in order to shield her from the photographers. Shouting angrily at the cameramen to back off, he held Polly tightly and dashed for the automobile, pushing aside those who tried to block him.

Enraged at being foiled in their attempt to get pictures, photographers surged around the car. Hoots and catcalls were heard, while many had their cameras smashed and their clothes torn in the confusion. Polly was ashen, her hands clenched around Gene's arm, and Tunney — a man so calm in the ring he seemed often placid — was red in the face, eyes flashing, having to restrain himself from physically lashing out.

"No! No! You won't move until we get pictures," yelled photographers blocking the car. "Signor Toonie! Signor Toonie!" yelled reporters, trying to grab his attention.

"Jeers and catcalls rang out! Excited men shook their fists at the couple!" said the New York *Daily News*, which had dispatched a reporter to Rome to cover the wedding.

"Something that looked mighty like a riot continued for a few moments," said the *Times*, "when the police interfered, arrested one photographer and re-established order."

Tunney's chauffeur sped off, knocking over several camera tripods. "Tunney and Bride Hissed" was the headline on the *Daily News* story. "Crowd Irked by High-Hat Ceremonies."

Later, at Gene's instruction, a guest released a photograph taken immediately after the ceremony, showing Polly in a long-sleeved gold-colored velvet dress with Venetian lace and wearing a silver hair net decorated with pearls. The wedding outfit had been made to look like the character Marguerite in *Faust*, the romantic opera by Charles Gounod, one of Polly's favorites. In the opera, the tender maiden Marguerite is loved by Dr. Faust during his one day of returned youth, the gift of Mephistopheles.

As Gene sped off with Polly, he carried in his breast pocket a crumpled postcard that had arrived the morning of the wedding. It had been forwarded from London's Savoy Hotel, first to Aix-les-Baines and Avignon in France, and from there to the American consulate in Naples and, finally, to the Hotel de Russie. The postcard was at least the fourth or fifth attempt by Bernard Shaw to contact Gene by mail or cable, though it was the first piece Gene had actually received. Rarely had Shaw had so much difficulty getting hold of someone he wanted to invite to lunch, especially one who seemed to pop up in the press daily.

> Just to say — in case you are at the Savoy — that I wrote to you from Geneva to c/o the American Express Co. 6 Haymarket Square and have had no reply. Tomorrow (Saturday) afternoon, I go down to Ayot St. Lawrence until Thursday next.
>
> G. Bernard Shaw.

TOP TO BOTTOM: CROWDS OF REPORTERS AND CAMERAMEN MOBBED THE WEDDING PARTY IN NAPLES, OCTOBER 1928; THE NEWLYWED TUNNEYS SPOKE BRIEFLY TO NEWSREEL CAMERAMEN AS THEY LEFT POLA, ITALY, ON THEIR WAY TO ENGLAND WHERE THEY WOULD MEET THE SHAWS, DECEMBER 1928. (TUNNEY COLLECTION).

CHAPTER 9

4 Whitehall Court

"Max Beerbohm & his wife are lunching with us today
at 1:30. So are Gene Tunney and Mrs. Tunney!!!"
G. BERNARD SHAW TO MAURICE BARING

"G.B.S., you know, loved prizefighters," said Max Beerbohm, England's favorite caricaturist and *bon vivant*. "He had a deep regard for prizefighters."
So it was no surprise to Max when, ten days before Christmas in 1928, his
friend Shaw invited him to lunch to meet the boxer who had become the toast
of Britain only months before. Shaw had been frustrated that he had missed
the earlier visit, all the more so because friends had told intriguing stories
about meeting the young man, even going so far as to say that the boxer
Tunney was Shaw's fictional Cashel Byron come to life. Shaw was delighted
by the unexpected attention linking him to a manly young man of action,
and had appreciated Tunney's remarks to newspapers on Samuel Butler's *The
Way of All Flesh*, but he preferred to make his own decisions regarding the
fellow's attributes.

"Tell Gene I will be delighted to meet him," Shaw had told the London
Daily Mail the previous August. "In fact, I have every intention of making his
acquaintance. We will meet as private gentlemen. I will discuss boxing, and
Gene will discuss literature, and we ought to get along very well."

In November, the head of London's Golden Square Throat, Nose and
Ear Hospital read in the *Daily Mail* that the playwright expected to meet the
boxer and wrote Shaw, suggesting the hospital sponsor a fund-raising dinner
for the two celebrities. Shaw's response was immediate.

"Mr. Tunney, who has been a specialist in traumatic nose and ear cases,
might entertain the proposal," Shaw wrote back. "But it is against my rules.
I am obliged in self-preservation to repel all attempts to exploit my publicity
for the relief of the rates and taxes, on which the cost of the hospital should
properly fall."

It had taken three months to set up a meeting. The newlyweds arrived in
London from Paris about a week before Shaw's luncheon, purposely coming
in late at night to try to avoid the press. A note from Charlotte Shaw was waiting at the hotel, saying how glad she and her husband would be to host them
both. "It will be quite a small affair as we live very quietly," wrote Charlotte.
She signed the note C.F. Shaw, but in parenthesis at the bottom, as if to be certain the Tunneys recognized their hostess, wrote: "Mrs. G. Bernard Shaw!"

Gene was anxious for his bride to meet some of his new friends and
concerned that reporters might spoil it. The people he wanted to know better

were not the sort who would endure what Gene called "the powerful numbing light of international publicity," and he worried that the press would isolate him from the very people he wanted to be with. These were people like Hugh Walpole, who didn't want to be followed by photographers or have dinner constantly interrupted by autograph-seekers, as had happened to him when he accompanied Gene on his earlier visit.

"It was so fine being able to see so much of you," Gene had written Walpole after his first visit to London. "I fully realize the loveliness of your friendship and value it beyond measure." He also promised that when they met again, "I will make every effort to keep it quiet and private."

"The former pugilist is on the warpath so far as the press is concerned," fumed a front page news report after word leaked that the couple had settled into the Royal Suite at London's opulent Savoy Hotel. A newspaper photographer telephoned Tunney asking if he could take his picture.

"No!" said Tunney curtly.

"I see you mean what you say," said the startled photographer.

"You are very perspicacious," replied Gene, and he hung up.

Gene found privacy by inviting guests to dine in his suite. Walpole, a New Zealander educated in England, liked boxing and opera and had spent three boyhood years only blocks from Gene's childhood home. He and Gene discussed old manuscripts (Walpole was a collector), the Great War (he had been decorated for rescuing a wounded man under fire) and the church (his father became Bishop of Edinburgh). Gene was eager to be associated with Walpole for the literary ideas and insights that the good-natured author was so willing to share.

Polly was interested in Walpole's research for what would become *Rogue Herries*, the first of *The Herries Chronicles*, and the publication of his new biography of the popular 19th-century novelist Anthony Trollope. (Two years later, Tunney accompanied Walpole to a lecture he was giving on the novel in New York City. The audience mobbed Walpole with books to be autographed, and in the spirit of being helpful, Tunney stood by his friend to ease the crush. Press reports claimed many attendees were surprised to find the autograph in their book was that of Tunney, *not* Walpole.)

The two friends discussed authors, including Somerset Maugham, who, after they met at Yale, had invited Gene to visit him on the Riviera. Later, when Maugham's scandalous 1930 satire *Cakes and Ale* was published, with a scathing portrait of a character based on Walpole, Gene wrote that Maugham's creativeness had come to an end: "Too bad, for he did do a few very good things. I shall never forget *Of Human Bondage*, though in my humble and entirely unliterary opinion, he slightly plagiarized Samuel Butler. Several of his plays were masterpieces, particularly *Rain*. It is pathetic that so brilliant a mind could become so poisoned with envy, vitriol and sheer malice. *Cakes and Ale* finishes him for all time as an artist!"

Walpole was unable to attend Shaw's lunch, though he offered the amusing tidbit that he and Shaw shared the same barber, the assistant hairdresser to King George V. He went on to tell them that the King and other royalty had patronized the Savoy so often that at one point, the hotel set up a special bell heralding their arrival. "Both the best and the worst place to hide out," observed Gene. "O, to be Lord of one's self, uncumbered [sic] with a name," Gene wrote Walpole, borrowing a line from Hazlitt.

Gene and Polly both hoped Thornton Wilder could meet them in London, but Wilder, already annoyed at being caught in Gene's limelight, was traveling in Europe. Gene had repeatedly assured Thornt that he would not discuss their friendship with reporters. "Do not unnecessarily disturb yourself about my reported interviews," he wrote Wilder. "You are a kindred spirit and our kinship started aeons and aeons ago on some spiritual plane of eternity. There is no measuring it by weeks or months or years. It seems to have always been. When I talk of friends for publication, I mean the 'Babbitt' type. I never discuss my *real* friends with news reporters; they are too sacred for that. The 'penny-a-liners,' as Schopenhauer called them, who would discuss our friendship in a light vein, don't even interest me…I am aloof. I am not interested in drivel, even if I happen to be the subject."

Polly was fidgeting, walking around the spacious hotel suite and looking down from the tall, heavily curtained windows across the low, peaked roofs of the West End. She stopped to do what she called cat stretches. Balancing herself in front of a wide desk facing outwards toward a commanding view of the River Thames, she put her arms over her head, standing first on one leg, then the other and, when finished, bent easily to touch her toes. She was trying to unwind before lunch with Mr. and Mrs. Shaw, and she had to find just the right outfit for a chilly December day.

She was, she admitted to herself, terribly nervous. This was her first social event as the new Mrs. Tunney, and she had no idea what to prepare for, except that it was a gathering with influential writers and friends of the Shaws. She had hoped that Thornt could have attended or even nice Mr. Walpole, people she *knew*. Polly appreciated that meeting Shaw was going to be a highlight of the trip for Gene, but she was worried about how she would handle it. Though a fan of his plays, she was acquainted with the playwright's prickly reputation for didactic rhetoric, and she was desperately concerned that she could be trapped in discussion without any notion of how to respond.

She had unkind memories of being ensnared in conversations in another time, when in the imposing living room at *Tighnabruaich* she would be dressed up with a big, floppy bow in her hair for guests and be told by the governess Miss Hilda "to sit, child, still as a turnip and talk only when ye be spoken to." Adults — even her mother, she thought — would look at her as if she were a rare insect while they waited for her to respond to something she either didn't understand or didn't hear in her nervousness. She always tried to smile or stuff a sweet in her mouth, and if she were lucky, Cot talked for her.

But Cot wasn't in London. Polly knew Gene didn't appreciate what it was like to be self-conscious and tongue-tied among strangers, and strangers for Polly were pretty much everyone outside of her immediate family. She didn't look nervous. She looked composed and ladylike, even regal. But inside, Polly was in a panic.

Gene, on the other hand, was electrified by the prospect of meeting Shaw and was not intimidated. "Social position, political prestige, financial power or the hurrahs of the crowd — none of it matters," said Gene. "The thing that matters is character," and he felt he could size a man up, that he was a good judge of character. Gene was more excited about the chance to become acquainted with Shaw than anyone he could ever remember meeting. Shaw embodied the kind of man he wished that he could become, and though he couldn't identify the reason, he told Polly that he felt that he knew Shaw through his writing more intimately that any other author he had ever read.

He had achieved his goal of accumulating wealth — he had $2 million in the bank — and marrying the woman of his dreams, but he wanted to become someone different from his public persona. He wanted to prove that he could remake himself, that he wasn't a person who affected a manner of culture just to impress others. He yearned to contribute to society, and he longed for the kind of lasting respectability that would come from being accepted by those he emulated — people such as Walpole, Wilder and Professor Billy Phelps. More than he wanted to admit, the barbs of the press had stung, wounding him deeply, and he saw a higher purpose in creating a personal life of achievement. He knew that there were detractors who felt he was a sham, a posturing Irishman in new clothes. His old Greenwich Village friends thought he was a snob for marrying rich and moving uptown with the Protestant Yankees, and some of the uptown crowd felt he should go back to the docks and the "lace-curtain" Irish. He was near the golden circle of America's power establishment, but also outside of it, a man between two worlds and a part of neither one.

Polly watched Gene pick up the telephone. "Victoria 3160," said Gene, speaking to an operator. "Mr. Shaw's flat, please." Charlotte Shaw answered, and Polly heard him say how much he looked forward to meeting Mr. Shaw, and that they would be at Number Four, Whitehall Court, at precisely 1:30 pm Polly clenched and unclenched her hands and then shook them out gently to relax.

Whitehall Court was "a palace of flats," a sprawling, four-story, turreted white stone apartment complex with steep roofs built at the end of the 19th century along the embankment on the River Thames in the style of a French chateau. The land had been given to the royal family of Scotland by the English Crown about 800 A.D., and the area itself was commonly called Whitehall or Scotland Yard because it was also the home of the metropolitan police force. The blocks were built with apartments of three or four bedrooms each. The Shaws had moved the year before from Adelphi Terrace to a spacious, five-room flat vacated by Bertrand Russell's former sister-in-law, the novelist Elizabeth, Countess Russell. It was surrounded by balconies on the corner of the fourth floor, overlooking the river.

Polly and Gene, driven by chauffeur, passed Buckingham Palace and approached the Shaws' apartment complex from Horseguards Avenue, driving past the Banqueting House, the only surviving fragment of the Palace of Whitehall, where King James I used to watch Will Shakespeare act in his own plays, and where, in 1649, King Charles I stepped from a first-floor window onto a scaffold, where he was beheaded. "History-rich London," said Gene. "It's like tripping through a library with figures larger than life. I need to read more history."

Alighting from their car and facing the imposing façade of Whitehall Court felt to Polly a little like arriving at court. She watched Gene pull down and button his suit jacket and take a comb from his pocket to smooth back his thick wavy hair, which had a way of flopping forward. A sign that he's a little nervous too, she thought. A liveried doorman saw the car pull up, bowed obsequiously and escorted them up the steps to the door. They entered a small lobby with a chandelier, Tiffany-style windows, marble tiles and wood paneling. There was even a fire in the fireplace to warm the space. The lobby reminded Polly of the apartments on Fifth and Park Avenues in New York City; the visitors' lobby, designated only for residents of one section of the complex, those at Number Four, kept a guest from being overwhelmed by the building's tremendous size.

Personal attention was immediate — nice, Polly thought with relief. When in doubt, she had always found the etiquette of ceremony and protocol reassuring. They were expected. A gentleman who seemed aware of the subtleties of English class distinctions bowed politely, identified himself as a footman and, as Polly squeezed Gene's hand for reassurance, escorted them upstairs to the Shaws' door.

"We are so pleased to finally be able to meet you, Mr. Tunney," Charlotte Shaw told Gene in greeting him. "G.B.S. thought he was jinxed because he kept missing you."

"From the moment Charlotte took my hand at the door, I felt at home," said Polly. Charlotte had all the qualities of a country gentlewoman, with masses of curling gray-brown hair and beautiful eyes, a tailor-made dress that might have been expensive but didn't look it, and the graceful movements of a natural hostess comfortable with her age and her household. "She was charming and dear, with wonderful manners. I was immensely impressed, being very young, inexperienced and out in the world. Charlotte put me at ease immediately. She was very warm, very motherly with me."

The apartment, bathed in pale afternoon sunshine, was exactly what the home of a famous writer should be, thought Polly, with piles of books and papers and writing instruments, tastefully furnished with portraits of Descartes, Einstein, Schopenhauer, Nietzsche and Strindberg. There was a grandfather clock ticking in the hallway, a clavichord with sheet music, landscapes by Sartori, a striking pastel of a young, green-eyed Charlotte Shaw, a bust of Shaw by Rodin, Chinese porcelains, beautiful, softly muted Oriental rugs and, in the sitting room, chairs at every angle filled with people talking.

The man they had heard so much about bounded toward them, all snowy-white beard, pink cheeks and sparkling blue eyes, looking for a moment to the astonished young Americans like an animated version of Uncle Sam, a caricature that had leapt from a wall poster so quickly that he was stripped of his red, white and blue clothes. He was as tall as Gene, though slender, with a ramrod posture that immediately reminded Polly to stand tall and keep her shoulders back. He looked so much like her beloved Uncle Pete that she was almost too startled to speak.

"He just breathed health and gaiety. He took Gene by the arm and they were immediately engrossed in conversation as if they'd known one another their entire lives," said Polly. "I was enchanted."

She was relieved that Charlotte stayed by her side. Polly said later that perhaps Shaw's experience of feeling awkward as a young Irishman in London society made both him and Charlotte particularly sensitive to making sure she and Gene felt welcome. For this, she was grateful.

Tunney's bride was almost as much an object of interest to Shaw as the groom. News reports identified her as an heiress, a relative of multimillionaire industrialist and philanthropist Andrew Carnegie. Carnegie was one of Shaw's models for the role of the wealthy Andrew Undershaft, the lead character in his successful theatrical production, *Major Barbara*, a play about wealth and poverty, business and salvation, pragmatism and idealism, a play meant to illustrate that the root of all evil is not money but the lack of it, because only money can provide food, education and housing for the poor.

Shaw agreed with Carnegie's view that surplus wealth was a sacred trust that its possessor is bound to administer in his lifetime for the good of the community and that ties of brotherhood should bind together the rich and the poor in fair and productive relationships. "There was a man, though some did think him mad, the more he gave away, the more he had," Shaw wrote, quoting from *Pilgrim's Progress*. Besides endowing free public libraries in the United States and the British Commonwealth, Carnegie also believed that no child should inherit a voice in a family business, an idea which may have inspired the Undershaft family tradition.

Shaw himself had married an heiress (though he had waited until attaining success before he did so) and significantly, his life's work reflected his observations of classes in Victorian society. He was acutely aware of the gulf between a man who started with poor roots and a woman who grew up in luxury. He admired those women who could defy social conventions while also remaining true to themselves, seeing in them the moral courage of Raina, the heroine in his play *Arms and the Man*, who befriends an enemy soldier and falls in love with him, or the wealthy Lydia Carew, who marries the boxer Cashel Byron.

Other luncheon guests included Maurice Baring, author of the memoir *The Puppet Show of Memory* and member of the highly visible family who owned the international merchant bank, Baring Brothers; H.G. Wells, science fiction writer nonpareil and contentious colleague of Shaw's at the Fabian Society; the leading Irish painter and portraitist Sir John Lavery and his wife Hazel, daughter of a Chicago industrialist and one of the most influential hostesses in Dublin and London; the inimitable critic and caricaturist from the *Saturday Review*, Max Beerbohm and his actress wife; the artist and writer John Collier, whose evocative painting *The Last Voyage of Henry Hudson* the young Tunneys had admired at the Tate, and Shaw's old friend and connoisseur of the arts, Sydney Cockerell, director of the Fitzwilliam Museum in Cambridge.

Almost immediately, the talk turned to the guests of honor and their ongoing efforts to evade the press. "It seems to take people a couple of days

TUNNEY WITH H.G. WELLS AND CHARLIE CHAPLIN, 1935 (CORBIS).

to make up their minds as to whether or not we are the *famous Tunneys* and by that time we are ready to leave," said Gene. "So I would say our 'incog' has been successful so far." (Tabloid stories told of the couple "standing in the moonlight" in Teruga, picnicking in Perugia and holding hands in Florence. "I thought on account of his going to Europe to marry, that maybe he was going to get a Shakespeare to marry them," quipped Will Rogers.) Polly was relieved when the talk turned to Gene and became less personal.

Gene basked in the attention, yet he remembered later being baffled as to why, when surrounded by intellectuals, his accomplishments in the ring and his observations on the pouring rain in Philadelphia ("wet resin made the slippery canvas feel like skating on ice") and running backwards ("five miles a day and you get proficient") were more interesting than the theatre or literature. He had known boxing his entire adult life and having saturated himself in it and learned all that he could, he had purposely left the ring behind and was now mentally galloping forward, exploring every new book and idea that came to him, trying to build on what he had already taught himself to make up for his lost education.

"I found in England that literary men and scholars in general were interested in the prize ring," Gene wrote. "The more classical they were, the greater their interest. This may seem strange, but their attitude toward pugilism was largely intellectual. Like the classical Greeks, they idealized the boxer as the well-trained warrior athlete. I found that when I wanted to talk about books, they wanted to talk to me about boxing.

"H.G. Wells was different. He wanted to talk about women."

For Gene, it was the beginning of a lifetime of grappling with balancing his past ring celebrity against his personal interests of reading, music, the arts and later, business. Astute as he was, he understood quickly that boxing was his key to meeting the people he wanted to meet. Politely, even eloquently, he played the part.

The questions about his career were relentless. What was Jack Dempsey like? Could Gene have gotten up during the Long Count? Had he really retired? Who will be the next champion? Did he ever see Joe Beckett in the ring? Why do Americans have sluggers, instead of scientific fighters? Why did he read books in training? Why didn't the American press take to him?

The saving grace was his host. Shaw was the only person at lunch, outside of himself, who appreciated prizefighting as a metaphor in a broader social, economic and historical context. Therefore, discussing boxing with Shaw was more than hammering Cashel Byron over the newswires, as they had done two years earlier, but was tantamount to talking about life. In addition, Gene saw immediately that Shaw actually enjoyed conversation about "the Game," and when Gene eagerly joined in, the playwright boldly seized center stage. Shaw liked boxing as he liked the theatre.

"He liked the language of it, the nuances of training, the skill, the masculinity, the personalities, the sense of being part of something unpredictable that had a beginning, a middle and an end. He was, surprisingly to me, a remarkably knowledgeable boxing fan," said Gene, who was astonished that Shaw had once boxed some himself.

Shaw recounted how he had become a pugilist through his old friend, the poet Pakenham Beatty, with whom he used to spar regularly. He called Beatty one of the most humorous and fantastic characters he'd ever known. They talked about the history of boxing and its earliest recorded use in literature, a conversation that tempted other guests. "Everyone joined in the discussion," remembered Polly, who was amazed to hear authors she knew discussed through the prism of the boxing world. It was a revelation.

Virgil's *Aeneid* has one of the earliest detailed descriptions of a boxing match, a contest between Dares and Entellus, said Shaw. Gene responded that he read and reread Greek and Roman histories and recalled Homer writing about boxers, about the terrible grinding of the teeth and the sweat and the great hearts who gave and withstood blows.

Shaw said William Hazlitt's 1822 essay *The Fight*, on the bare-knuckles battle between Thomas "the Gasman" Hickman and Bill Neate, was a classic. A surprised Gene agreed, saying that he always carried a copy of it in his traveling bag. They discussed fighting as depicted in literature by Victor Hugo, William Thackeray, Conan Doyle and Charles Dickens.

And, of course, said Gene, there was Mr. Shaw's own *Cashel Byron*, to whom he paid tribute for best describing the scientific art of "slipping a punch." Saying that slipping a punch and countering was the principal reason for his own effectiveness in the ring, he quoted the sentence — perfectly, Shaw said — which described the move: "Cashel's blows were never so tremendous as when he turned his head deftly out of harm's way, and met his advancing foe with a counter hit." Gene turned his head and shoulder as if deflecting a punch, then brought his hand around to demonstrate.

Shaw beamed quite happily and seemed to enjoy the conversation, Polly recalled, though she, too, was perplexed as to why so many learned people with much to offer in terms of current affairs and literature would want to discuss the sport of boxing.

Shaw told Gene that he had been following his career in newspaper reports and motion pictures of his prizefights from the time Gene had beaten Georges Carpentier in 1924.

"I'm astonished," said Gene. "But why that fight? That fight was not my best."

"You won me over because of one particular point," said Shaw. "When I saw the motion pictures and observed Carpentier bounce right-hand punches off your jaw — plenty of them — I thought, 'Aha, there is a coming champion. He has a jaw of iron.'"

"I have no reason to be flattered by this," said Gene. "Getting pummeled with anybody's rights is no satisfaction to a ring man who knows how to box. Carpentier had a good right hand, sharp and hard, and he hit me with it more than once. But if I had been in condition, I should have won quickly, not in the 15th round."

"What do you mean?" asked Lady Lavery, the picture of elegance in a long shawl draped around her body. She became famous as the face adorning the Irish pound and 10 shilling notes that carried a portrait of her painted by her husband. Polly thought her one of the most beautiful women she had ever met and was stunned later when Lady Lavery told her she would like to attend a prizefight and asked Polly if she had done so. Polly smiled and shook her head "no."

"My training for Carpentier was all off," said Gene. "There was no help for it. I had to make the light heavyweight limit of 175 pounds, when actually I had grown too big to be a light heavyweight. I had to take off pounds. For a final ironic touch, the scales in my training camp turned out to be faulty. I discovered this when I weighed in on the afternoon of the fight and was several pounds below the light heavyweight limit. In fact, I had taken off seven pounds the day before the fight. I was badly over-trained, one of the worst things in boxing."

"You were not in the pink," said Shaw.

"No," said Gene. "I was more like the sere and yellow leaf."

Shaw explained to the guests that "pink" is a term derived from the old days of boxing when a fighter stepped out of a cold bath — never a hot bath, which was considered debilitating — and the trainer judged the condition of the man's body. A boxer trained to the right point of physical conditioning would emerge from cold water a glowing pink.

"And you, G.B.S., you are always in the pink?" offered Max Beerbohm, the caricaturist.

"G.B.S. was born pink," replied an amused Lady Lavery.

Gene said he once arrived in the pinkest of the pink in Pittsburgh for a fight and nearly blew it. It was his second bout with Jack Burke, a boxer who carried the same name as the boxer Shaw had used as a model for Cashel Byron. Jack Burke was a ring name and there are at least three Burkes. In 1893, one of them, not Shaw's Burke and not Tunney's Burke, fought the longest recorded glove fight in boxing history — 110 rounds, lasting seven hours and 19 minutes. Ring names serve the same purpose as stage names in the theatre and are usually taken from a popular fighter who became champion. There were, for instance, two Jack Dempseys. The man Gene fought, William Harrison Dempsey, took the name "Jack" from a great middleweight of the late 19th century.

Gene said his first bout with his Burke, which he won, had also been his first professional fight in Madison Square Garden. The second fight against

Burke, in Pittsburgh, turned out to be tougher.

"I was fit and ready, but it was a broiling hot day, so I stopped and had a tall glass of ale. After my walk, I put away a big porterhouse steak and another tall glass. The result," he went on, "was several pounds of extra weight and a complete waterlogging. It is hard for the layman to understand what it means to a boxer to be a mere few pounds overweight."

"What happened?" asked Shaw.

"I couldn't do a thing in the ring," said Gene. "I couldn't get out of my own way. At the beginning of every round, he would walk out and nail me in the jaw. He could hit, I assure you. All I could do with Burke was to stay in close and avoid the haymakers and at the same time keep him busy in-fighting."

At this, Gene got up to demonstrate what he meant. To the amusement of the guests, Shaw stepped forward to be the other man "in the ring" to demonstrate in-fighting. With Gene on one side and Shaw on the other, they moved in on each other close enough to wrestle but in fact were acting out a fight at close range, with each man feinting in an attempt to try to get in position to land a short, punishing blow. There was much laughter at this exercise.

"Along about the seventh round, I began to feel fresh and lively," said Gene, continuing his narration as he moved quicker, bringing more laughter from among the guests. "I had fought myself into condition and sweated out the excess fluid. After that, I had no trouble. Bam! I knocked him out." With that, he moved his right fist to within two inches of Shaw's chin as if to punch him out. The playwright threw his head back and laughed, greatly enjoying his role in the demonstration.

Before lunch was served, the honored guests were ushered out onto a balcony that encircled the flat to "taste the view," as Charlotte put it. Ahead was the Thames; to the right across the trees on the Victoria Embankment, one could see Westminster Bridge, Big Ben and the Houses of Parliament along the river, with the towers of Westminster Abbey just beyond. "Has G.B.S. told you about Big Ben?" inquired Sydney Cockerell, who was standing alongside. "If not, he hasn't had time yet. It's one of his favorite stories."

"Please," said Gene, "tell us."

"Big Ben is the nickname of the bell in the Clock Tower. There are many versions of how the name came about, but G.B.S. takes the view that it's named after a 19th-century boxer with Shaw's ears, that is, ears that stuck out like sails," said Cockerell. "Big Ben" Caunt, 6 feet 3 inches, fought his last fight in 1857, a bare-knuckle fight that went 60 rounds.

Below the balcony and along the embankment was a promenade with rows of stately plane trees and statuary. The embankment was built on land reclaimed from the river to ease traffic congestion and hide the main London sewer system. Cockerell said he could remember the odor of fermented sewage that in past times was so horrific Parliament occasionally had to recess. They looked down on flower beds, now fallow in winter, a curving walkway, street lamps and, almost directly under the Shaws' apartment, a statue of William Tyndale, the 16th-century scholar who was strangled and burnt at the stake for heresy for being the first to challenge the Catholic Church by translating the New Testament from Latin into English so that common folk could read it. Inscribed on the statue was a verse from Psalms: "The word is a lamp to my feet and a light to my path."

Charlotte said their move to Whitehall Court the year before initially was unsettling. But, she said, the new flat had more sunlight, expansive views and even a restaurant in the building. And, said Charlotte with sparkling eyes, for the first time they had a bathroom in their apartment, instead of having to use chamber pots.

At lunch, Gene sat across the table from Shaw, totally engrossed. Polly knew that Shaw, like the poet Shelley, was vegetarian and watched when he was served what looked like a haystack of carrots and turnips while the rest of the party, including Mrs. Shaw, had meat. She made a mental note to ask Mrs. Shaw about it because her mother was fastidious about food, and Shaw's choices appeared to keep him radiantly healthy, buoyant and exceptionally fit.

As the light of the winter afternoon faded, changing the colors of the dining room and softening the aura around the guests, Polly felt she had known these people her entire life. They stayed at lunch a long time, and no one cared. No butler hung over them, and no one rang a bell under the table, which in Polly's growing up seemed always to signal haste in marching on to finish the meal.

The host had an actor's ability to call attention to himself and to regale his audience with wit and stories, to hold center stage. He raised his eyebrows in mock horror when Gene mentioned Hollywood and burst into song with a few bars of "It's a Long Way to Tipperary" when Gene said he had been to the Dublin races. Yet he never showed a hint of condescension toward others, and Polly and Gene were amazed at how relaxed the Shaws made them feel and how generous in spirit they seemed.

"These were very interesting people and we were included as if we were among our closest friends," Polly recalled. She was also surprised, and impressed, that her husband and the playwright had seemed so quickly to form a bond, and initially she amused herself by wondering if it was based on the Irish gift of gab and a bit of blarney.

Tunney and Shaw's immediate affinity for one another at Whitehall Court reflected also an instinctive recognition that each had successfully won the struggle to become someone by overcoming hardscrabble Irish roots. Aside from their shared humor, which was considerable, both were optimistic, self-educated and driven. They instantly liked and trusted one another, and although competitive with others, the difference in their ages and their fields of expertise freed them from competing with each other. Tunney became one of the few people outside of the playwright's elderly contemporaries who treated Shaw as an equal, without deference. It was a trait that distinguished the boxer and pleased the playwright.

"Tunney is a remarkable man," the painter Sir John Lavery had told the *Evening Standard* after he had asked Gene to sit for a portrait the previous August. "I saw a man of perfect physique, with a face so sensitive that I found it hard to realize that he was the champion heavyweight of the world. As a subject for a portrait painter, he would be wonderful, but as a model for a sculptor, ideal. I thought that here indeed was a favorite of the gods."

The artist told Gene that he had finished the work and planned to exhibit it. Shaw, overhearing, put down his fork, quickly turned toward Polly, and with the forceful direction of a strict but kindly professor, said emphatically, "My dear, you must have it. Go tomorrow, before you leave." Polly felt she had been commanded.

"Mr. Shaw often gets painted and bronzed," Charlotte told Polly. "You might have to get used to it."

Polly bought the portrait before leaving London. "Per Mr. Shaw's instructions," she always said, with a twinkle.

Cockerell captured Polly's attention during lunch by talking about a nun who devoted her life exclusively to prayer and monastic scholarship while secluded in the confines of a Benedictine abbey behind stone walls and locked doors. Cockerell said he visited Sister Laurentia Margaret McLachlan by appointment, and they conversed through an iron grille that divided a small, bare visitors' room. He said Sister Laurentia possessed one of the most incisive, wise minds he had ever encountered. Polly had visited abbeys and was fascinated, so she asked if one day she, too, might visit. Cockerell then mentioned he had introduced Sister Laurentia to Mr. and Mrs. Shaw as well.

"To *Mr.* Shaw?" she inquired. "But...isn't he an atheist?"

Cockerell admitted he wondered initially how they would get along, but then he smiled, and added that G.B.S. was not always what his reputation suggested. He pointed out that just as he was surprised to learn before lunch that Tunney considered Saint Francis his favorite saint (as Cockerell himself did), one could not always presume to know who public people are in private. Cockerell was a specialist in ancient

SIR JOHN LAVERY'S PORTRAIT OF TUNNEY (PRIVATE COLLECTION).

manuscripts, and he told Polly he applied the same approach to people as to medieval documents: look beneath the covers.

It was twilight and distant lights could be seen across the river by the time the guests moved from the table into the sitting room for coffee and tea. Max Beerbohm walked to the window with Gene and listened to him extol the red-gold reflection of the setting sun along the Thames. Beerbohm's humor, tongue-in-cheek drawings and parodies of pretentious excesses of the day had caused Shaw to name him "the incomparable Max." But Beerbohm knew nothing about prizefighters or boxing and could, when he wished, be biting and sarcastic in his observations. "Charming man," Beerbohm said later of Tunney. "Delightful man. Not at all what you would have expected. I mean, you would never have guessed his profession from his conversation. It was so literary, you know.

"Do you know, Mr. Tunney took me by the arm and led me to the windows and compelled my attention to the beauties of the sunset?" said Beerbohm. "I had never — no, I think I had never before met anyone so *militantly* aesthetic. I felt I could not reach his level, I could not match his appreciation."

The friend to whom Max told the story, S.N. Behrman, wrote that Beerbohm leaned forward, noting that "when Max reached the climax of a story, the little pauses, the little intakes of breath were not hesitations; they were beautifully timed dynamics of crescendo. 'You know,' he said, 'I cannot be considered a coarse person...and yet...you know...I had to strain every nerve...to meet...*that* sensitivity.'" Notwithstanding his sardonic view of the boxer's sensitivities, Beerbohm did invite Gene to visit him in Rapallo, Italy, where he lived.

It would not be the only time Gene's eagerness to share his awareness went unappreciated by the social circle he sought to impress.

Several years later, at a dinner hosted by New York columnist and drama critic Heywood Broun, Gene arrived with several expensive bottles of wine to demonstrate what he had learned in Europe. Broun was dressed in a yellow silk pajama top over an old sweatshirt and looked, said his son Heywood Hale, as if he could use lectures on the niceties of life.

"Tunney, full of his new learning, launched into an oenological ABC that was punctuated by the command that we were all to wash out our mouths with black coffee in order to clarify the palate," wrote Hale. "We were at last allowed to sip the wine and had its virtues explained in technical terms that made me feel that I was taking part in a laboratory experiment."

The elder Broun remained silent until ice cream arrived for dessert. By this time, said his son, Tunney was demonstrating how brandy should be sniffed before tasting. "Heywood suddenly and shockingly picked up his snifter and dumped the golden liquid into the puddle of ice cream that he then began to stir into an alcoholic goop." There was a stunned silence. Afterward,

Broun told his son, "I could hardly be expected to take instruction on wine from a *fighter.*"

Darkness had fallen over London by the time the other guests had departed Whitehall Court. Shaw rose from his chair, clapped Gene gently on the back and smiled, beckoning him to follow. Gene had assumed he would meet a world-famous writer with a brilliant mind, but he had not expected a cheerful, kindly, gracious man who seemed more like a neighbor and who appeared to expect from him only that he be himself. Polly and Gene had offered vivid descriptions of their honeymoon retreat on an island in the Adriatic, and they were touched when Shaw suggested that he and Charlotte might even visit them.

Shaw invited Gene to visit his study, with its big, flat-topped desk, filing cabinets, bookcases and stacks of books, including the Encyclopedia Britannica. There were dictionaries, Bibles in French, German, Italian and Spanish as well as English, and copies of Shaw's plays and books. In short, it was a working writer's study. A smaller desk in the room was used by Shaw's secretary. A Remington typewriter, the same model that Gene had bought for himself in 1925, was on a typing table near an inkpot. Gene was amused to be told that Shaw couldn't change the typewriter ribbon by himself, and he offered to put on a new one.

"Can you really write here?" asked Gene.

"I write anywhere," said Shaw. "On railway carriages, buses, in restaurants, backs of theatres, walking in a field — anywhere." He told Gene he carried a notebook wherever he went. "You might try it too," he suggested.

"Oh, I already do," said Gene. And he showed Shaw the black notebook of words he kept in his pocket. He turned to the page on which he had written the last two lines of Tennyson's *Ulysses*: "Made weak by time and fate, but strong in will / To strive, to seek, to find, and not to yield."

Shaw smiled and without hesitation quoted the lines just preceding it in which Ulysses refers to his old sailors with whom he will take his last voyage: "...and tho' / We are not now that strength which in old days / Moved earth and heaven, that which we are, we are."

A few weeks later, the former amateur boxing champion turned writer-journalist, Norman Clark, ran into Shaw on the street in London. "He seemed very favorably impressed by the retired champion," wrote Clark. Thinking that what Shaw had said could be added to an article he had written, Clark wrote asking to publish his comments. Shaw wouldn't hear of it.

"It is quite out of the question for me to give to the press anything that passes between me and my private guests or to criticize them in public in any way," Shaw wrote. "Besides, you have not got the hang of Tunney at all."

Almost no one, Shaw told Charlotte, has the hang of Tunney.

CHAPTER 10

Coldest Place We Ever Struck

"There are a number of questions I wish to ask Tunney.
One is whether he taught Mr. Shaw the jack-knife dive,
the dive in which Gene was most proficient."
WALTER TRUMBULL, COLUMNIST

"It was a fairy tale," said Helen Sligo, Polly's friend and classmate. "We sailed and swam, and Gene and Mr. Shaw walked for hours. I was from a family of modest means, and I never expected to have the chance to live in a high-class resort with so many important people. For a girl like me, who had been working in the lunchroom at Schrafft's, it was the dream of a lifetime."

In April of 1929, the stock market crash was still months away, and prosperity could be read in new neon signs from the Thames to Times Square. The newest dance craze was the Charleston, television was in its infancy, Popeye the Sailor and Tarzan debuted in the comics, and the first telephone was installed in the White House. Herbert Hoover was inaugurated as president, the Boston Red Sox announced they would play on Sundays, and Hemingway's *A Farewell to Arms* was finished in Paris. There was much to feel good about.

In Europe, the archipelago of Brioni, comprising 14 green-jeweled islands in the north Adriatic Sea, was a favored destination of wealthy vacationers. The largest and only developed island, referred to as Brioni, boasted the longest tournament golf course in Europe, with its greens and tee-offs constructed of compacted sand, as in India, to save water. After tours in India, Burma and other points east of the Suez, British families often returned home through Brioni, seeing it as a rest stop before a return to the more rigid social hierarchy of the homeland.

Austrian industrialist Paul Kupelweiser purchased the islands in 1893 to turn them into a luxury resort for European royalty, aristocracy and literati. The area's persistent problem had been malaria, and Kupelweiser himself had barely survived the disease. To protect his investment, the new proprietor asked Dr. Robert Koch, a Berlin bacteriologist renowned for isolating the bacteria that caused tuberculosis, for help in eradicating the *Anopheles* mosquito. Koch's instructions to fill in the breeding places of the mosquito, a revolutionary idea at the time, wiped out the malaria and led to new research on how to control disease.

By the time Koch won the Nobel Prize in 1905, Brioni had gained a reputation as a health Mecca. The irony of Shaw's visiting a place made famous by a doctor would not be lost on him. The playwright's 1906 dramatic satire *The Doctor's Dilemma*, which confronts moral and ethical issues in the worlds of science and art, was written when Koch's discoveries were headline news.

Visitors to Brioni, who came as much for the island's perceived health benefits as for the extravagant amenities, included the Archduchess Marie Josephine, mother of the last Austro-Hungarian emperor Karl, the Archduke Franz Ferdinand, Kaiser Wilhelm II, and later on, authors Thomas Mann, James Joyce and Lady Nancy Astor. During one week in 1911, there had been 16 princes and princesses and 15 counts and countesses on vacation there at the same time. By the 1920s, a count, countess or prince was so common that one just assumed any guest to have the title. Helen said people called Mrs. Lauder "countess" because she was so secure in her wealth and position that she looked and acted like one.

Vacationers were offered polo matches, tennis, bicycling, boating, sailing, fishing, skeet and pheasant shooting, horseback riding and swimming. The island's charm lay in its captivating natural beauty, its soft, dry air, and its many extensive ruins, from Neolithic settlements and Roman villas to medieval churches.

"In Brioni, there are no villages, no factories, nothing to remind one of life's tedious civilization," boasted a brochure. Pathways cut through the evergreens around the edge of the island, and walkers could peer into shallow waters to observe sponges and shells on the seabed. The sea, always crucial to Brioni, played a dual role as moat and bridge to the world. Throughout its history, and until an aerial bombing in the Second World War, a two-mile waterway known as the Fazana Channel helped keep invaders at bay.

Polly and Gene were, in 1929, Brioni's most famous long-term guests. Brioni and the Istrian coast reminded them of Maine, with islands of undulating, tree-covered hills and sailboats and fishing vessels. Its weather was more Mediterranean than Maine's, and when a rare heavy snowfall fell during the winter of 1928-29, freezing the small harbor and inlets, local residents were astounded. Pipes froze and drifts were so high that gardening tools were used to dig out roads and pathways. Gene endeared himself to the island workers by helping them shovel. The harsh winter had led into an unusually cold spring.

"Everything was beautiful," wrote Anne-Marie Lenz, the wife of the island doctor, in her diary. "The young ex-boxing champion was unusually simpatico, his nature and face were childlike and gentle. Polly was beautiful and delicate. It was nice to see them so young and so happy."

Gene had told the Shaws that Brioni was the only place in Europe where he had found privacy and that he could live in peace without the meddling presence of reporters and photographers. This impressed them. Charlotte Shaw liked the independence of travel and felt fresh scenery was vital for her husband's health by offering a diversion that would curtail his workaholic writing schedule. Shaw had hated his seven-week holiday the previous summer on the sweaty, crowded French Riviera, calling it a purgatory and a horrible hell-paradise. In deciding to go to Brioni, he looked forward to swimming

THE TUNNEYS IN ONE OF THE ONLY CARS ON BRIONI,
USUALLY RESERVED FOR ROYALTY (TUNNEY COLLECTION).

in the warm Adriatic and taking long, uninterrupted walks. Brioni, Gene assured him, was nothing like the Riviera.

Using Brioni as a base, the Tunneys made side trips in Europe. In January, Polly and Gene skied at St. Moritz ("the social life had us hanging on the ropes," and longing for "quiet evenings and engaging silences," Gene wrote the author Walpole.) In early April, they visited Spain on the recommendation of Ernest Hemingway, the author Gene had met and liked so much in Paris. A big man with a punch, Hemingway fancied himself a boxer, and the two maintained a close friendship until Hemingway's death in 1961. Despite their relationship, Gene felt the novelist sometimes got carried away with his obsession for fisticuffs.

On one occasion, they were chatting at Ernesto's favorite *El Floridita* in Havana over whether a rough-and-tumble street slugger could, as Hemingway claimed, beat a professional boxer. Gene told him about "Fingey," a friend from the docks who had lost the thumb of his left hand but continued to fight. Fingey's four fingers were like steel. "He would get in a brawl with somebody," said Gene, demonstrating an overhand right, "and when the sucker looked up, Fingey would come in low with that left and dig his fingers into the fellow's groin. When Fingey got a man like that, the poor fellow toppled face forward," said Gene.

"Try it again," Hemingway asked him.

"I was merely demonstrating, of course," said Gene later, "but when I went in with my left hand, Hemingway shot his right elbow into my mouth. If I hadn't had strong teeth, he would have knocked them out." Gene shoved Hemingway against the wall and threw a short left, "which I pulled at the last fraction of a second and laid against his chin. Then I did the same thing with my right. Bang! Bang!"

"Hemingway went white," said Gene. "It was the only time I ever saw the man flustered." Tunney returned to his hotel with a badly bleeding mouth and a blood-soaked tie and shirt.

When Polly and Gene extended their honeymoon travels to Seville, the heartland of Spanish bullfighting, Hemingway set them up to visit the bull-fighter Algabeno, who had appeared as a minor character in his first major novel, *The Sun Also Rises*. Algabeno kept a ranch outside Seville where Gene was invited to prove his courage by facing a young bull in a *tientas*, used primarily to test the young calves, not the guest. *Tientas* helped determine which young bulls were kept for the ring.

Tunney took a lesson in cape and sword handling from the bullfighter, and according to the Paris correspondent of *Corriere Istriano*, Tunney "bravely dispatched a calf with a single dramatic thrust of the sword." This would be a difficult feat for a novice, even a man as quick and adept on his feet as Gene, and it was more likely a blend of fact and fiction created by Hemingway, who fed the yarn to correspondents from a Paris café.

The story, like other news about the boxer, spun out of hand, and what started as a stop at a ranch turned into a trans-Atlantic challenge to Spain's national ego. "Madrid newspapers have published protests against the reports issued abroad that Gene Tunney went into the arena and killed a bull," said the Associated Press. "Tunney no toreador, says Spain," read a headline in *The New York Times*.

Will Rogers added his own *bon mot*: "Bullfight season opened in Madrid Sunday with a doubleheader. Gene Tunney threw out the first bull."

On Monday, April 15, the Shaws left London, bound for Brioni.

"All day yesterday I could think of nothing but: 'As there seems to be plenty of room in the box / I might as well take some additional socks,'" Shaw wrote Nancy Astor. "Brioni Hotel, Brioni, Istria, Italy, is our next address. It was recommended to us as a desert island. We learn now that it is one of the most overcrowded 'resorts' on Earth. I wonder how long we will be able to stand it."

"Shaw off to Tunney Isle," spouted a London headline. Shaw's travels were covered as extensively as Gene's, and there was considerable speculation as to why the world-famous playwright and the former champion would get together. It was assumed that it had something to do with *Cashel Byron's Profession*, possibly a play or movie based on the novel.

The weather in Brioni continued to be unseasonably cool for April, with temperatures in the low 40s and 50s, and more rain than was normal. *Boras*, the cold, biting winds that whirl like dervishes across the northern Adriatic, were frequent, slicing through the body like pricks of icicles. Spring blooms were delayed, and fishermen complained that even the fish hid at the bottom of the sea from the cold. Gene had a passing, worrisome thought that the Shaws might be disappointed in the weather and might even blame him for overselling Brioni as an idyllic island of warm seas and sunshine. "But it's barely spring weather in Maine, and probably even in England," said Polly. "It may change by the time they arrive, and even if not, surely Mr. and Mrs. Shaw, who travel abroad often, will be prepared for the worst."

The temperature was in the 40s on April 18. Gusting winds blew white-caps across the water, tossing around the boat bringing the Shaws from the mainland like a teacup. Water-sodden and weary, they arrived at the dock and were escorted by carriage to the hotel, where they were given a spacious two-bedroom suite with a large balcony facing a wintry sea. "This is the coldest place we ever struck," Shaw wrote the composer Albert Coates. He would write actress Molly Tompkins that "the *bora* was the most horrible wind that ever blew, even in Italy."

After settling in, the playwright met Gene in the lobby, an expansive space not unlike the great hall of a Mediterranean manor house, with pillars, rococo plaster decoration, arched doorways and a peaked ceiling. Large plants in ceramic pots defined seating groups, and dozens of stuffed leather couches and wicker armchairs were strewn with foreign newspapers and magazines, giving the appearance of a men's club on a rainy afternoon. The many terrace doors, usually open to allow in breezes, remained closed against the wind, and the stifling aroma of tobacco provided ample evidence that the weather had confined guests indoors.

The two strolled off to plush armchairs set in a distant corner, facing away from other people, and as far away as possible from the lingering smell of cigarettes and pipe smoke, which they both loathed.

Shaw said the most horrific smoke-filled evening he had ever spent was with Lee Simonson, a director of the Theatre Guild, who visited him in London to discuss Guild business. He said that he and Charlotte nearly died before it ended. "You must give up smoking," Shaw wrote Simonson afterward. "You smoked 117 cigarettes in two hours, and you would have smoked 118 if I had not stopped you once. Where do you expect to go when you die — how do you expect to spend the brief and stupefying remnant of your days — if you give way to such reckless self-indulgence? You are worse than anyone I ever met."

Smoking cigarettes was socially acceptable, even for women, but that didn't deter Gene from campaigning for a smokeless world either. As champion, he turned down $10,000 to endorse a well-known cigarette brand because

TUNNEY TALKING WITH G.B.S.
AND CHARLOTTE ON THE QUAY
IN BRIONI (TUNNEY COLLECTION).

he felt that it might encourage youngsters to smoke. Once invited to speak at a boxing writers' dinner, he devoted his entire speech to the health hazards of tobacco. He chided friends who lit up in his presence. "The evils of smoking are not well understood," he lectured regularly. "Smoking is the most insidious, filthy, degrading habit that the human race has ever developed."

As Shaw and Tunney sat with their backs to the lobby, only the tips of their heads were visible and they could have been any two men talking. An Italian reporter caught sight of them and surreptitiously took a seat behind a plant nearby to try to record their conversation. He caught enough of what they said to write a story for the next day's *Corriere Istriano*.

"Despite their age difference, there was no lack of warmth in the conversation between the two noted personalities," the reporter wrote. "The two vacationers found themselves chatting with an amiability that is not characteristic of Anglo-American relations."

"Is it true about your meeting with the actress Pola Negri?" asked Gene, grinning. The newspaper called Tunney "playful" and sometimes "impish."

Shaw gave a gentle tap to his companion.

"Yes…yes, dear Gene. I have met and spoken to her. She is such a charming creature, but somewhat bizarre." Negri was a Polish film actress who achieved notoriety as a femme fatale in silent films and was, in 1929, one of the wealthiest and best known actresses in Hollywood. Her vamp's style and romantic affairs with notable actors such as Charles Chaplin and Rudolph Valentino ensured her place in the public eye. Her lunch with Shaw, for which she had dressed in black silk and a gray fur coat, had made headlines in the newspapers. Negri saw herself as the playwright's perfect Cleopatra and had pursued Shaw for permission to turn *Caesar and Cleopatra* into a film, with her as the star. Shaw did not like American directors and was never enthusiastic about having Hollywood turn his plays into movies.

"And may I ask…it is said that you agreed to the actress's request?"

"I could not hurt her with my refusal, even though I have heretofore been against converting my works for the cinema," said Shaw. "I had to surrender to her gentle siege."

"So Pola Negri will be your Cleopatra?" asked Gene.

"Yes. She will film my *Caesar and Cleopatra*, and she told me that in the process, she will even go to the desert." At this point, Shaw laughed and enthusiastically patted his leather armchair. "Can you imagine my following her, at my age, which calls for padding and soft armchairs?" he said. (The film was made 16 years later, without Pola Negri.)

The correspondent said the two changed subjects and Gene asked the playwright about his writing, but their voices softened and the newspaperman could not hear their conversation.

Before he arrived, Shaw had told Gene that while on Brioni he expected to finish final revisions for *The Apple Cart* and also wanted to write a preface for the letters of the actress Ellen Terry, who had died the year before. The Ellen Terry project particularly interested Polly because she had admired the actress and her mother raved about seeing Terry on the stage. In addition, her relative Andrew Carnegie had once offered Ellen Terry a carriage ride in New York's Central Park, which in family folklore indicated he might have wanted to be a suitor. (Terry became ill, and the carriage ride never happened.)

The correspondent heard both Tunney and Shaw speaking louder.

"For now, my dear," said Shaw, "I am enjoying a well-earned rest in this enchanting refuge where I am beyond the reach of indiscreet gossiping voices and the harassment of journalists in search of words to fill newspapers."

"Ah! They are an ugly breed, indeed," agreed Tunney, shaking his head.

The reporter, fearful that he had been found out, wrote that he quickly moved away and left them alone.

The Tunneys and Shaws were staying in adjacent luxury hotels, and Polly's mother had moved to a palatial villa about 25 minutes away on the other side of the island. This had allowed the newlyweds privacy, yet also the proximity to arrange social gatherings and sporting activities. Gene invited the Shaws to the villa for tea the next day.

To Shaw's dismay, the next day was even colder, but sunshine splashed across the sea, wrapping the island in a cobalt blue ribbon like a brilliant jewel. On the carriage ride to the villa, the Shaws would have had their first view of the expanse of the island: pines, graceful holm oaks shaped like gigantic deep green mushrooms and paths lined with towering cypress etched against the blueness of the sea. Scrub of the macchia stretched across the hillsides, resembling Kenya's Masai Mara, and herds of deer roamed freely across the paths of the island as if they were on plains of the savanna. They would have passed Roman ruins and seen the sun-bleached marble columns of the Temple of Venus and the remaining terraces of a sprawling, first-century Roman imperial villa. Shaw was amused to learn that the crafty Roman owner also had built a winter house with its back to the northeast and the sea as protection against the *bora*.

Villa Punta Naso was situated alone on a small, nose-shaped peninsula that jutted like the prow of a ship into a wide bay. Surrounded by the sea on three sides, it offered complete privacy. Stone walls and a wrought-iron gate protected the only entrance. It was one of the grandest residences on Brioni — "an Italian palace" said Gene — a four-story Italianate showplace built of stone from the island quarries that had once supplied marble to build the imperial *palazzi* of Vienna. There were Doric columns, two wide porches so that one could move with the sun or shade and, inside, high ceilings and an exuberance of ornamentation with plaster medallions and baroque cornices.

The villa had been built by the brother of the island's owner, Paul Kupelweiser, for his wife, but she found it too big and the location too windy.

It was given to a niece who didn't like it much either and finally rented out to Princess Elizabeth of Austria, who spent three summers there. The Tunneys were residents for nearly a year.

"You must be Mr. and Mrs. Shaw," said a surprised Helen Sligo, meeting the Shaws on the path. She introduced herself as the bride's classmate, traveling with Polly's mother as a companion and occasional secretary. Tiny, with wide, cheerful eyes and a happy disposition, she was everyone's friend. Helen instinctively made a small curtsy, then, realizing that Mrs. Shaw seemed eager to rest, she dropped her basket and turned to escort them back to the house: "I'm taking the boat to Pola to pick up some special food and supplies. Might I get you something?"

"No, no, my dear," said Shaw. "Except maybe warmer weather."

"It's been beastly," said Helen. "I hope you've missed the worst part. They say it's supposed to warm up." Helen helped Mrs. Shaw up the stone steps and left them at the door. She was surprised at how nimble and energetic the playwright seemed to be, but worried that Mrs. Shaw, wearing a coat, a squishy hat that hid her face and a heavy scarf around her neck to protect against the chill, seemed to walk much more carefully and slowly, almost like an invalid.

The villa's large main salon opened with windows to the sea on three sides. A porch extended the view on one side toward a loggia and gardens that formed a canopy of cypress, cedar, giant cactus and bougainvillea. Tapestries covered the walls, and a *seicento* chair covered in fine Brussels tapestry was set alongside dark wicker armchairs and large *Frau* chairs and fine Italian leather couches. The entrance hall tiles were patterned after the black-and-white designs from the Roman ruins in nearby Verige Bay, and Oriental carpets covered the floors. There were large Italian vases and decorative wine jugs, a painting of the Madonna over the fireplace, stacks of books on side tables as well as on a long library table, and silver candlesticks on the mantel. It looked well kept up and lived-in.

"Hello, hello, hello!" said Shaw in greeting. Polly gave Charlotte a warm embrace and said how honored they were to have them visit, and Gene said that their arrival signaled a turn in the weather. Mrs. Lauder, Polly's mother, agreed with Charlotte that the "turn" was still not summer-like, and when the subject of swimming came up, all but Gene and Shaw shuddered at the very thought of it.

From somewhere deep in the house, a liveried butler in black jacket and bow-tie and two maids in starchy white aprons arrived with a trolley of sweets, sugary nougat cake, small cheese sandwiches, pots of strong, steaming tea and porcelain cups. Polly had included hot water and lemon for Shaw, some milk if he wanted it, and fruit tarts as well as fresh fruit. Not an English cream tea but a sumptuous afternoon repast. Shaw clapped his hands, and Gene smiled, delighted.

"Mr. Shaw was in wonderful humor, and he and Gene told stories and laughed, making the rest of us laugh too," recalled Polly. "I enjoyed the conversations we had because Mr. Shaw would tell jokes. He would make fun. He always had a twinkle in his eyes, a spark that I think was the Irish in him. Gene had it too."

In the beginning, Polly noticed that Shaw seemed to look at Charlotte when he talked, except when he was conversing to Gene. "Instead of looking at the rest of us, he would look at her. A little bit of shyness, as though he were addressing things to her, but he also wanted us to hear what he was saying. And maybe he would gain a little more confidence when he would look at her, and he would get encouragement from her in telling a story. It was extraordinarily interesting." This was not something that Polly had noticed in London, and she decided that Shaw was simply timid with new acquaintances.

Polly's intuitive feeling that Shaw was somewhat bashful never changed, and since she was shy herself, she tried to take extra care in listening when he talked so as to encourage him.

"My father died when I was young so that I never saw my parents get old together. I didn't realize until we spent all that time with the Shaws how much I might have missed. The little things that add up to a life, the jokes, the way my father might have taken his tea. Mr. Shaw often had a camera with him, and we talked about my father, who was a serious amateur photographer and had his own photography studio in the house." She noticed that on excursions, Shaw seemed to use the Leica as a shield, holding it in front of his face whenever he did not want to be recognized. He told her that looking through the viewfinder was like looking through "a peephole."

"There was always a very important closeness between Mr. and Mrs. Shaw," she said. "Mr. Shaw was much older than we were, of course, and he seemed courtly and old-fashioned in a gallant sort of way. They were terribly affectionate to one another." He helped her in and out of boats, opened doors for her, and they sometimes sat side by side, almost touching, the "gestures you notice as a bride. They had a devotion that was no less intense for being virtually unspoken, and that, of course, was an inspiration for us."

"Automatic writing? You used automatic writing for *Saint Joan*?" asked an incredulous Gene. Automatic writing, much talked about in the 1920s, was material that supposedly flowed from the writer's hand without conscious thought. Some people thought it was linked to mysticism and the ability to channel thoughts, especially spiritual feelings, from the mind to paper. On occasion, both Shaw and Charlotte referred to themselves as mystics.

"I have an Ouija board," said Polly's mother, who enjoyed the thought that she could channel spirits. Ouija boards, called "talking boards," were

SHAW, HAVING TEA ON BRIONI, WITH POLLY'S FRIEND AND CLASSMATE HELEN SLIGO, STANDING, AND POLLY'S MOTHER KATHERINE ROWLAND LAUDER (TUNNEY COLLECTION).

much in vogue. "Does that mean I can do automatic writing and write a play?" she asked, laughing. Shaw's sister Lucy had experimented with Ouija boards and Charlotte said that she, too, had used one, but she thought they would be useless in writing a play.

"We had a good deal of talk about automatic writing," said Polly. Shaw said that he had written *Saint Joan* rapidly, with such ease that he considered it automatic writing. Shaw used historical records of the trial as the basis for research for the play and sometimes dismissed his own hand in the end result. "Historical plays hardly count," he wrote; "the material is ready-made." He said the words came "tumbling out at such a speed that my pen rushed across the paper and I could barely write fast enough to write them down."

In the following days, before other events took over, Polly, her mother and Helen Sligo, with Gene and the Shaws, shared tea and talk most afternoons. Conversation never stopped, said Polly. When Gene and G.B.S. were not at tea, they were walking, swimming or sharing meals. They often had lunch and dinner together.

"I would catch a glimpse of them walking in the distance or having lunch alone or sitting together in the long lobby — their heads always bobbing and their hands moving and Gene more engrossed that I had ever seen him, or ever saw him after," said Helen, who knew Gene all her life. "It was the intensity of their interaction which caught me. They talked nonstop to each other, always alone, of course. They were almost never in a group, unless it was with the family."

In the rain, Shaw and Gene walked with caps; in downpours, they reluctantly carried umbrellas. It didn't stop the occasional newspaper reporter coming from the mainland in an effort to determine what the two were doing. But on an island with more than thirty miles of wandering trails and hidden coves, it was difficult to locate two men who didn't want to be found. Both Gene and Shaw were fast walkers, matching each other's stride easily, and both had contempt for a prying press. When they showed up together to watch a round of polo or golf, they would often be gone again before someone could find them or take a photograph. They enjoyed outwitting the curious and took boyish delight in winning the reporter's game of hide-and-seek.

They became almost inseparable. Tunney was so "handsome & gentle & babyish that it refreshes one to look at him," Charlotte wrote to Nancy Astor. "He takes G.B.S. for long walks (his boast is that you can walk eight miles on the island without repeating yourself!) & gazes at him, like a large dog at its master."

Shaw had suffered debilitating migraine headaches. "He lived by the rules of the perfectionist," as Gene told him. He encouraged Shaw to relax and breathe to speed up his blood circulation while walking, which in turn would help diminish the headaches. Instead of a leisurely 90-minute walk away from his desk, Gene encouraged him to walk briskly for 20 minutes a day. Gene's instructions to Shaw were to inhale deeply through his nose for 12 paces, hold his breath and exhale slowly through his mouth, repeating the process 15 times to sweep impurities from his body. Doing this together proved laughable, and Gene, using an old boxing phrase, said they finally "threw in the towel," though Shaw said he practiced on his own, and it helped him.

Even in cool weather, their favorite morning exercise was swimming. Whenever there was no rain, even if there was no sun, they swam in the sea, sometimes near the Saluga, the public beach and bathing facility. They also swam off the broad rock ledges below the villa, where no one could see them from a passing boat without using powerful binoculars. "Following a cold shower each morning, the former world's heavyweight champion and the Irish playwright glided easily through the water for long distances," said one newspaper report. "Shaw, despite his 72 years and flowing white beard, was an excellent swimmer."

Gene had always felt at home in the sea and was a strong swimmer who often swam miles, even in Maine's cold, rough Atlantic waters. He said that Shaw was so relaxed in water that he seemed to be floating in space, serene and utterly quiet, in a place with no gravity.

"A favorite turn to their exercise was to cease all muscular effort and float, faces upturned to the warm sun, taking life as easily and placidly as the isle itself," said an Associated Press story. "Sunbaths on the beach, with the sand sometimes piled high about them, followed the excursions into the water."

The image of two grown men digging holes in the beach and building sand castles might have seemed too incredible for a reporter to mention, but the mounds piled high around them did have the effect of cutting off the view of cameras.

Sometimes they swam to a float to chat quietly as the water rocked them back and forth like a hammock. Shaw talked about his childhood summers in Dalkey, on the coast south of Dublin, and how he would race to the top of a hillside of gorse and watch clouds float through the valleys below him to the sea, feeling that he could fly. Gene talked about how he used to dive off the wharves, sometimes plummeting 30 feet through the air with his arms at his side, foolishly coming dangerously close to breaking his neck. Gene told his friend about the long trails through the woods in the Adirondacks, with no cities, no people and no sound but birds, crickets and the wind.

"You can almost hear the soughing of the wind across those great open spaces," Gene once told a Cleveland, Ohio, reporter as he looked out his hotel window toward a park. "I always stay here," he said, "so that I can train along the edge of that picturesque little lake. There is something in me that responds to the windswept spaces."

TUNNEY AND SHAW LEAVING A SPORTING FIELD ON BRIONI. OPPOSITE, TOP
TO BOTTOM: TUNNEY AND SHAW AT A POLO MATCH; TUNNEY PLAYING GOLF
UNDER THE WATCHFUL EYE OF G.B.S. AT FAR RIGHT. (TUNNEY COLLECTION)

The reporter thought him "the weirdest pug that ever climbed through the ropes," but Gene meant every word of it. His sensibilities were deeply romantic and easily moved by the smells and sounds of nature. Shaw saw an optimism of spirit and an inner calm in the younger man, and this was undoubtedly one of the traits that drew them so closely together.

"All my life I wanted to grip the essential poetry of living and it has always eluded me," Shaw said late in life. "I wanted to be a Shakespeare and I became a Shaw."

Sometimes, Gene said, he and Shaw didn't talk at all. They lay on their backs in the water in harmonious silence. "I feel that Shaw is someone I have known all my life," Gene told Polly.

"Let's sail to Rovigno for lunch," said Polly, eager to suggest an outing for Charlotte. "Just the four of us." Charlotte was promised that she would not have to navigate the steep cobbled roads to visit the baroque cathedral which dominated the town, its bell tower a copy of St. Mark's in Venice. The short trip by boat was seen as a refreshing change, a chance to see a still thriving seventh-century fishing harbor. The day was calm, the sky clear, and the tables set in the sunshine at a harbor restaurant were so protected from the wind they felt they were sitting cozily in front of a warm fire.

"The local wines are excellent," said Gene, pleased to be host and priding himself on his recently acquired knowledge of wine and the area itself. He took a bottle of wine from the waiter and poured glasses for Charlotte, Polly and himself. As they held up their glasses for a toast, Shaw held out his empty wineglass and said that he, too, would like to taste the wine.

"But you don't drink," said Gene matter-of-factly. "How can you possibly pronounce a wine good or bad when you don't even drink?"

"I always taste them," said Shaw. When Gene looked doubtful, Shaw said, "For 30 years, Charlotte and I have entertained guests and served wine with meals. But Charlotte knows nothing of wines and leaves the selection to me. With no tobacco or meat to mar my palate, I have the most excellent taste in wines." Gene poured Shaw some wine, which the playwright sipped, then smacked his lips. "Charlotte complains of our wine bills, because I only order the very best!"

Gene regaled Shaw with stories of a long weekend when, as a houseguest of William Randolph Hearst at San Simeon, he joined actors Charlie Chaplin, Mary Pickford, Douglas Fairbanks and other Hollywood guests in an impromptu party about 2 am in the castle's gigantic kitchen. "Old man Hearst woke up and came roaring into the kitchen in his bathrobe to tell us to shut up and go to bed. NOW! House rules, he said. We obeyed like sheep."

In the moment of silence that followed, as they sipped the wine and Gene wondered if his selection met Shaw's criteria, Shaw cleared his throat. He said Charlotte had persuaded him to bring up something he had thus far avoided.

For a moment, Gene couldn't breathe as he imagined what might derail this new friendship. Since childhood, meals had been a source of unexpected anxiety, and the long shadow of the brooding, dictatorial Red could be counted on to hang over any worrisome discussion.

"Charlotte thinks it's time that you stopped calling me *Mr.* Shaw," said the playwright. "All my friends call me G.B.S." Gene later remembered being pleased and also touched that Shaw made such an effort not to embarrass him for not picking up on the change himself. Being invited to call his friend G.B.S. made Gene feel included in an inner circle, and by association, he felt it also kept him firmly tethered to the umbrella of friendship and away from the self-seeking sycophants he knew circled around the playwright. Gene welcomed the familiarity, but in talking to them directly, Polly mostly stayed with "Mr. and Mrs. Shaw." It felt right to her.

Accepting Shaw's story that he was a teetotaler who only sipped wine was a different matter altogether. Never one to accept an explanation at face value, his teasing nature led him to concoct a prank to test Shaw.

Gene found mischievous pleasure in practical jokes. He once shut up a boorish member of a fishing party in the Bahamas by having a cable sent to the man saying that there had been a fire at his house in New York. On one son's birthday, he promised to pick up a party magician at a train, and then called home, his voice disguised as the magician, and said the birthday show was off. He created a conspiracy with friends to mail to a general at the Pentagon pictures in unmarked envelopes of one of the general's most ardent critics, driving the general's office into frenzy. Required to fill out a police registration form on a visit to Germany in late 1929, he gave his correct name and his address as New York, but then — apparently unable to endure prolonged paperwork without poking fun at the system — he entered his nationality as Senegalese.

Using the name Signor J.N. Pesera, that of the villa's cook, Gene wrapped a case of cordials and wrote a note in broken English to Shaw proclaiming his great and undying admiration for the world's best-known playwright and going on to say that he knew that no true full-blooded Irishman could be a teetotaler and to relish his stay in Brioni. Shaw replied the same day.

Dear Sir
I appreciate your kind intention in sending me a case of wine, but I must return it unopened, as I drink nothing but water. May I add that as I am here on a holiday, I prefer to leave my public character behind me, and to be treated as far as possible as a quite private and unknown individual.

Faithfully,
G. Bernard Shaw

About a week after the Shaws arrived, Polly's mother and family left for a tour of Europe, and the newlyweds moved into the villa. Polly had been troubled by stomach pain, and the island's Dr. Otto Lenz diagnosed her with scampi poisoning and prescribed several tonics and rest. Scampi poisoning was not uncommon in the Mediterranean, and Polly's favorite *involtini di prosciutto agli scampi* (scampi wrapped in prosciutto) was a specialty on the Istrian coast. Not wanting to delay her mother's departure, she didn't mention it. Nor did she tell her husband. This was relatively easy, because Gene was now spending virtually all of his time with G.B.S.

No one, least of all the doctor, thought there was any cause for alarm.

TUNNEY AND SHAW SMILE FOR THE CAMERA WHILE CHARLOTTE CHATS WITH FRIENDS. TUNNEY WROTE ON THE PICTURE THAT THEY WERE ATTENDING PONY RACES (TUNNEY COLLECTION).

CHAPTER 11

He was the teacher, I the pupil

"Once we took a trip to the Galapagos Islands. While fishing
off the ship, he read Bulfinch's *Mythology* on the way out
and Darwin's *Voyage of the Beagle* on the way back."
COLUMNIST CHARLES MCCABE ON TUNNEY

Shaw and Gene were strolling along the quay toward a path that skirted the
public bathing beach and curved along the shoreline to the opposite side of the
island. In a picture taken that morning, several hotel guests whiz past on bicycles, and a fisherman on the seawall trolls his lines and smokes cigarettes. It
was unseasonably cool: "Another summer day in Shangri-la," quipped Shaw.
The steel-white glare of an overcast sky made them squint. Both were dressed
in wool knickers. Shaw wore a white sweater, carried a fat book under his arm
and sported a floppy, tan-colored hat that shaded his eyes. Gene was checking
his pockets for pencils and notebooks.

"Richard Strauss has arrived," said Shaw. "Would you like to meet him?"

Gene yanked his hand out of his jacket, stopped on the path and gazed at
Shaw. "Would I like to meet Richard Strauss, the world-renowned composer
of *Der Rosenkavalier, Death and Transfiguration, Don Juan, Salome* and
Elektra?" he said, mimicking the question. "You know I would!"

Music, in all its variety, was a favorite topic for both G.B.S. and Gene,
and it had quickly become the basis of one of their many dialogues. Gene's
earliest memories were of Gregorian chant at Mass, and of his mother playing
hymns and Irish ballads on her upright piano with her most prized possessions, sheet music, at her side. Shaw could recall his own mother sitting at
the Broadwood piano on Synge Street singing at concerts held in their heavily
draped drawing room. By age 12, Shaw could sing or whistle all the principal
works of Handel, Haydn, Mozart, Beethoven, Rossini, Bellini, Donizetti and
Verdi.

By nature, Shaw was equally artistic and logical, a forceful and distinguished speaker and debater, but he was also a frustrated schoolmaster at
heart, and Gene became his most willing pupil. Despite, or perhaps because
of, the 41-year difference in age, the playwright and the boxer found the mental energy to enjoy hours together at a time. Charlotte said she had rarely
known anyone to keep her husband away from his desk longer. "In the evening, Shaw and Tunney invariably dined together," noted an Associated Press
report, "but neither in the dining room nor in their walks was anyone able to
ascertain just what the topics of conversation were." They remained distant
and declined to talk to outsiders. The playwright, approached by one correspondent, said there was nothing he had to say and that his coming to Brioni
was "solely to seek an isolated and tranquil spot."

In private, there was no pretense between them. They were frank and straightforward. Gene's friends rated sincerity and ingenuousness among his foremost character traits. He was unpretentious and never used evasions or deceit. However, in public, when they were on stage, affectation sometimes crept into both their conversations. "When you ask what kind of guy Gene is," said an acquaintance, "you've got to specify where — and when. In public, he is apt to make high-sounding speeches. But in a small group of people, he's interesting and genuine. And there's nobody around who's been more generous to guys who need help." Likewise, Shaw's flippancy and contrariness in public, and his predilection for seeing and believing the opposite of what other people saw and believed, had earned him a reputation quite at odds with the gentleman Gene knew when they were alone. It was the private man that each came to know and befriend.

"Gene possessed a vigorous intensity and he soaked up information like a sponge," said his friend Sam Pryor. "He was smart. He wanted to be with the top minds, and if he had a choice between a social engagement and seeing someone who could teach him something new, he always went with the new. He was different that way." In his pursuit of learning, Gene was like a hound on the trail of a fox, with no barrier too high to distract him. He said he emerged from afternoons with G.B.S. feeling enlightened, acquiring information from stories that Shaw wound around readings, books, personal experiences and an older man's sense of history, conjuring up meanings that were so relevant to his own life that it was like listening to Socrates.

Polly said her husband learned from Shaw avidly and that he thrived on music — particularly opera — because it conveyed private feeling and sentiments that he could not easily put into his own words.

Not even the grandest books have the impact of song and story combined because music appeals to the soul, Shaw pointed out to Gene; song expresses the joy and sorrow of the world, and like a religion, music gives comfort. Shaw had been a leading music critic in London for six years (1888-94), taking the *nom de plume* Corno di Bassetto (after the English basset horn), and his collected writings filled 2700 pages, the equivalent of half a dozen books. Inspired to do better than the conventional music criticism, which was academic to the point of being unreadable and often nonsensical, he became what W.H. Auden said was "probably the best music critic who ever lived," writing in lively language that even a parlor maid could understand.

Gene had liked Strauss's *Elektra*. "Emotional and unforgettable," he called it, adding that it completely transformed Sophocles's take on Homer's tale into a harrowing but passionate *opera noir*. When *Elektra* had first been performed in London in 1910, Shaw vigorously defended Strauss against the critic Ernest Newman, who claimed much of the opera was "like a huge volcano sputtering forth a vast amount of dirt and murk."

"Human emotion is a complex thing," Shaw wrote Newman, in a letter to *The Nation*. "There are moments when our feeling is so deep and our ecstasy so exalted that the primeval monsters from whom we are evolved wake within us and utter the strange, tormented cries of their ancient struggles with the Life Force. All this is in *Elektra*." The feat was beyond all verbal description, he said. "It must be heard and felt."

In 1929, Richard Strauss, the man Gene was to meet, was the preeminent composer in the world, having inherited the mantle of Richard Wagner. In Vienna six months earlier, Gene and Polly had seen half a dozen operas, including some by Strauss, Mozart's *Abduction from the Seraglio* and Wagner's *Das Rheingold*, the last "conducted by [Wilhelm] Furtwangler, who did it in a most finished and thrilling style," as Gene wrote in a letter to Thornton Wilder. "One does not have to have your appreciation of music, Thornt, to be moved by such heavenly rhythm." Gene always said that Wagner's music "wept."

Shaw considered Wagner an unparalleled literary musician and said the secret of his genius was that unlike the music of most composers, his was full of unbridled passion, yearning and love. After seeing *Tristan and Isolde* at the Bayreuth Festival, Shaw called it "an ocean of sentiment...universal in its appeal to human sympathy." He said the performance was in sharp contrast to "the scratch representations we are accustomed to in London, at which half the attention of the singers are given to the prompter, half to the conductor, and the rest to the character impersonated."

They talked about how Wagner transformed musical thought in the 19th century through his continuous and interlocking melodies, creating emotionally dramatic expression that was new to listeners and outside the formal opera structure of the period. Wagner's *Ring of the Nibelungs*, the four-opera "Ring" chronicle — still considered one of the monumental achievements of Western classical music — was one Gene would see in its entirety many times in opera houses all over the world.

From their first outing together, Shaw sang on walks, telling Gene that he regarded singing as a happy, stimulating and healthy exercise. "I had sung like a bird all through my childhood," he said. As they strolled along narrow island pathways, Shaw would explain a passage and then sing it in a rich baritone voice, demonstrating in a few bars the differences between composers and styles. He cited Handel's use of a half close (imperfect cadence) for his *Hallelujah Chorus* as an example of how a man of genius can pick "a commonplace out of the gutter and take our breath away with it." He liked Beethoven's Symphony No.3, the *Eroica*, he said, because it expressed the drama of the French Revolution, and the music captured for him the moods of Beethoven's turbulent Bohemian spirit.

But nothing in art, said Shaw, is better than Mozart's best. Everyone else, he said, seemed like a bungler in comparison. In his early boyhood, Shaw said he had the good fortune of learning thoroughly Mozart's *Don Giovanni*. "Mozart alone is completely self-possessed; his gentleness and touch never desert him," wrote Shaw. "He is economical and practical, under the same pressure of inspiration that throws the titan into convulsions. This is the secret of his unpopularity with the titan fanciers and his popularity with the truly inspired."

"You can only imagine," Gene later said of these encounters. "Two Irishmen in knee breeches — singing!" Actually, he said, only G.B.S. actually sang. "I hummed off-key." His acquaintance with the world's great works of music was incredible," Gene recalled. "He knew every note of Wagner and frequently sang passages to differentiate one from another as we wound our way through the lovely trails of Brioni." They discussed harmonic syntax, rhythms, progressions, questions about whether a piece can be overscored (with "too many notes," as the Emperor said to Mozart), instrumentation, and the role of a conductor in capturing the composer's intent.

Shaw sang while sitting on the rocks near the villa or walking on trails and once while standing in the lee of a small hillock overlooking a wheat-colored meadow, only to realize too late that several women riding bicycles had stopped to listen. The women clapped and giggled, delighted to have heard the impromptu performance. Ever the showman, Shaw made a courtly bow as if he were in a concert hall.

"The critics approve," said Gene, who had been watching "from the wings" under a tree.

Only criticism inspired by personal feeling was legitimate, said Shaw. "People have pointed out evidences of personal feeling in my notices as if they were accusing me of a misdemeanor," he wrote. "Really fine artists inspire me...when my critical mode is at its height, it is passion: the passion for artistic perfection — for the noblest beauty of sound, sight, and action — that rages in me." Richard Strauss, for one, was highly sensitive to critics, Shaw warned Gene.

Shaw and Gene met Strauss while he was standing on a gravel walkway in front of his large, Mediterranean-style hotel chatting with several friends. Shaw made introductions in German, as interpreter. The musician did not speak English and the only German Gene knew was *Danke schoen*. There were smiles and handshakes, and the assembled guests chatted amicably until they were interrupted by a tourist asking to take a photograph.

As the group politely turned toward the camera, Strauss backed away, whispering loudly, "*Nein, nein!*" The agitated composer retreated to a distant shaded area and Shaw followed. When they returned Shaw nodded good-naturedly, and the tourist snapped a grainy, out-of-focus photograph that shows the creases in Shaw's pants better than any of the faces. In the photograph, a tall, angular Strauss, dressed in a suit and tie and sporting a beret, stands rigidly between Gene and G.B.S., who is holding a small flower in his hands.

A puckish Shaw told Gene later that Strauss hadn't wanted to be photographed with a boxer. He said that Strauss felt his image as the supreme musical artist of his age would be — and here G.B.S. chuckled as he struggled to find the right word in English — *missverstanden*/misunderstood. "Misunderstood!" he said, laughing. He thought he would be "ruined. Made a laughingstock!" if he were seen with a prizefighter. G.B.S. said he assured the composer that his friend was not a typical fighter but an artist-athlete in the

GERMAN COMPOSER RICHARD STRAUSS, SECOND FROM LEFT, STANDS BETWEEN TUNNEY, FAR LEFT, AND SHAW IN A FUZZY PHOTOGRAPH TAKEN BY A TOURIST (TUNNEY COLLECTION).

Greek tradition, and that if anything, being seen with Tunney had upgraded Shaw's image.

On another occasion, Gene and G.B.S. passed Strauss sitting alone at a table on the hotel's verandah and joined him. For Gene, a man who now could draw upon works of literature from memory and recognize the sublime notes of the grandest music, being with Shaw and Strauss was humbling. "I was overawed," he said. "A ring fighter sitting there with the world's greatest living masters of literature and music." These were geniuses able to capture the heartache and joy and the poetry of life in words and music, messages that would make the heart swell and give voice to the hopes and struggles of millions of people. He also sensed, with some sadness, the enormous gulf between them and himself, and he yearned anew to make a larger contribution with his life.

A portly press photographer popped up behind a large trellis of yellow flowers at one end of the verandah. He was struggling to focus his bulky 4-by-5 Speed Graphic while fending off the hotel manager, who was waving angrily in the universal message of stop-what-you-are-doing-and-go-away. The photographer shouted at the manager loudly enough for other guests on the terrace to hear clearly. "Move the two old guys! I need a picture of the champ!" Gene was mortified. Shaw laughed and translated for Strauss, who was perplexed as to why a prizefighter could be of more interest than two famous artists. The photographer was driven away, but a crowd had already gathered.

One of their favorite hideouts during walks, and a place they could count on to be deserted, was the Church of Saint Mary, a fifth-century basilica and monastery, one of the island's oldest temples of Christian thought, now a pile of stone almost hidden off a pathway of towering cypresses and holm oaks. Some of the thick walls had been preserved in the dry Adriatic air. Gene found the symmetrical simplicity of the façade appealing. According to anthropologists, the church had been constructed out of portions of abandoned castles from the mainland and had once been a masterpiece. Loose stones bleached white by the sun littered the ground.

"We're sitting where an army sat," said Shaw during a visit to the ruins. They were resting on stone ledges and talking about the Great War, about conflict and aggression and man's inability to stop wars in spite of what they felt was his fundamentally charitable nature. Shaw said that the human costs of the Great War had depressed him beyond endurance and bitterly disillusioned English society, and he was losing faith in political solutions for lasting peace and prosperity for the millions of impoverished, downtrodden people. A humanitarian, pacifist and socialist, Shaw saw the world was not moving in his direction. The rich were getting richer and more powerful politically, and the poor were weaker and disenfranchised, and no government seemed to care.

History repeats itself, he said, and men have never learned how to resist the desire to control other men. Shaw gave as an example the Treaty of Versailles, through which the victors of the war were humiliating Germany and making its citizens feel they were the enemies of mankind. First in warfare and now in peace, the Allies were crushing Germany, he said, adding that the reparations Germany had to pay France and England would keep Germany the beggar of Europe and lead to another war of incalculable repercussions.

Gene was aware that in 1914 Shaw had enraged Britons when he wrote *Common Sense About the War*, an essay taking a neutralist-pacifist position in which his paramount concern was for the lives of all human beings, not victory for either side. The war, he said, had been avoidable, its existence proof of the bankruptcy of the political system. Against a highly charged backdrop of self-righteously patriotic Englishmen on the eve of the Great War, Shaw found himself the most unpopular man in Britain.

As a patriotic Marine, Gene had been disappointed when he wasn't made a machine gunner. But in his travels around France and Germany following the armistice, he saw the aftermath of the brutal trench warfare that marked World War I and left tens of thousands of French, British and American soldiers wounded and maimed for life. He was deeply troubled by the waste of lives and stirred by Shaw's conviction that mankind had to resolve conflict before it started.

In Shaw's view, the League of Nations should have been given authority with claws sharp enough to stop renegade nationalism and governments from ganging up on each other through secret treaties. "I wrote Bertrand Russell that our job is to make people serious about the Great War. It was the monstrous triviality of the damned thing, and the vulgar frivolity of what we imagined to be patriotism, that gets at my temper." The current generation had not only lost faith in God, Shaw said, but had lost faith in Man and that's why so many were so unhappy.

"How do we wipe out war?" asked Gene. "Even the Church has sanctified aggression." This statement was borne out by their surroundings: the Byzantine army and the Knights Templar had sought refuge at Saint Mary's. "Mankind throughout history has shown a preference for hostilities to protect itself," he said.

"True," said Shaw, insisting that people allowed themselves to be romanced by military conflict, like the poet Rupert Brooke who had glorified England's patriotism and chivalry prior to the war in which he died. Man, Shaw insisted, was not predisposed to evil and sin and controlling the other fellow. Shaw said we must rid ourselves of the dark side, which seeks to dominate and seek revenge, or we would annihilate ourselves before another century was out. He said it had become so common to say that the next war would destroy civilization that no one even listened anymore.

"But how can we change man's basic nature to dominate or destroy?" asked Gene.

It's all in one's point of view, said Shaw. Our thinking about who we are, and who our enemies are, must be reconsidered, he said. If we continue to operate in a "survival of the fittest world," we will destroy ourselves. We must change the model. To know where the other person goes wrong is not as important as knowing where *we* go wrong. Live and let live.

"But how?" asked Gene. By education and enlightening ourselves, said Shaw. Through practicing tolerance continuously, by realizing that we're all in this world together and that the ultimate object of life cannot be conflict — us versus them — but the acceptance that both exist together at the same time as part of the process of life in nature. Then, said Shaw, it becomes common sense not to attack and dominate other cultures or people, because "they" are "us."

"You've read about Mahatma Gandhi," said Shaw, speaking of the British-educated Indian barrister jailed for leading nonviolent protests and civil disobedience against his colonial masters in India. "An eye for an eye makes the whole world blind," wrote the political and spiritual leader, preaching that all violence was unjustified. He wrote that he was prepared to die for many causes but said, "I'm not prepared to kill for them." Shaw said he was supportive of Gandhi's teachings.

Gene picked up a small, rounded stone, worn down by weather and perhaps by the feet of years past, and tossed it back and forth in his hands in the same way he used to squeeze hard rubber balls to strengthen his hands in training. A million times he had squeezed those balls, he said. Besides hardening his knuckles, it allowed him to think. He had come to regard these long hours with Shaw as "a post-graduate course in the art of living and thinking."

They spoke of the developing world around them and of man's emergence. Science had shown life beginning as an amoeba some three and a half billion years ago and evolving from water to land through the amphibious stage to becoming man as he is today. They talked about man's future hopefully in the millennia to come.

They had conversations about the new universe of Albert Einstein, the brilliant mind reader of the cosmos. Shaw was fascinated by Einstein's revolutionary theories of General Relativity and Quantum physics, which appropriated the 300-year-old laws of Isaac Newton in which the universe was based on predictability, constants, certainties of time and space and formulaic order. It had been the foundation of Western thinking.

Shaw was enthralled with Einstein's discovery of a whole new way of looking at reality — a curvilinear universe, warped space, the bending of light rays, absolute truths giving away to contingent truths, curved lines replacing straight lines and interdependency substituting for constants in time, space and matter. All motion now was relative to different frames of reference. Shaw envisioned it as a symbol of human possibilities. He saw it as a way to expand human consciousness. Einstein's theories encouraged Shaw to use different points of view in his plays, stimulating disputation and repartee among his characters and creating a unique Shavian dynamic.

The play *In Good King Charles's Golden Days*, one of the scripts Shaw later sent to Gene, includes a scene between Charles II and his queen, Catherine. The queen is shocked that there are 50 religions in England besides Catholicism. Charles, the relativist, is pleased by the variety. Catherine, the non-relativist, wonders if Charles has a conscience because her conscience, which she says came from her Catholic God, makes it clear that consciences must be the same.

Charles replies, "No two consciences are the same. No two love affairs are the same. No two marriages are the same. No two illnesses are the same. What is right for one is wrong for the other."

Shaw's plays, particularly those written in the 1930s and 1940s, reflect his world travels, his honoring of human differences and his celebration of diverse human truths and moral behavior. Shaw said that as a young man, he felt, as Gene must have, the need to bridge the gulf between the limitations we experience in ourselves and that power beyond ourselves that incessantly drives us forward to forge an individual path to betterment. He said his study of Percy Shelley, the romantic poet, set him on a track.

"And Shelley was your pivotal influence?" asked Tunney, surprised that a poet who had aroused him also affected Shaw.

"I learned from Shelley first," Shaw said. "Shelley, whom you know well, was more than a lyrical poet. He was a philosopher and an atheist, a social and political revolutionary." Shelley had a soaring spirit, and though he did not believe in a personal God, he had a paramount devotion to man and nature. The epilogue to *Prometheus Unbound,* in which Shelley champions free will, goodness, hope and idealism in the face of what the poet perceives as state tyranny and Church oppression, is the essence of his writings:

> To suffer woes which Hope thinks infinite;
> To forgive wrongs darker than death or night;
> To defy Power, which seems omnipotent;
> To love, and bear; to hope till Hope creates
> From its own wreck the thing it contemplates;
> Neither to change, nor falter, nor repent;
> This, like the glory, Titan, is to be
> Good, great and joyous, beautiful and free;
> This is alone Life, Joy, Empire, and Victory.

Shaw had postulated that there was on Earth a compulsion for betterment, a natural propensity to improve the lives and surroundings of Man.

It was not blind evolution that produced Man, as Darwin posited, said Shaw, but a universal will that allowed man to muddle through from the molecule stage and ascend to superiority over other species. Shaw called it "Creative Evolution," with its agent, "the Life Force." Its purpose wasn't to focus on what people were as much as what they could become.

"You see," said Shaw, "my instrument of the Life Force, the aspiring man who knows that the world can be improved, is not what you might refer to as a satisfied man. He does not accept being held down by family or society. My aspiring subject is not a contented fatalist, accepting himself and his limitations just as they are, in order to have peace of mind, knowing that he is a weed and not trying to be a rose. The superman-to-be will always be trying to improve himself in one way or the other and will settle for a sunflower if the rose is unreachable, but will never accept being a weed."

He said that, in practice, the Life Force meant Man could change himself to meet every vital need, "and that, however long the trials and frequent the failures may be, we can put up a soul as an athlete puts up a muscle." Shaw championed those who were self-empowered and relentlessly determined and who were most like himself, and he had at times a fanatical devotion to those he considered kindred spirits. When he came across an incarnation of the Life Force, he embraced it zealously, as he embraced Gene. In his play *Man and Superman*, Shaw identifies the philosophic (superior) man as one who "seeks in contemplation to discover the inner will of the world, in invention to discover the means of fulfilling that will, and in action to do that will by the so discovered means. Of all other sorts of men I declare myself tired."

To Shaw, life was about aspiring, emerging, but not fully arriving if it meant spending the rest of one's days in irresponsible merrymaking and contentment.

On Brioni, it was not uncommon to hear peacocks rustling in nearby bushes or to share space with herds of pale yellow fallow deer. Exotic African animal life had been imported by the island's owner as a way to entertain guests, and Shaw and Gene shared their walks with zebras and antelope as well as with hawks, green cormorants and hundreds of wild ducks, sea-swallows and gulls.

Shaw spoke of Jean-Baptiste Lamarck, the 18th-century French naturalist who first formulated the idea that the environment itself forces and shapes evolution. Lamarck theorized that in early times, the giraffe, by trying to feed from the highest branches for the choicest leaves, had, by conscious effort and will, lengthened its neck.

Although the theory was later disproved scientifically, Shaw metaphorically adapted it to humans and said that he felt man could, through sheer will, rise above his circumstances if he wanted to and tried hard enough. Where there's a will there's a way. "Can a scientist disprove that?" said Shaw. "Can a scientist study under a microscope an iron nerve, a fanatical conviction, a man's willpower?"

Shaw encouraged Tunney's aspirations toward bettering himself intellectually and culturally, and Tunney's presence gave Shaw a brace of reality by carrying him away from what many saw as the fantasy of the theatre and the characters that inhabited it. Shaw seemed to thrive in the presence of someone younger who had lived as a man of action, a man capable of taking another life with his bare hands, yet one who purposely chose not to maim opponents in the ring. A highly principled, well-spoken prizefighter who sought answers with scholarly intensity, Gene acted on willpower and intellect conjointly, never held back a question or opinion, was honest to the core and quoted the poets fluently. G.B.S. was delighted that Gene was a prizefighter, but more delighted that he was not typical at all.

Shaw lived in his mind and was attracted by his physical opposite in Gene. Both appreciated the "otherness" in each other. The fascinating contrast in their existences — the boxer with his shadow of a violent life against Shaw's cleanliness and humanitarianism — added to the mysterious paradox of their friendship. In Gene, Shaw found a character too incredible to have written about, and this amazed and satisfied him.

For his part, Gene thoroughly enjoyed G.B.S. as a person, finding him not only a walking library but a good listener and a thoughtful observer with whom he could share confidences. "If for nothing else, I am grateful to the profession of boxing for enabling me to know the witty, wise and altogether kindly Bernard Shaw," Gene wrote years later. "The world is aware of his encyclopedic genius. I know also his generosity, affability and charm."

One day, after a long talk about shadow boxing, in which Gene described how boxing one's shadow increases a fighter's alertness, balance and agility in the ring, they began a friendly spar. Playing hard to reach and not wanting to actually hurt his friend, Gene backpedaled over some tree roots and tripped. Convulsed in laughter, he accidentally fell down on some rocks, ripping his trousers. Gene, whose natural coordination and grace had been honed by thousands of repetitive motions of his sport, gestured generously with his entire body and held his arms open in a sign of defeat.

"Down for the count!" said a delighted Shaw. An observer said that both Shaw and Tunney were so demonstrative that watching the two friends together from a distance was "like watching windmills...their hands and heads never stopped moving."

Gene said that Shaw had a soft singsong Irish accent (a Protestant accent, Shaw reminded him) and their conversations were always so relaxed and jovial that it was easy to forget that Shaw's meanings were heartfelt and that this saintly person was the same Bernard Shaw who publicly provoked so many. "He was charming and entirely unaffected alone. I never heard him utter a foul word," said Gene, "nor raise his voice in anger, despite pouring rain, wind, cold sea waters, several missed meals and the occasional inconveniences of getting lost." He said Shaw's serenity was absolute; it came from the very marrow of his being. That serenity was sustained throughout their debates on questions of the unknown, discussions for which Gene had a particular appetite.

Gene had told a reporter that the day after winning the championship, he pored over the *Meditations* of Marcus Aurelius, the emperor who didn't believe in an afterlife and wrote, "We live for an instant, only to be swallowed in complete forgetfulness and the void of infinite time." While Gene realized that Shaw rejected the standard Church of God, he saw that Shaw had an educated disbelief in God and an unlimited capacity for hope and optimism that Man could achieve a God-like state. For his part, Gene offered that he particularly liked the *Confessions of Saint Augustine*, a classic of Christian dualistic theology which recounts the saint's struggle to achieve a life of spiritual grace.

"Shaw was in his element with a sympathetic pupil who needed to learn," said Shaw biographer Michael Holroyd in an interview with the BBC. "What Shaw didn't like was dry, academic teaching. Shaw liked almost outdoor teaching, spontaneous teaching, the magic of teaching rather than a more rigid, academic way of going about things. He would have had a really perfect pupil [in Gene] and he would have learned something at the same time, and that's a very good relationship. The best relationship is when the teacher also learns something."

When Gene returned at night, Polly said, he would sit in a chair and recount his conversations, sometimes stopping to reflect and almost too excited to speak. He learned so eagerly, she reported, it was "like a wolf crunching up bone." He emptied his pockets of papers, which were full of notes and diagrams, and he would sometimes take out his books to look up a passage or to write one down.

"I do think Mr. Shaw was wanting to give or pass on his knowledge," said Polly.

Gene ordered books from London, and with those he'd brought with him on his honeymoon, he began to build a library at the villa. He bought titles that Shaw recommended, including Shaw's *The Perfect Wagnerite* and *The Quintessence of Ibsenism*, H.G. Wells's *The Outline of History*, Ibsen's *Emperor and Galilean*, and Thomas Carlyle's *On Heroes, Hero-Worship and the Heroic in History*. One of the traveling trunks Gene had shipped to Brioni held not clothes but well over 150 volumes. He gathered so many more books that when they were shipped off the island, it took two horses hooked to a sled to pull the trunks.

Shaw was a clever, well-informed businessman and was impressed by Gene's winnings from the ring. Until the 1920s, boxing had rarely been a ve-

CARICATURE BY MIGUEL COVARRUBIAS OF SHAW AND TUNNEY WITH JIM TULLY – A
JOURNALIST WHO HAD INTERVIEWED BOTH – PUBLISHED IN *VANITY FAIR* JUNE, 1930.
THE ARTIST USED BRIONI AS BACKGROUND BECAUSE THE TWO FRIENDS' TIME THERE WAS
SO WIDELY PUBLICIZED (USED WITH PERMISSION OF MARIA ELENA RICO COVARRUBIAS).

hicle to financial independence, but Gene had made and kept more money than anyone else who had ever retired from the ring. "I wrote a letter to Norman Clark," said Shaw, "and told him you won because you had the good sense to win!" (When a reporter called Shaw biographer Archibald Henderson for comment on the friendship, the author guessed that it was based on money. "That always impresses Shaw," he said. "No boxer since Tunney has qualified so well for the playwright's esteem. The golden age ended with him.")

Like Shaw, Gene had been a negotiator. As champion, in addition to demanding and receiving 50 percent of the gate receipts, Gene had helped the promoter Tex Rickard devise what amounted to playoffs between boxers to create a ladder to the title. Shaw insisted on 15 percent of the box office receipts for his plays, even if it meant closing a production. Both of them supervised their own business affairs, and both gave money to needy causes or friends but insisted on anonymity for fear of becoming a mark.

"It may seem scandalous," wrote Shaw in discussing the distribution of wealth in *The Intelligent Woman's Guide to Socialism*, "that a prizefighter, for hitting another prizefighter so hard at Wembley that he fell down and could not rise within ten seconds, received the same sum that was paid to the Archbishop of Canterbury for acting as Primate of the Church of England for nine months."

Shaw said he would defy anyone to estimate the merits of individuals in terms of money alone. "I have two friends: Dean Inge and Gene Tunney," he told biographer Hesketh Pearson. Inge was the Dean of St. Paul's Cathedral in London. "What auctioneer is going to value their relative worth in pounds or dollars? At present, Gene can buy Dr. Inge up to ten times over without overdrawing his bank account. Is that distribution an ideal one?"

Gene said that boxing's ultimate value was not only in its monetary rewards but in the way it taught one how to stay in control when an opponent throws everything he's got, as well as how to handle life's ups and downs, the wins and the losses. One's gameness in the ring reflected how game one was in life, he said. In a similar vein, Shaw wrote that "fearlessness may be a gift or it may be learned but more precious is the courage of endeavor, of refusing to let fear of discrimination or intimidation or lack of money or worry of what other people might say halt one's forward motion and lose one's moral compass." Or, said Shaw, as the Roman poet Horace wrote, "It is courage, courage, courage that raises the blood of life to crimson splendor."

A private person who tended to keep his own counsel, Gene was eager for Shaw's encouragement and validation. After concentrating on boxing for ten years, he found himself trying to redefine his life. He felt that he was too well known and that it was too late to go to college. (When he had floated the idea that he might study at Oxford or the Sorbonne, the press had a field day). Shaw was, however, delighted to help Gene realize his natural potential.

He explained how he himself had gone from unsuccessful student to clerk to unpublished novelist to theatre art and music critic to writing political tracts for the Fabian Society and, finally, to success as a playwright. In addition, he had defeated a mortal shyness around people to become one of England's finest orators.

"We are not here to fulfill life's prophesies and fit ourselves into puzzles, but to wrestle with life as it comes. And it never comes as we expect it to come," the playwright wrote in *Simpleton of the Unexpected Isles.*

No matter how much Gene would learn, no matter how many speeches he made or how much writing he did, he would always be first a boxer in the minds of the public, Shaw said. "Boxing was what you did," said Shaw. "But boxing is not what you are." He was like Eliza Doolittle in *Pygmalion*, Shaw said, a person of character and personal magnetism totally unrelated to his original place in the social order; he could move comfortably in any social class. The contrast between the gentlemen in their finely tailored suits and the pugilist in his sweaty trunks is only cosmetic, Shaw said. As Professor Henry Higgins tells the street urchin Eliza in *Pygmalion*:

> The great secret, Eliza, is not having bad manners or good manners or any other particular sort of manners, but having the same manner for all human souls; in short, behaving as if you were in Heaven, where there are no third-class carriages, and one soul is as good as another.

On one sunny afternoon before leaving the ruins of Saint Mary's, Gene noted that the dramatic setting of ancient crumbling stone, combined with the history of the old basilica could make it a stage set. "Why, this could be a setting for a play," said Gene, gesturing toward the walls with a flourish. Shaw nodded good-naturedly.

"Let's call it 'The Master and the Boy,'" said Shaw.

"I suppose I'm to be the boy?" said Gene.

They laughed and discussed whether they should make a film of the Master and the Boy, star in it themselves and include a boxing match. "I can see it on the marquee already," said Gene, and he wrote the name in a notebook to be sure he remembered.

"I think of Shaw as the most considerate person I have ever known," wrote Gene. "He was helpful, directing me aright on questions of literature, music, art, thought. He was patient with me, and would go back over some difficult exposition, repeating it to be sure I'd get the full import. No period of my life was more valuable than this. It was like a matriculation in a cosmic school. During long walks we took together on Brioni, he was the teacher, I the pupil."

CHAPTER 12

Doctor's Dilemma

"As a matter of fact, the rank and file of doctors
are no more scientific than their tailors."
G. BERNARD SHAW, PREFACE TO *THE DOCTOR'S DILEMMA*

By the last week in April, with the Tunneys moved into the big villa, Polly was adjusting to her first chance as a bride to run a household. She had just celebrated her twenty-second birthday, and she "had never been happier." She felt like a romantic heroine in a grand Italian opera. She prepared menus, gathered flowers to decorate the rooms, directed the staff, and, ever eager to put her own mark on the villa, she bought colorfully painted Italian china to replace the more formal dinnerware favored by her mother. The Shaws had come for teas and dinner, and they were expected for the weekend. But on Saturday, April 27, the stomach pain she had tried so hard to ignore had worsened. Polly could barely get up from bed and couldn't descend the stairs.

"It will be fine," she gamely assured Gene, and she agreed to remain in bed for the day as the doctor had already advised her to do. "It's just a cramp." Gene sent for Dr. Lenz anyway. The doctor reiterated his diagnosis of scampi poisoning, but he agreed to confer with area doctors. Gene urged Polly to let him try to notify her mother who was motoring through Europe, but Polly adamantly refused, saying that it would only alarm her unnecessarily. Her mother, she said, had little tolerance for illness and would expect an adult daughter to make her own decisions. She made Gene promise to leave her mother alone.

Polly remained in bed, looked after by the villa staff, and Gene, thus reassured, departed and went off to entertain the Shaws.

The doctor's wife wrote in her diary that one of the vacationing doctors thought it sounded like intestinal flu or a virus. A medical professor from Trieste, knowing that Shaw was on the island, joked that it was "a doctor's dilemma," a reference to Shaw's play about doctors who claim omniscience in human matters, including life and death.

The next morning, Sunday, April 28, Polly was doubled over in pain and had been unable to sleep. Gene contacted Dr. Lenz to come again, exerting him to reconsider his diagnosis and strongly urging that Polly be moved immediately to a mainland hospital. But on examining the patient, Dr. Lenz said that she now had a fever and as her pain was more serious, it would be ill-advised to move her at all. She was better off remaining where she was.

The doctor used the island's phone to consult once more with doctors on the mainland, and their assessments concurred with Dr. Lenz: the poisoning that wracked the patient's body had to run its course, and the patient needed to be kept as still and comfortable as possible and should remain in bed. Dr. Lenz, well aware that Polly's health was not only of paramount concern to her husband but was now becoming a matter of discussion throughout Brioni, was solicitous and attentive and promised to check on her again in the evening. Guests on the island had begun to gossip about the beautiful *americana* who had succumbed to illness on her honeymoon.

Despite Polly's encouragement that her husband keep to his daily schedule, Gene canceled his swim and walk with Shaw. Becoming the focus of attention was something Polly never liked. She believed illness was the most intimate and private of human conditions and felt that word of it to any but the closest members of the family would have a negative and distressing effect on others. She was desperate to prove that she could overcome the illness on her own. She was sorry that Shaw's plans had been disrupted, and she would have been mortified to learn that anyone other than Gene knew she was ill. Polly spent an uncomfortable day in bed sleeping and reading poetry, but she couldn't eat, and she drank broth only when Gene spooned it into her mouth.

Polly's confidence that she could overcome medical matters on her own was heavily influenced by her belief in alternative and natural therapies that stressed the right food and exercise. She didn't like doctors and didn't like to take medication of any kind, and she had been fortunate in enjoying good health ("except for a teenage fat period") all her life. "Pooh — pills!" she always said, laughing. "They never help." She liked to collect local herbs or over-the-counter rubbing lotions and used whatever worked best, making her own healthful choices. In this regard, Shaw concurred.

"Doctors do more damage than good," Shaw had heartily agreed over dinner. He joked that since they were confined to a resort created by a doctor and a businessman who saw profit in turning a mosquito-infested island into a spa, good sense should warn them that they would be lucky to survive. When men die of disease, they are said to die of natural causes, said Shaw; when they recover, which they mostly do, the doctor gets the credit for curing them. In surgery, he said, operations are recorded as successful if the patient gets out alive.

"Fortunately, I've rarely needed a doctor myself," said Gene. "Just a broken nose and a few scrapes, and Polly is as healthy as an ox."

"Mother would agree with you," Polly told Shaw. "She's a Christian Scientist and doesn't believe doctors help her at all. I've read," she said, "that Lady Astor is a Christian Scientist, too."

"Are all rich American women Christian Scientists?" asked Shaw.

"Oh, no," laughed Polly. "I hardly think so. My mother just feels that homeopathic treatments often work quite well. She believes in a strong mind-body connection and feels healing and faith are related. But I think she would go to a doctor if she had a really serious medical problem. She's still an Episcopalian."

Shaw, she said, smiled. He told a story of a Christian Scientist who meditated over his own mother as she lay dying, but she died anyway, eventually, "as we all will do. I am old," said Shaw, "I'll go first." He told them that only a couple of months earlier, he had tried a new American treatment for spider bites, and despite Charlotte's skepticism, it worked.

"You have to believe in it to make it work," said Polly.

"Yes," said Shaw, "maybe you do."

"A toast," said Gene, raising his wineglass. "To good health!" Hear, hear, Shaw replied, and they all clinked their glasses together and laughed. Nothing is more dangerous than a poor doctor, Shaw wrote, not even a poor employer or a poor landlord.

On Monday, April 29, Polly had a burning fever, hadn't been able to eat for the third day, hadn't slept and had vomiting and diarrhea. She was too weak to walk to the bathroom by herself, and she looked ever more pale and frail. There was no doubt that she was desperately ill, and Gene's pulse quickened with concern. He sent for the doctor, then sat on the bed beside her to try to soothe her.

While holding her hand, her wedding ring slipped off her finger and rolled onto the sheets. He caught it in his hand and held it. She seemed to be losing weight before his eyes. He put his hands around her wrist and was startled that his once robust and athletic wife, a woman who could swing a tennis racquet and row a boat as well as any man, felt barely more alive than a stick of wood.

Gene and G.B.S. had joked about their skepticism of doctors, but Gene's past experience had been far more positive than Shaw's and, he felt, possibly more enlightened. He had read enough medical books to feel that he could diagnose some illnesses himself. When as a teenager he accompanied his Greenwich Village doctor on house calls, he often assisted in medical procedures, including childbirth and setting broken limbs. The doctor had encouraged him to think about medicine as a career, and if there had been money for education, Gene said he would have considered it.

Dr. Lenz arrived to check the patient, and it was immediately apparent from his furrowed brow and serious tone of voice that he was more concerned than he had been previously. The doctor said that he would cancel his office hours and move into the villa, to monitor the patient more closely and to be nearby if he was needed quickly. "It's just a precaution," he told Gene. While this was meant to relieve the anxiety of his patient as well as her husband, Gene did not see it as a good omen. Nor did he any longer believe what he was told.

Shaw had thus far done almost no work on his holiday because he had been spending his days and evenings with Gene. He told Charlotte that he was worried about Polly, but he took the time to catch up with neglected paperwork at his desk. "I have begun to work at the Ellen Terry preface," Shaw wrote that morning to his secretary, Blanche Patch, "but am leaving it to gad about the island on every pretext. The terrible *bora* has ceased blowing now for some days and some glorious *looking* weather has ensued; but it is not real summer yet."

By afternoon, despite the presence of the doctor, there had been no change in Polly's health. Dr. Lenz looked more worried and seemed more unable to provide answers to Gene's increasingly pressing questions, even though he remained loyally near enough to the patient to try to provide comfort. In his mind, Gene saw himself in a pretty bedroom with a beautiful girl. But it was a disquieting scene. He and Polly were trapped with maids, cooks, butlers, a well-meaning but ineffective doctor, and a problem — the first he could ever remember having that he could not solve by taking matters into his own hands.

His anxiety increased, and his imagination ran wild, triggering grim scenarios over which he would have no control. He paced, but movement, which usually tempered his restlessness, did not help. He could feel tension building in the pit of his stomach, rising into his shoulders and gripping his neck in a vise. Polly was given sedatives but each time Gene looked at her, she seemed to have faded more into the white sheets, her eyes sunken into her sockets and her skin translucent and fragile as gossamer. She occasionally opened her eyes slightly and tried weakly to smile, but she could barely speak. Gene held her hand and gently wiped her feverish brow. With each hour he read on the doctor's face that whatever devil had taken over Polly was further out of his control, and he remembered a Psalm he used to repeat as a boy: He will not fear evil tidings; his heart is steadfast, trusting in the Lord. Trusting in the Lord.

Dr. Lenz tried to be reassuring, saying that Polly's body was young and strong, and she would fight off the poison ravishing her system.

"And if she can't?" asked Gene.

"The consequences would be grave, indeed," said Dr. Lenz. "I will pray for her."

The doctor's lowered eyes told Gene what he needed to know. Almost unable to breathe, unable even to consider the consequences or show his fear to Polly, Gene excused himself and walked down the broad staircase to the villa kitchen. Pesara, the usually chatty cook, urged him to sit and offered him some food, which Gene refused and pushed away. Then, bowing slightly, Pesara handed him a small box that he said had come from friends at the hotel.

Gene sat down in a wooden chair at the long sturdy table, nodded and, smiling kindly at the obvious efforts to sympathize, took the lid off the box. On top was a piece of Italian lace floating like a delicate cobweb against a black background.

Some moments are etched in utter stillness as if all clocks, all noise, all movement, all life has been suspended, captured as a stark black-and-white image taken by an unknown photographer of pain so profound it seems to belong to someone else. It's always the seemingly ordinary that becomes extraordinary in life: looking down at the brown scuffed shoes of his brother Tom when he was told that John was dead, the night wind and the prickly holly Gene remembered backing into when she first said "I love you," the powdered smell of resin on the canvas in the seventh round. Such moments are but milliseconds yet can linger in memory for a lifetime of love or grieving, the moments ripping through consciousness to feed joy and despair.

It was such a moment when Gene looked at the open box, with the little square of lace placed neatly on top. Gene knew he would never forget this kitchen or this table or this small box. The big straw broom hung in the corner behind the stove. Dishes were stacked in a pile beside the sink. Damp dishtowels, probably left by a cook, lay crumpled on a chair waiting to be hung up to dry. A large bottle of olive oil, its top off, sat on the counter beside a knife and a basket of onions. He had been meaning to ask about that olive oil, why when it was used every day the bottle never emptied, and for a second, he chastised himself for thinking about such a trivial and mundane kitchen matter when so much else was at stake.

Unable to stop himself, he reached in to finger the contents of the box and realized that his hand was shaking. "I am never fidgety," he wrote. "I can sit quietly without nervous motions." He was always proud that he had mastered the art of repose. He could be on airplanes that were buffeted by gale force winds and nearly crashed and continue reading, his self-control so powerful that he appeared never to notice and seemed oblivious to the panic of others. Twice, he nearly drowned in deep ice-covered waters, but with his great strength and composure, he hauled himself from the brink of death up onto the ice and saved his life. The exception in surrendering to his feelings would always be the crisis on Brioni.

Gene pushed the lid of the box aside, removed the lace covering and took out a small black pillow, a cushion so black that it seemed to weigh down his fingertips. Stitched to the black felt was a black-and-white picture of the Virgin Mary that looked cut from a prayer book, a Virgin who seemed to be crying; perhaps the sender had added the tears. There was a blue crocheted pillow the size of a stamp with another Virgin, also with black tears, holding the baby Jesus.

The sentiments of the little box were becoming obvious, and Gene began to sweat, but Pesara stood watching and so he nodded and continued his horrible unearthing of objects that he didn't want to see and couldn't bear to comprehend. He picked up a handmade red paper heart folded neatly in half as if one-half of the heart had already been torn asunder. A handful of saints' medals were tucked on the sides. There were handkerchiefs for weeping, the kind he had seen at funerals in his family: a white embroidered handkerchief, a purple handkerchief with gold threads, and handkerchiefs with white and black borders. There were dozens of pieces of paper with words written in Italian, each folded carefully. Prayers, said Pesara. He offered to read them, but Gene saw a hand-cut paper cross and a rosary with black beads that had been well used and knew that he had had enough.

He found he couldn't go through the rest. Replacing the black felt pillow neatly on top underneath the lace, he removed the rosary.

"*Kyrie, eleison*," he intoned silently, hearing the echoes of Latin liturgy as he fingered the dark beads.

"*Christe, eleison.*"

"Hail Mary, full of grace," he murmured, tucking the rosary back into the box. "The Lord is with thee."

As a fighter, Gene had known fear — not fear that he told his mother about and certainly not his father, who would have taken it as cowardice and a lack of manhood. As a young fighter, he had been terrified of meeting professional boxers in the ring, terrified that he would meet the same end as the handsome hero of Jack London's *The Game*, who dies in the ring on the eve of his wedding, fighting his last fight. In the final page, the bride Genevieve kisses the lips of her beloved, and collapses, sobbing, rocking her body in pain. After reading the book as a teenager, he had given up fighting altogether for months, until the need for money and encouragement from his brother John pushed him back into it.

"I can remember praying that morning as fervently and humbly as any man ever has," he wrote of one of his first professional bouts against a tough, seasoned veteran of the ring. "I prayed that in the fight that afternoon I might not be permanently injured when I was knocked out. I didn't ask that I might win. I took it for granted that I'd be knocked out, and I was terribly afraid of being hurt for life."

As a boy Gene, crossed himself before daring deeds like swinging on buoys or diving from ship's ladders into the Hudson River. At one of his first professional fights, he instinctively made a sign of the cross while standing in his corner before the opening bell. "So you need God to win, do you, Gene?" snickered a reporter who saw him. "Well, the fans are looking for a slugger who can win on his own." The pious gesture had become a ring superstition, and some boxers who were not even Catholic crossed themselves like a good luck charm, but Gene never again made a public display of his faith.

While training to meet Dempsey for the first time, he had awakened one night and felt his bed shaking. "It seemed fantastic," he wrote. "Ghosts? Then I understood. It was I who was shaking, trembling so hard that I made the bed tremble. I was that much afraid. The fear was lurking in the back of my mind and had set me quaking in my sleep, the nightmare thought of myself being beaten down by Dempsey's shattering punches. The vision of myself bleeding, mauled and helpless, sinking to the canvas and being counted out. I couldn't stop trembling."

Before the fight in Chicago, Gene had gone to church to pray, then he pinned to the shiny blue robe he wore into the ring a medal of Saint Francis, the saint that reminded him of towering pines, singing birds and the power of faith. "I had to close the doors of my mind to destructive thoughts and divert my thinking to other things. Prayer and faith were pillars of strength to me." Gene had escaped serious and life-threatening injuries as a boxer and had retired virtually unscathed, a quality of life he attributed to his belief as well as to training.

While in London and visiting Shaw, he had been invited to present a soccer trophy to the British Royal Marines on behalf of their American counterparts. There was sadness in Britain at the time because King George V was gravely ill, and Gene unexpectedly and rather boldly set aside the sporting speech he planned to deliver. Stepping to the podium, he looked out over the audience of 7000 Marines lined up in formation, 14,000 eyes focused on him. He closed his own eyes for a moment, then asked them to join him in silent prayer for the King's recovery. "As in one motion, the endless lines of heads were bowed. I have never known a more fervent moment of supplication." But even the memory of that collective outpouring of emotion did little to quiet him.

The horrible reality was that Gene felt he had touched death in the ring, and it haunted him. His beloved brother had been given to the earth before Gene knew he was gone, and he had helped his family bury his father. But he had also lost two opponents, two men he hardly knew, and the memory of touching them raced back into his mind with every heaving breath that Polly took.

Herman Crossley had been an able-bodied Englishman in September of 1921. Gene had whipped Crossley so badly that the man's seconds called a halt to the bout in the seventh round. Crossley fought again but died suddenly six weeks later of complications from pneumonia. A tragic fluke, Gene was told. He had nothing to do with it. Then, three days before Christmas of the same year, he fought Eddie O'Hare in Madison Square Garden. He had looked forward to fighting Eddie because he was fast, clever, and a hard hitter, a promising boxer Gene felt he could learn a good deal from because Eddie had served Dempsey as a sparring partner. He knocked Eddie out. A few weeks later Eddie went to Maine to recuperate from his injuries. The talented Eddie went tobogganing, struck his head on a tree stump and died of a broken neck after somersaulting into a pile of snow.

Two good men. He had shared their space, fought their fight. Could he ever be sure his hands had not played a part in their untimely deaths? Was it possible that two bad beatings in the ring had no consequences?

"Christe, eleison…"

In the back of his mind, the hooded memory of death and despair took root, and he felt fear gnawing at his body. Questions chased each other around and around in his head. How did Polly become so ill without him realizing it? What should he have done, what should he have noticed? Why didn't he realize that while he was out walking and swimming and enjoying his life that Polly might have been wasting away, beginning to wither? Why, with all his money and connections, couldn't he get her the medical treatment she needed? It was entirely his fault. He was to blame. He was sure of it. Gene felt as if walls were closing in around him; he felt as close to panic as he had ever been in his life. He sat in a chair beside Polly and laid his head on the bed, his arm protectively across hers. "I was dejected…forlorn…on an island in the Adriatic. Had I been in the United States I would have known who to approach for medical advice, but there on the island was but one poorly prepared physician."

Toward evening, Dr. Lenz told Gene he would stay the night. Then, with all the care, concern, and delicate, well-meaning words in English that he could muster, the kind Austrian doctor who had been optimistic only 24 hours before and who had said that healing was a matter of time for a young and vibrant woman, told Gene that he now felt his patient's life was in the balance. It was possible, he said, that she might not recover. He told Gene that he should be prepared for the worst. It was in God's hands, he said.

Gene took a rosary from his bedroom dresser and pushed it deep into his pocket.

He had only one person to turn to, and he practically ran across the island.

CHAPTER 13

Saint Rocco Prayers

"I know Gene Tunney quite well. He is a serious
Roman Catholic with literary tastes."
G. BERNARD SHAW

Menacing clouds raced across the leaden sky like dark silk in the wind, and
the weather, which for several days had been mild, was turning colder again.
The two men walked along the broad quay, bent toward one another in conversation. The Adriatic slapped quietly against boats secured to the heavy iron
moorings, and lights from the fishing village of Fazana could be seen across
the channel. Behind them there were occasional far distant sounds of music
and merriment, probably diners going to and from one of the restaurants, a
reminder that in a seaside resort, there were others in a holiday mood. It was
the end of April, and May would signal a new surge of wealthy Austrian and
German tourists.

"A German lunatic asylum," Shaw had called Brioni a few days earlier,
and they had both stopped, almost overcome with laughter at the joke.

For the merrymakers in the distance and the fishermen at home, it was no
different from any other night. Nor was there anything to distinguish Shaw
and Gene in the dark. Up close, they would have been about the same height,
Shaw with a white beard, a cap, a walking stick and, like the younger Gene,
wearing tweeds. They could have been mistaken for father and son. Gene
walked with his hands pushed deep into his pockets where his fingers occasionally touched the rosary. His shoulders were stooped. He no longer had
the upright, easy gait of an athlete, certainly not that of a man who had been
boxing champion of the world only months before. A stranger wouldn't have
bothered him this night, for he was a man in anguish. He had thought his
toughest battles were behind him in the ring, and now he knew, with a cer-
tainty he could barely put into words, that they had only just begun.

The older man did most of the talking. Bernard Shaw was known for
talking. But the 72-year-old sage, known to be one of the most loquacious
people in the world, must have regretted not having more words to offer.

It had initially seemed such a clear-cut diagnosis: the young Mrs. Tunney
had scampi poisoning, a common tourist ailment along the Adriatic, and the
doctor would treat her. Nothing seemed too amiss, even when the pain came
back, for hadn't Mrs. Tunney indulged herself with scampi again? It would
get better with bed rest, the doctor said, adding that some cases take longer
to cure.

In hindsight, Shaw, always a skeptic about doctors playing their all-know-
ing roles, felt that maybe he should have asked questions or pressed Gene to

seek more answers, and maybe he should have anticipated earlier what none of them could have known. Too late, the medical man said she was far more ill than he realized and that she was in severe pain, too feverish to be moved, even if he had somewhere to move her. Desperate as he was to offer hope, the doctor had told Gene that a cure, her very survival, was out of his hands.

As they talked, a ribbon of red-orange burned briefly through the overcast sky, signaling the setting of the sun. The two watched the light fade and disappear across the water, then turned and walked back through an approaching night heavy with the sweet scent of jasmine, which they didn't smell, and with storm clouds above that they didn't see.

Taking care to avoid the pathway that led to laughter and music, they walked farther from the water, behind one of the hotels where workers would have been seen dumping trash and tidying up from the evening meal; still unseen, they walked beneath a canopy of pines that cast dark shadows against the already darkened grass.

A band was playing at the open-air ballroom called the "bull ring," a large, circular dance floor sunk below ground and surrounded by tiers of tables under striped umbrellas and illuminated by lights in brightly colored paper lanterns hanging in the trees. The bull ring was popular at teatime, and Gene felt a pang of remorse remembering how happy Polly had been to introduce the Shaws to the afternoon music. Shaw had even suggested they have a turn on the dance floor.

Nearby was the Gothic-style St. German church, dedicated to a brave citizen who, at the end of the third century, dared to object to a local administrator about intolerance toward the Christians and was sentenced to death. The original 15th-century frescoes had been damaged by fire and replaced with copies. Black-and-white mosaics from the ruins of the imperial Roman villa on the seaside had been installed in the floor of the church to protect the artwork from the elements and the ravages of saltwater. Shaw and Gene had walked through the church earlier in the week, commenting on how much it needed repair. Something about the simplicity of the whitewashed stone interior reminded them of Gregorian chant.

"The nuns taught us that music was proof of God's existence," said Gene, "And I think what I most enjoyed in church was the music. The Mass was sung, of course. Can you imagine?" he said, throwing his head back and laughing. "It wasn't until later that I realized even *Methodists* had music."

"The New Testament says they sang at the Last Supper, before going to the Mount of Olives," said Shaw. "To hear echoes of the chant is considered a blessing, and you don't need be in church to hear it." Shaw hummed a passage from one of Joseph Haydn's Masses that Gene didn't recognize. But he told Shaw that day, not for the first time, that he wished he could sing too.

St. German's was at a crosswalk where party-goers might mingle at night, so they didn't stop. They didn't wish to see anyone.

Farther up the hill under the trees, in an area now in darkness, was another church, a simple stone building with a high-peaked roof, smaller than a suite in the hotel and about the size of a cowshed. It was ruddy gray, streaked brown with the rivulets of past rain, and plain and windowless, except for a small opening so high up on one wall that it would have been impossible for anyone to actually see through it. Saint Rocco's Chapel looked as if it had grown organically out of the ground like a large boulder, rooted into a spot on the hillside between a row of cypress with no plan of function beyond providing shade on a hot day should a wandering animal or worker need a place to rest. It was too small to be used as a regular church, and it was rare these days that someone would bother to step inside.

It was named after the French nobleman who distributed his wealth among the poor and took an oath of poverty, then set out on his pilgrimage to Rome at a time when all of Italy was stricken with a deadly plague. During his travels, Saint Rocco cured many people, but he, too, contracted the plague and died. The chapel, a tribute to the saint who saved lives, had been built on Brioni in 1504 as the plague ravaged Italy, to offer sanctuary for prayer and to harbor grieving souls.

Shaw pushed hard against the old wooden door with his shoulder and it creaked open.

They stepped over the door frame, one after another, and went inside, standing in the near darkness, the small space still as a tomb and just as silent. The only sound was their breathing. Fumbling for a moment, they located matches and votive candles on a table beside the door, in the same place where Gene remembered he had always found candles and matches in a Catholic church. Do they always put them there, he wondered? Does Rome tell them even where to put the matches? Shaw closed the door behind them, and Gene lit two candles and carried them to a plain wooden chest that doubled as an altar at the front of the chapel.

It smelled musty, as if no one had visited for a long time, and the thick stone walls held the cold of the winter in them, though Gene hardly noticed.

They sat down together on a long wooden bench.

Gene had told his friend that it had been a very long time since he had been to confession or attended Mass. Shaw seemed unconcerned with this revelation and had been the one to suggest going into the church.

"You may have left the church," Shaw said, "but the church would not leave you."

"I am one of those people who believe in prayer," said Gene.

"Then you must pray," said Shaw.

Earlier that evening, Gene had come to Charlotte and G.B.S. almost breathless, interrupting them as they prepared for dinner alone. Gene had told them, hardly believing his own words, that the doctor now said Polly might not

SAINT ROCCO'S CHAPEL ON BRIONI WAS BUILT IN 1504
ON THE LONGEST NIGHT OF HIS LIFE, GENE CAME TO
PRAY, WITH G.B.S. BY HIS SIDE (TUNNEY COLLECTION).

survive, and the Shaws sat speechless as he poured out his heart, frantically trying to explain how little he had done to save her and how he could never live without her. She was his Juliet, his goddess Selene, his ideal, and the only woman he had ever loved or could love, a soul mate who shared his deepest dreams and knew his heart as no one else. She loved poetry and music and she loved him. He couldn't live without her, and he was unable to speak of the unbearable burden to him should she be lost.

Gene wept, trembling, his wide shoulders heaving and tears cascading down his face, unable to stop himself and too grief-stricken to be embarrassed at his complete loss of control. He bared his heart as he had never done to anyone before, and he hung his head and said he was sorry, so very sorry, but that he had nowhere else to turn. He was alone. He would give his own life, his fortune, all his worldly goods if need be, to save his bride. Shaw rested an arm on Gene's shoulder and listened. And when Gene's torrent of despair subsided, Shaw suggested they take a walk. "Walking," he said, "always helps me think." So they had left on their walk along the quay, and Gene went — almost meekly, like a child, it seemed — so desperate was he to have someone help him cope with the nightmare that was careening out of his control.

There was no script for despair. Shaw had been at the bedside of his sister Lucy, holding her hand, when she died. Her thumb straightened, he wrote, and then she was dead. He had sympathized with those whose loved ones were slain in the Great War. When J.M. Barrie wrote Shaw about the loss of his adopted son George, the model for Peter Pan, Shaw wept. "Such waste," he muttered to Charlotte, "such utterly damnable waste." By the time he reached his seventies, the death of friends was not uncommon.

But he had never been in the middle of a life-or-death crisis — on stage, so to speak — for that bellow of raw agony and intolerable heartbreak when one is suddenly aware that death in its steady stealth to snatch a life may not be stopped. Shaw couldn't remember when he had held a man weeping uncontrollably, pleading for divine intervention. And he couldn't remember when he himself had been the sole person available to offer solace, when there had been no one else to turn to, no churchman or family to take over, as they always did. They were on an island far from home and none of the usual polite behaviors applied. They were stranded in a critical drama filled with despair and tension, without an ending. A beautiful, young life was in the balance. If the tables were turned and it were G.B.S. or Charlotte struggling for breath, what would one expect from the young Tunneys?

Charlotte had been kind and sympathetic, putting her arms around Gene, offering water and tea and listening in her gentlewomanly manner. She understood instinctively and immediately that Gene needed to be with someone, and in particular, needed to be alone with G.B.S.

In the dark shadows of Saint Rocco, under the high ceiling and exposed beams where the candlelight barely flickered, Gene knelt. He made the customary sign of the cross, with the fingers of his opened right hand on his forehead, "In the name of the Father," he murmured, then, touching his heart and sweeping his hand from left shoulder to the right, "and the Holy Spirit," and bringing his hands together, "Amen."

He slipped the rosary from his pocket and, kneeling on the cold stone floor, he began moving his lips in silent prayer as the beads slipped through his fingers, words that he had said every morning and every night of his childhood. His mind flashed with memories of the melodious chanting of the priests, the familiar cadence of the Latin liturgy that had always touched him for its purity and goodness, making him feel connected spiritually to all that he felt was gratifying, inspirational and holy in life. In the presence of God and Shaw, he bowed his head and prayed for Polly.

The man who sat beside Gene, his walking stick laid quietly along the plank that served as a seat, was not an easy man for most people to understand. He had scandalized the Church by declaring it to be a contradiction in terms, was frequently referred to as an atheist and had even called himself an atheist, because he disagreed publicly with church teachings that he felt forced people to blindly accept superstition instead of encouraging a broader search for truth. He railed against theologians and disputed the moral authority of religious leaders. Yet he always packed his Bible in his suitcase, and he was more familiar with the teachings of the Old and New Testament than many preachers.

He didn't record what he was thinking. He might have thought of the child in himself who had seen God in his garden in Dublin at age 3, the Lord's Prayer that he used to ward off storms or the time that he dreamed he had died and gone to heaven, to "a waiting room with walls of pale, sky-coloured tabbinet and a pew-like bench running all around, except at one corner, where there was a door. I was," he wrote, "somehow aware that God was in the next room, accessible through that door."

As a boy of 13, Shaw had prowled through Dublin's National Gallery for hours, memorizing details of 17th-century Italian religious paintings with his only friend, a chubby boy with black curly hair named Matthew Edward McNulty. During winter's dank and chilly months, the museum's two-story main gallery was illuminated by more than 2000 flickering gas burners, casting an almost ethereal light against the parade of angels and cherubs and Virgin Marys. Gigantic plaster casts of Grecian sculpture, gladiators and lions marched along the walls. There were few places in Dublin as visually invigorating to an inquisitive young mind, and in time, the youthful Shaw had memorized every painting in the museum, from Giovanni Lanfranco's dramatic *Last Supper* and his *Multiplication of the Loaves and Fishes* to Giulio Cesare Procaccini's *Glory of Charles Borromeo*.

Shaw told Gene later that he couldn't remember when he had sat alone in a church beside a man whose every breath pleaded deliverance for a loved one, a young man with a strength of character he had come to admire but who had been blindsided by the devil he least expected on the person he loved most. Shaw couldn't help but be touched by the simplicity and enormity of the circumstances, and he was profoundly moved that he was included in a hallowed moment of such singular magnitude. Here was a man kneeling beside him — including him in his circle of complete trust and confidence — and lifting his heart and mind to God, praying with a total lack of hypocrisy and a genuine belief that the church of Saint Peter would hear. Here was a man reaching alone into the great unknown toward the essential meaning and mystery of the transcendent God, the most private, powerful and least understood of human communications, and he was unwavering in his fortitude and purpose.

Shaw's comments later indicated that he found his friend's faith in the divine almost overpowering, and he would have known that sitting on that stiff, cold bench offered him a unique glimpse of something bright and hot and fearful — man's deepest beliefs and purpose in communion with the universe.

Shaw sat like a shadow in the pew, almost motionless, perhaps as a result of being forced to sit in church as a child with his ankles laced together in silence. "I had been told to keep my restless little limbs still all through those interminable hours; not to talk; and above all, to be happy and holy there and glad that I was not a wicked little boy playing in the fields instead of worshipping God," he wrote. The only sounds were the click of the rosary through Gene's fingers and an occasional intake of breath, but even that was muffled, so bent was Gene's head against his chest.

Shaw kept his own thoughts. He might have remembered Victor Hugo saying, "Certain thoughts are prayers. There are moments when the soul is kneeling no matter what the attitude of the body may be."

If Shaw thought that sitting in that dark, frigid little church was unusual for him, he never said so. If he thought that it was useless, he never said so. Later, he made frequent mention of prayer to his friend Sister Laurentia, writing that, "I don't mind being prayed for. When I play with my wireless set, I realize that all the sounds in the world are in my room; for I catch them as I alter the wave length receiver — German, French, Italian, and unknown tongues. The ether is full of prayers, too; and I suppose if I were God, I could tune in to them all. Nobody can tell what influence these prayers have."

What Shaw said afterwards, what he told Gene and what he told Polly, was that he had prayed for a miracle. "A miracle, my friend, is an event which creates faith," Shaw wrote in *Saint Joan*. "That is the purpose and the nature of miracles." Years later, he would write, "Prayer consoles, heals, builds the soul in us; and to enact a prohibition of prayer, as some secularists would if they had the power, would be as futile as it would be cruel."

The two remained in the church until Gene's knees gave out, until the sounds of night had taken over the sounds of evening, and until the candles died, leaving tallow spooled on the altar. In praying, Gene regained his strength of conviction that he, and Polly, could overcome the ordeal. He thanked Shaw for being with him, and placing his hands over his friend's hands in the silence that followed, he felt a thickness rising in his chest, a sensation he would always associate with deep and lasting affection. It had been for Gene a coming home, and the emotion was so overflowing in him that knowing his friend understood made him unable to speak of it, even in the dark. No more were they the famous author and the boxer whose winnings and wedding had been news worldwide. If such details had been important to their relationship at all, it would never matter to either of them again.

Neither remembered when they left the church. Shaw walked part of the way back to the villa with Gene until, when they reached the fork in the road where the Temple of Venus stood, where Romans had prayed to their own gods, he was persuaded to return, lest a trip in the darkness could cause him to fall.

On the way back, Shaw cut into a meadow where an ancient olive tree stood distant and alone, its silvery leaves rustling against the increasingly gusty night wind. The tree was more than 1500 years old, a squat, straggly, bushy thing that in surviving plagues and wars and generations of onlookers had not grown as much in height as in circumference, with many gnarled off-shoots of its original trunk, as if it had knowingly kept itself grounded to the earth for safety. In Homer's *Odyssey*, Odysseus crawls beneath an olive tree, and some claim that the olive trees in the Garden of Gethsemane date back to the time of Jesus. In the New Testament, an olive tree symbolizes salvation.

Shaw snipped off a twig and stuck it in his pocket.

The temperature was dropping and a storm was coming.

CHAPTER 14

Tipping Point

"What a mystery friendship is! One of those subtle and beautiful forces that glorify life. And how strangely and delightfully different one's friends are one from the other."
DAME LAURENTIA MCLACHLAN

Shaw might well have thought of his friend Sister Laurentia as an anchor for his conscience.

The holiday on Brioni was not going at all the way he expected. In fact, from a purely objective and analytical viewpoint, almost every conceivable thing had gone wrong, and there were good and sensible reasons to depart as quickly and diplomatically as possible. In trading stories about Hollywood, Gene had used cowboy slang of the American West, and though he couldn't remember the exact words for a gunslinger having to get out of town fast, Shaw thought the notion of it applied perfectly.

He wasn't getting any work done because he was spending so much time with Gene. He had not made enough progress on final revisions for *The Apple Cart*, and the Terry preface was sitting unfinished on his desk. He thought the weather was overall rather horrendous, certainly not the summer weather he had expected, and he missed the gregarious nature of a city, for its noises and traffic and smells of real people.

Even Charlotte said she thought the island was boring.

If it hadn't been for Gene and Polly, the Shaws agreed that they would have left long ago.

The day before, as Polly's condition had worsened, Charlotte and G.B.S. had discussed the option of leaving so they wouldn't become embroiled in someone else's problems. They knew they easily could have apologized for being a distraction and in the way and departed for Pola, a short boat ride away, or Dubrovnik or Venice, where they planned to move on to anyway before returning to England. Once ensconced in a more suitable place, they could have written, sent cables, ordered flowers and expressed frequent and stirring concern for the health of the patient — something they were both exceptionally practiced at doing.

Shaw was known to deluge his friends with advice. "The first rumor of a crisis in the life of a friend or acquaintance would stimulate Shaw to a string of admonitory letters or postcards, always glittering or entertaining, usually grossly misinformed regarding the nature of that crisis, insolently confident that there was an easy way out of it which only he had thought of, and inappropriately cheerful in tone, even jaunty," wrote the novelist Rebecca West.

"It was like being serenaded on the banjo throughout the dark night of the soul."

There was clearly no familial obligation that they remain on Brioni. Though they now knew the young Tunneys extremely well, they had been barely more than acquaintances before they arrived. The weather was poor, the swimming was cold, and the unpredictable rain and winds interfered with walks. In a note to his secretary, Shaw complained about the "bitter *bora*" and said, "There is nobody here that we know except Gene Tunney. A settled melancholy, peculiar to the place perhaps, devours us."

Many, faced with such a troubling scenario, would have opted to leave the young couple to the doctors and the highly attentive staff of the villa and the hotel, and for that, they wouldn't be faulted. The Tunneys had garnered tremendous affection during their visit, and virtually anyone on the island would have been willing to step in, eager to attend the famous boxer in his hour of need. It wasn't like the Christmas of 1927, when they had been snowed in for 18 days at Clivedon, the Astors' vast 19th-century Italianate mansion overlooking the Thames. Then, there had been a houseful of maids, valets, cooks, coachmen and other guests caught up in a kind of gay adventure of being snowbound, all with nothing to do but attend splendid meals, read books, exchange witty stories and share spirited conversation around the roaring fire in the great wood-paneled library. It was, Charlotte wrote, "a wonderful & impossible dream" and she and G.B.S. had become, as a result, much better acquainted with the Astors.

On Brioni, there was no lure of adventure. There was no protocol for a childless couple in their 70s jumping into the role of parents or caretakers during a life-threatening crisis for an ailing bride and her husband, who were not related to them in any way. It undoubtedly seemed somewhat like finding a shipwreck at your door and having to decide on the spot how much personal effort to expend as Good Samaritan when you knew help could, and undoubtedly would, be found elsewhere if you didn't allow yourself to get any more directly involved. What would they be able to do anyway? Gene and Polly would have been grateful that they came at all.

The trouble was that both Charlotte and G.B.S. *liked* the young couple and were genuinely worried and affected by the dilemma.

In early April, as they were preparing to depart for their trip, Charlotte's younger sister Mary "Sissy" Cholmondeley had died, leaving Charlotte devastated and in a state of nervous exhaustion. Shaw had felt that the trip to a sunny climate would be especially restful for Charlotte and would divert her attention to the sort of vacation that she especially always enjoyed. If he was worried that a new life-threatening crisis would unleash more anxieties and impair her own recovery from grief, he was proved wrong. To see "little Polly," as she called her, so vulnerable affected Charlotte deeply. Despite herself, Charlotte felt bound to Brioni.

Shaw also knew instinctively and beyond any doubt that he was needed and that in his staying, he could make a profound difference in the quality of the outcome, no matter what it might be. He realized that the sincere young man who had accomplished so much was desperately lonely and frightened and that all of his fame and new wealth amounted to nothing in the face of such possible loss. Gene seemed to hunger for his support and presence perhaps more than anyone Shaw had ever met.

Shaw liked to pride himself that he kept his feelings under wraps and maintained a discreet emotional distance from other people. But somehow — perhaps in being captive on an island — he had become intimately connected to the Tunneys. As he expressed it in later conversations, this feeling was apparently as unexpected as it was welcome. Gene would not ask him to stay, of course. But could a moral man live with himself if he knew he could have made a difference in a life and hadn't bothered to try? A year later, Shaw would tell an American interviewer who pressed him on the point that he had not planned to stay on Brioni but realized that his friend was in a "low mental state," and had changed his mind. He had then switched the subject and declined to elaborate.

Sister Laurentia would have known that he would do the right thing.

And Shaw knew there was only one thing to do. It may have surprised him, but he told Charlotte before going to bed that they had no other options.

THIS PHOTO OF TUNNEY WAS CHARLOTTE'S FAVORITE PICTURE OF HIM, AND REMAINS ON DISPLAY AT SHAW'S CORNER, THE PLAYWRIGHT'S HOME, WHICH IS NOW A MUSEUM IN AYOT ST. LAWRENCE, HERTFORDSHIRE, ENGLAND (TUNNEY COLLECTION).

CHAPTER 15
Polly's Miracle

"You can pray away your terrors, if you have enough faith."
GENE TUNNEY

The storm came in over the mountains from the northeast in darkness with the fury of a *bora*, whipping up whitecaps along the rocky coast, driving water over the seawalls and dumping shells and debris on the lawn at the villa. Small boats and dinghies were overturned and ripped from their moorings. Leaves and branches blew off trees and rainwater drove divots the size of rabbit holes into the sand greens on the golf course. Lounge chairs left outside at the villa slammed against columns of the loggia. At the "bull ring," the striped umbrellas that were not tied down were tossed and wrapped around the bandstand like mangled spaghetti.

Inside Villa Punta Naso, the situation was grim.

A weary, worried Dr. Lenz stationed himself in the big second-floor hallway to be nearer the sickroom. He sat quiet and solemn in a large leather chair, reading and occasionally pouring coffee into a cup from a pot on a small table. Gene was in the bedroom with Polly, and at intervals, Dr. Lenz knocked and went in to check on his patient, changing the moist towels that he hoped would help bring down her high fever. But her fever barely fluctuated. The fever wasn't the worst part, of course. Dr. Lenz was worried about the unrelenting, knifelike pain in her lower abdomen and his inability to ease her discomfort. There was no doubt in his mind that her condition was grave, but he had no idea what to do.

Lenz felt as bad as a doctor can feel. Trained at one of the finest medical institutes in Austria, he was a man now in his 50s, and most of his medical experience had been delivering babies, consoling elderly islanders and treating viruses, food poisoning and the occasional broken limbs. Seriously ill patients were sent to the mainland, and island guests rarely were ill at all. He had been proud of his profession and, until young Mrs. Tunney's misfortune, of his reputation as the island's only doctor.

It was a job he had coveted. Lenz had first visited Brioni on holiday from Vienna almost 30 years before, in 1900, bringing with him a friend he hoped to cure of typhus. They had arrived in winter, in the middle of the night, and when morning came, he had his first view of the blue sunlit sea, a moment that so thrilled him he eagerly accepted a job two years later as the island doctor. Over the years, in his spare time, he had explored every ruin and every path and had even had time to write a guidebook for tourists. He considered his role in the island's development and as medical advisor to so many important people, including European royalty, the achievement of a lifetime. This was the most serious crisis of his medical career. He was devastated that he had no idea how to help Mrs. Tunney, and he did not understand what he could have done differently.

In the bedroom, Gene paced, held Polly's hands, stroked her forehead, her arms, her legs and talked quietly, then paced more as she dozed in a feverish delirium. He was focused and dry-eyed, the fear and realization that he could lose her buried deep inside him. All his willpower and positive thinking were directed at saving Polly. The rosary he had taken from his bedroom and carried to Saint Rocco was still in his pocket, and sometimes in his pacing, he instinctively dug his hand down around the small purple beads, their rough surfaces reminding him of his faith as he fingered the gold crucifix. Not 24-carat gold, of course, because he couldn't have afforded it in 1919. He had bought the rosary as a Marine, when he had been given a leave to fight an exhibition in Paris. As a favor for the priest at his camp, he had stopped to buy altar linen and had just enough money left over to buy his first real purchase in the capital.

Gene read poetry that Polly would recognize if she were listening, and he hoped it would calm and center her and give her strength. Shakespeare always did.

> Shall I compare thee to a summer's day?
> Thou art more lovely and more temperate.
> Rough winds do shake the darling buds of May
> And summer's lease hath all too short a date.
> So long as men can breathe or eyes can see...
> So long lives this, and this gives life to thee.

He talked to her about their plans to take an apartment in Paris for several months. They both liked Paris, and he reminded her of how well she knew it, and how much she looked forward to the small cafés in the Rue du Faubourg St-Denis, covered with art nouveau plasterwork and mirrors and hat stands, and how much she relished the leisurely freedom of walking cobbled streets and visiting the Louvre and Versailles again.

He talked of how they had evaded the press by changing clothes, wearing sunglasses and using the back door of the hotel, and how the French actually believed they were English because Polly, giggling, assumed a haughty British accent while Gene wore an ascot and used a walking stick. One of her first trips as a small child had been to Normandy with her mother, and she wanted to return. He had promised they would do that too. He knew she would remember that Hemingway had invited them to revisit Paris, and Wilder and Walpole both had written that they might come to Brioni during the summer. And he talked about the pin feather brooch.

"Remember all the trouble we caused with the pin feather," he said, smiling at the memory. Gene's first gift to her had been a gold pin feather brooch he had designed himself at one of Fifth Avenue's finest jewelers. It was meant to be a discreet symbol of their love that she could wear pinned over her heart, keeping him close. "Birds of a feather," they had lovingly called one another. Gene was proud that the brooch was unique. She loved it.

And then her mother had found out and was furious at the impropriety of a young woman accepting such an expensive piece of jewelry from a man who wasn't her husband. "Adhering strictly to convention, she insisted that it be given back to me," he said. Luckily, Cot had stepped in, pleading for consideration, and had somehow convinced their mother that the pin feather was a substitute for an engagement ring that Polly couldn't wear in public. Then, in the summer, Polly, who never misplaced anything, lost the brooch. As a surprise, he ordered a new one, an exact replica of the first pin feather, and he had a friend deliver it to her in a black velvet case the day before she boarded the ship for Italy.

Polly woke to the sound of his voice. Gene held the brooch up for her to see, then pinned it to her pillow. She smiled and tried to move her hand to touch his:

> She was a phantom of delight
> When first she gleamed upon my sight;
> A lovely apparition, sent
> To be a moment's ornament...
> A perfect woman, nobly planned,
> To warn, to comfort, and command;
> And yet a spirit still, and bright
> With something of an angel light.

Windows rattled in the villa in the darkness as wind and rain swept over the peninsula. The house was only yards from the shoreline, and the bedroom faced the sea like a lighthouse on the rocks. The crashing of the waves on the rock ledges in the darkness sounded like thunder. Fires had been lit in the villa's big fireplaces, but it still felt cold, damp and dreary.

Gene told Polly that he had seen G.B.S. and Charlotte the night before, and that they wished her well soon. She seemed to smile again, whispered that she was glad, then drifted off again into a feverish delirium.

Sometime during her sleep, Polly remembered kneeling during her wedding at the red plush-covered *prie-dieu* before Michelangelo's *Madonna*, a moment imprinted deep in her heart. She wanted never to forget the shadows cast by the tall white roses on the parquet floor, the Italian dust motes dancing in the Italian sunshine pouring in through the windows like a heavenly signal, and the sweet, sticky smell of the orange blossoms Gene had given her at the altar.

As newlyweds, they remained side by side, their knees bent together, their arms touching, and unexpectedly — as a gift to her — their friend John

McCormack started singing, at first so softly she strained to listen until she recognized the familiar tones of *Ave Maria*, his unaccompanied tenor voice so gentle and melodic it sounded like a love song to the Virgin. Steadily rising in volume, McCormack's great voice soon filled the rooms around them and tumbled through the doors into the halls of the hotel, through open windows into the streets beyond, ending with a rousing fortissimo that could have filled any opera house in the world.

Kneeling there in her wedding dress, her back to the small circle of her dearest friends and family, she fought back tears and had to clasp Gene's hand so tightly that her ring bit into the flesh of his hand. There had been a hushed silence afterward, and she knew she would never hear the *Ave Maria* sung that way again. Hearing *Ave Maria* echo through her sleep, she said, carried her to a soft and peaceful place and comforted her.

Since childhood, Gene had learned to banish fear and darkness by reading, praying, and taking any action needed to affect the outcome and return his mind to equilibrium. Sitting on the edge of grief, unable to move, was not an option he ever could have imagined he would accept. He felt tightness in his throat, shortness of breath and a raw emptiness in his stomach as waves of tension and panic drove through him: "The day is done, and the darkness / Falls from the wings of night."

The unthinkable was happening. He rested his head on the bed and lost track of all time. He knew that he could not let her out of his sight. If he slept at all, he didn't remember. He didn't remember what day it was, nor did he care. He was infected by a crushing listlessness, and poems of death and darkness kept entering his mind. He tried to remember if there was a normal poem. "Yea, though I walk through the valley of the shadow of death, I will fear no evil: for thou art with me..." and he struggled to believe.

> Out of the night that covers me
> Black as the pit from pole to pole
> I thank whatever Gods may be
> For my unconquerable soul.

"The husband has the duty — *duty*!" Signor Brofferio had emphasized — "of protecting his wife." The jolly Brofferio had been specially designated by the Governor of Rome to solemnize the wedding, and he spoke his instructions seriously in heavily accented English. "He has the duty to keep her with him and administer to her everything necessary to the needs of life in proportion to his substance." Afterward, Signor Brofferio had clasped Gene's hands in his and given him the gold pen used to sign the marriage documents. "Remain in Italy and yours will be a long and happy marriage. *Buona fortuna*!"

The boat from Pola was late that morning due to the wind and rain, but it carried mail and supplies for the island, as well as two men who had arrived in Pola on the overnight train from Berlin. They had come with their wives for what they hoped would be sunshine on the most popular island resort along the Adriatic coast. Both carried black leather medical bags.

Dr. Fritz Meyer, immaculately dressed in suit and tie, was a professor, one of the most respected doctors in Berlin and the personal physician of the American ambassador. Fritz had been having trouble with his gall bladder for more than a year and knew that he should get some rest. But he didn't dare leave Berlin on holiday without a surgeon. In the event that any further gall bladder trouble developed, he wanted to have his own doctor handy to operate. He had never trusted provincial hospitals and local doctors, least of all in Italy. He prided himself on German medical training, unlike that of the Italians who, it was rumored, casually sipped *caffe corretto* — black coffee with a heavy dose of grappa — during hospital rounds.

With Brioni as the lure, Fritz coaxed his own doctor, Dr. Arthur Waldem Meyer, son of the Viennese professor Hans Horst Meyer and one of the most famous surgeons in Germany, to go on vacation with him. Plans were made and canceled several times in April and they had just about given up the idea to go at all. A.W., known for his research as well as his pioneering surgery, was in great demand, and time off was difficult to arrange.

On Monday, A.W. contacted Fritz and announced it was "now or never — let's go." He canceled the rest of his week's schedule so they could arrive in Brioni on April 30. "It just came to me to do it," A.W. said later. "I felt driven." When they arrived in Pola, Fritz took a look at the inclement weather and suggested they spend the day in Pola, a city with infinite resources to amuse. It was only at the urging of A.W. that they decided to continue the journey. They arrived in Brioni on Tuesday morning.

The boat sloshed into the pier in driving rain. While it was being secured to the moorings and luggage was being loaded into a covered carriage for the short ride to the hotel, the doctors waited under cover, chatting with their wives. They saw a figure from the hotel race down the pier carrying an umbrella, his red jacket flapping in the wind.

"*Buon giorno*," said the slender young man, stepping aboard and out of the rain as he caught his breath. He had the steely, dark eyes of someone old beyond his years, and from his dress, he was clearly a hotel employee. "Are you Dr. Meyer, sir?"

"We both are Dr. Meyer," the two doctors replied, smiling in spite of themselves.

"Dr. Otto Lenz sent me. There's an emergency with a guest. Maybe you can help?"

As surprised as they might have been, the doctors readily agreed. Sending their wives ahead to the hotel, they climbed into an automobile, one of the few on the island. The car was used only for state visits, said the hotel man. The doctors found themselves being driven on a roadway wide enough for only one vehicle, with no others, or even people, in sight. They were going across the midriff of the island to a *palazzo*. Their driver seemed to know very little except the patient's name, but he said everyone was worried about *l'americana*. Dr. Lenz, he said, had stayed all night at the villa.

The Meyers met Dr. Lenz at the door, and as they removed their wet coats in the hallway, the three men introduced themselves. A.W. Meyer asked Dr. Lenz how they could assist and the island doctor briefly explained the patient's history. A.W., sensing the haste, declined coffee and Lenz led them up the broad staircase to the bedroom by the sea. A.W. immediately recognized the tall, muscular man holding the young woman's hand because he had seen him frequently in newsreels and German magazines, though he had already been told the name of the patient. As the more experienced surgeon, and a man practiced in interpersonal as well as medical skills, he made a slight bow and moved efficiently to the bedside.

Polly was lying on her side. Her abdomen was swollen. According to Gene and Dr. Lenz, she had been unable to eat or walk without piercing pain for several days, and had had fits of nausea, vomiting and diarrhea. She was dehydrated and feverish and so terrified of the cramp-like pain twisting through her body that the look in her eyes made clear she feared moving even a muscle.

Speaking softly to the patient, Dr. A.W. Meyer took her temperature, smiled, examined her abdomen, had a few words with Polly, listened to the history of her ailment from Gene and Dr. Lenz, and then, patting Polly's hand, gently excused himself. He rose, motioned to Gene and the other doctors, and then turned and walked briskly into the hallway, with the rest following.

The patient, the surgeon Meyer said in a hushed voice, needed an operation immediately. Switching to German, which the other doctors spoke but which Gene did not, he used the words *sterben* and *Tod*, to die and death. Continuing in English to include Gene, he said there would be risk with surgery but a much graver risk without it. Without an operation, he said she would almost certainly perish within hours.

Perish? *Perish*? Even as he heard the doctor speaking, Gene's head throbbed with the ramifications of it, that such a soft, simple, gentle-sounding word could mean the end of a life. The end of Polly. The end of a future. The termination of a beloved's existence equal to six letters that he could look up in a dictionary or write in his book of words.

She was too sick to move, continued Meyer, even to the hotel. As Gene would learn, A.W. Meyer was one of Germany's most prominent surgeons, a doctor of considerable renown in Europe, and a specialist in complications of acute appendicitis, which was his diagnosis. In 1929, appendicitis was often fatal. Gene still had on his desk a news clipping mailed to him four months earlier saying that Tex Rickard, the showman and promoter who had staged five-million-dollar gates, including the two Gene had fought against Dempsey, had died in Miami Beach of complications following an appendectomy. Antibiotics were not yet available.

"We need a table," said A.W. "Is there a dining room?"

The kitchen, suggested Lenz, could be closed off.

With its big stoves for boiling water, its sinks and its tiles that were washed daily, the kitchen could be wiped down quickly and sterilized as much as possible. Dr. Lenz and Fritz Meyer took over the job of organizing a makeshift operating room. By his every move, A.W. signaled that time was of the essence: he and Gene rushed to prepare the patient.

Fritz pulled off his jacket, rolled up his shirtsleeves and hurried to the kitchen carrying the medical bags to begin setting up an operating theatre. At the time Fritz, the ambassador's doctor, was too busy to find irony in the fact that the surgical implements that he and A.W. had carried with them in case *he* needed surgery were being put to use on a patient before they had even checked into the hotel. Rain pelted the windows of the villa and the heaving of the sea could be heard outside, but there was no time to listen to any of it. Candelabras were brought into the kitchen to add light. *"Madre di Dio,"* whispered Signor Pessara over and over. *"Madre di Dio."*

"Boil water," Lenz shouted to the surprised cooks. "As much as you can, in every pot you can find. Now! *Presto! Presto!"* Maids, white-faced with alarm, with sheets and towels cascading from their arms, dashed in from the doorway that led into the dining rooms. "Sterilize the table first, then down with the sheets. Sheets on the floor and on the table. Hurry. *Beeilen Sie sich!"*

The old kitchen was soon unrecognizable, and except for the cooks and maids surging through it, occasionally bumping one another and speaking in frenzied whispers, it might have been an abandoned house closed for winter, with white sheets protecting every exposed surface. It had become an operating room, the doctor's utensils laid out on a breakfast tray with scalpels, scissors, retractors, probes, forceps, clamps and a bottle of chloroform. The cabinets, floor and table were scrubbed and covered, hiding the old Italian tiles. Pots of water boiled on the big stove and towels and torn sheets were stacked on the kitchen counter to be at the ready. Two elderly maids who had been midwives were assigned to remain in the kitchen to assist, and the rest of the help was excused to the back of the house.

Clump. Clump. Clump. His slow, steady steps sounded like the cadence of a military honor guard marching toward a tomb, the approach of reluctant duty. Gene could be heard descending the front staircase, bearing in his arms, as if she were a child simply going to sleep, the patient, his bride. It was the heaviest burden he had ever carried, and he knew then that his view of life would be forever altered by the outcome. He held her tightly, talking quietly to her, as if he would never let her go.

A.W. Meyer remembered that the young man's eyes were red and he looked as if he had not slept and might have been crying. The doctor made a mental note to keep the husband at a distance during the surgery, lest he cry out or faint and fall, creating an additional problem for the doctors to handle.

Gene laid Polly on the kitchen table, the same table he had sat at only the day before, opening the small box of religious relics, a moment that now seemed so distant it could have been another lifetime. He tried to drive from his mind the recurring image of the black felt pillow with its sad-looking Virgin, but trying to erase it seemed to make it loom larger and blacker and sadder.

Polly had been told they would operate in the kitchen and even in her delirium, it struck her as amusing. "Plopped down," she said, "just plopped down on the table like a dish of spaghetti." A little cold, too, she remembered thinking. She felt so tired that when one of the doctors Meyer leaned forward to ask her to breathe the chloroform, she only blinked and nodded. She looked at the curved ceiling with its cornices and drawings of little fishes and wondered why she had never noticed it before. The chloroform invaded her nostrils and mouth; it was the worst thing she had ever smelled. "I had frightful pain. I breathed and went off in a horrible state of pain and bad smells," with Gene, she recalled, holding her hand.

At the hotel, Shaw and Charlotte were told that two German doctors had arrived on the morning boat and been taken immediately to the villa to see Mrs. Tunney. At this, they were greatly relieved. They asked if there were any news, but there was none. Shaw apparently thought it best to wait at the hotel and decided to try to get some work done at his desk.

The horrible weather continued — this was the worst day of the month, he was told — and if he had been in the frame of mind to make quips, he most certainly would have done so. He found in his jacket pocket the small twig he had plucked from the old olive tree the night before, and he tucked it into his private copy of *Erewhon*, one of his favorite and most valued books.

By late in the day, Polly was sleeping in her bedroom. Dr. A.W. Meyer said the operation had been the best they could do under the circumstances and that the next few hours and days were critical. He ordered that one of the midwives and a nursing nun from a convent on the mainland be assigned to remain by her side. He had drained the gangrenous abscess, caused by an old inflamed, untreated condition of the appendix, and said she should remain in bed for four to six weeks. If she recovered well, a second operation to remove her appendix would be necessary before she left Europe. The doctors Meyer planned to remain in Brioni on holiday and would monitor her condition.

A solemn and exhausted A.W. told Gene that Polly remained gravely ill but would have died "a most painful and mysterious death" if he had failed to perform immediate surgery. He said that though it was uncharacteristic of him, he planned to visit a *Priester*, a priest. He said he did not believe in miracles but felt that he had been destined to meet this patient at this time in this place. He said he felt he had been chosen to save her life. "For a doctor," he said, "there is no greater calling."

"Mrs. Tunney's Life Saved," read the headlines when word of her operation leaked out. There were stories from Brioni, from Pola, Berlin and Rome.

"Mrs. Tunney's life was saved by the chance fact that two Berlin specialists were spending a vacation on the island of Brioni," reported the Associated Press. "It was said that only their immediate skill saved her life."

The *Havre Daily News Promoter* printed a story saying that "so serious was Mrs. Tunney's condition that it is felt that her life was saved only by the prompt intervention of two Berlin specialists."

"Two Berlin Doctors Save Tunney's Bride on Remote Italian Island by Hasty Operation," headlined *The New York Times*. The paper carried an unidentified wire service story from Rome saying the attack "developed quite suddenly in an acute form, and she was considered in danger for some time."

The stories noted that Shaw was visiting Tunney, and several reported that he stayed at the villa during the operation. Gene had been so frantic over the outcome of the operation — according to A.W.'s account, he had wept throughout the procedure — that he couldn't say later who was there, and Polly said she never knew.

By early afternoon, the rain had stopped and Shaw, restless and possibly lonely without Gene to accompany him, went to Pola by boat to have a walk. As the largest city on the Istrian peninsula, Pola had been an important base during Roman times, and it had a wealth of ruins spanning six centuries, including a remarkably well-preserved amphitheatre — designed for gladiatorial contests — that held 20,000 spectators. The narrow *calli* of the old city radiated out from the ancient forum, the town's central meeting place. The only visible remnant was the Temple of Augustus, erected around the time of Christ. Shaw passed a coffeehouse that advertised itself as having been patronized by Irish writer James Joyce, who once taught English in Pola, and on the way back to the harbor, he stopped to go into the city's cathedral, which dates to the fifth century. He went into the church and sat alone.

Several people reported seeing Shaw on his walk, but none disturbed him. He would write later that he had to go to Pola to escape the park-like atmosphere of Brioni, which he loathed. "As I am neither a golfer nor a polo fan," Shaw wrote, Brioni "was a prison to me. I cannot stand being confined to a park, however picturesque; and from time to time I had to make a dash over to the mainland to get into streets of all sorts of people and limitless roads."

In the evening, with Polly still sleeping, A.W. Meyer stopped by the villa to check on the patient and found Shaw was already there visiting. The doctor said he would wait until the patient woke to examine her.

The moon was out, flushing the villa's small peninsula with light. A worried Gene couldn't sit down and continued to pace in the garden — "to pace anxiously in the moonlight," reported A W — his face raw from exhaustion and eyes red from concern. Gene had lost all sense of time, all memory of everything but the immediate urgency of saving Polly, and he wouldn't believe the crisis was past until she woke. He ignored Meyer's suggestion that he rest, and he refused food and drink. He was a man obsessed, said Meyer.

The doctor and the playwright settled in the big sitting room and got out a chess set to move pieces around. While Gene walked, they chatted enthusiastically in German and English about eugenics, a subject that never interested Gene but which fascinated Shaw and Meyer. In the 1920s, eugenics was presented as the study of hereditary improvement of the human race by selective breeding so that people with the best genes would reproduce and thus improve the species. They occasionally looked up and saw Gene, his hands dug into his pockets and head down, coming in and out of the shadows as he walked in circles along the rocky sea ledge, around the loggia and the garden and past the large windows where they sat moving pieces around the chess board.

Before midnight, Polly weakly opened her eyes. She was weary and frail but made a small smile. She was awake barely long enough for the doctor to examine her, but Gene's relief was immediate. He leaned over to kiss her forehead, then held her hand tightly while the doctor finished his examination. She drifted off to sleep again almost immediately.

Gene was suddenly giddy with joy, "like a big boy," the doctor recalled. Gene couldn't stop talking and smiling. He hurried through the villa profusely shaking hands and thanking the staff who had helped through the ordeal, then sat at a table in the sitting room with G.B.S. and A.W. Meyer to eat great helpings of pasta, almost dizzy in his lightheartedness, unable to sit still and emotionally drained from the easing of the burden he had carried within him. The shock of how narrowly Polly had escaped death jarred his mind and left him breathless. He didn't remember later his walk in the garden, and he lost track of how long that night G.B.S. and the doctor had stayed with him.

The arrival of the doctors was a miracle, said Gene. "A miracle!" Yes, said the doctor, "It was a miracle we saved her." Meyer told Gene she could not have lasted more than a few hours, and that even as he was operating, he worried that he might be too late and he could lose her.

On being assured that the worst was past, G.B.S. told Gene that he and Charlotte would remain on Brioni until Polly was better. Gene meanwhile located Mrs. Lauder in Europe to share news of Polly's operation but reported that she was now recovering, and there was no reason to worry. He urged her to finish her trip, optimistically stating that by the time she returned to Brioni in May, Polly would be well. The Shaws, he said, promised to be with them until her return.

In remaining, Shaw almost overnight accepted the cloak of paterfamilias as if he had borne it his entire life. The Shaws, old enough to be the parents or grandparents of the couple, became de facto family, and they conducted themselves on every level as if they were close and caring relatives.

A daily pattern was established.

G.B.S. would walk to the villa after breakfast, taking a brisk 25-minute swing past the great ruins of the ancient Roman villa. Regardless of the weather, G.B.S. and Gene usually went for a swim in the bay off the long limestone ledges beneath the villa and then walked the paths of the island.

Charlotte stepped into the role she assumed so well at home, masterminding the household, watching over the nursing care, instructing the maids, keeping the villa quiet. She freshened flowers, directed the laying of the firewood — the Italians were horribly haphazard with fires, she said — and blocked well-meaning but inquisitive visitors. When Polly wasn't sleeping, Charlotte stopped in to see her, sometimes bringing books, many of them her own. "She was so nurturing, so reassuring," said Polly. "One felt so looked after. She was very motherly." Much of the time, Charlotte knitted and read in the great downstairs parlor, leaving Polly to rest and, mostly, to sleep. She occasionally took a nap herself. "The island is dull," Charlotte wrote Shaw's secretary, Blanche Patch, "but that is good for us! Mrs. Tunney has been very ill and given us a great fright but we think she will be all right now."

Charlotte ordered special foods brought in from Pola, and knowing that Polly especially liked vegetables, she ordered them prepared as she did for G.B.S., making soups and mashing potatoes and carrots. One afternoon, when Polly's scar itched, Charlotte picked *aloe vera* from the garden and together they dabbed the sticky sap of the plant on her stomach, laughing at what the strict German doctor might say about herbalist remedies. On another day, when Polly yearned for something warm to drink, Charlotte gave her Shaw's Instant Postum. Charlotte fluffed pillows and, when it was sunny and mild, opened windows to let in the sea air.

"She was as dear as if she was my family," said Polly. Though 50 years apart in age, their upbringings had been similar. Charlotte, like the young Polly, had grown up in a household of servants, had learned to ride horses from her father's stable as soon as she could sit and had a governess to teach her at home. Charlotte spoke German, French and Italian and delighted in Polly's stories of boarding school at Versailles. She was also a tough taskmaster. Familiar with the running of a big house, Charlotte brooked no infractions. The Italian help called her Signora *guardia* (policeman) behind her back.

"Mr. Tunney is a most wonderful help," Charlotte would write Blanche Patch. "He takes Mr. Shaw off to the polo ground, or the golf course, or sailing, or something, and so keeps him from writing, which is splendid."

Four days after the operation, the nurse raised Polly's head in bed for the first time, and G.B.S. visited the patient with Charlotte and Gene. Sunshine slipped in through the half-closed shutters and columns of light flickered against the ocher walls and fell across the foot of her bed. A large vase of red roses from her mother took up most of one dresser top, and a basket held stacks of letters and cards.

"You gave us quite a scare," G.B.S. told the patient. With her head propped up in bed with pillows, the frail Polly looked young enough to be a child. "I'm much too old to go through it all again."

Polly remembered his gentleness and said tears had come to her eyes because he seemed to care so much. There was "such compassion, such a depth of understanding." G.B.S. and Charlotte "somehow communicated what few other people could." The Shaws, she said, "were amazingly kind and tender."

Fumbling in his tweed jacket, he took out a thick book with a maroon hardback cover.

"It's by one of my favorite authors, who also happens to have played a significant role in your husband's life — Samuel Butler."

The book's edges were worn from travel. The novel, one of Butler's best-known works, was entitled *Erewhon*. Shaw was giving it to Polly, he said, because he hoped he would never, never, *never* again go through with Gene the terrible worry of losing her. He had inscribed the book carefully with flourishes, the words dramatically spaced as if the inscription were a title page to a play, or to a life:

> *To Mrs. Gene Tunney*
> *in the hope that*
> *she*
> *will take the precepts of this little book*
> *to heart*
> *and*
> *Never Again*
> *commit the crime of being ill at Brioni*
> *or anywhere else.*
> *from*
> *G. Bernard Shaw.*

Intrigued that it could be so important to Shaw, Polly asked him to tell her the story.

Erewhon, written in 1872, is a satire exposing the hypocritical attitudes of capitalistic Victorian England, especially to illness. After the passage of the Contagious Disease Act in 1864, the sick in England could be given compulsory medical exams and removed from their homes to be kept under surveillance by the police or by philanthropic societies. Prostitutes suffered the most from such legislation, which was largely enacted as a reaction to an increase in the incidence of syphilis. The legislation was repealed in 1886, partly as a result of attacks by people like Butler, but the continuing poverty and disease led Shaw and members of the Fabian Society to proclaim that socialism was far better suited to the care of needy citizens than was capitalism.

The story itself revolves around a sheep farmer named Higgs, a hero who, as Shaw pointed out, had the same name as the head gardener at his country home in Ayot St. Lawrence, "Harry" Higgs. In Butler's novel, the fictional Higgs sets out to visit a forbidden country, and after a dangerous journey, he wakes one morning surrounded by beautiful shepherdesses. They take his belongings, give him a medical exam and throw him in jail. There he learns that he has come to Erewhon (an anagram for Nowhere), a utopian society whose social issues parallel England's. In this country, illness is considered a crime. Even sad people are imprisoned, for distress is a sign of misfortune and people are held responsible for actions that lead to their illness or grief.

"How dreadful," said Polly, who was thinking that such a tale would be hard to digest, even in the best of health. But she was fascinated with Shaw's enthusiasm for an unconventional satire on the follies of English thoughts and behavior.

On the other hand, continued Shaw, people in *Erewhon* who rob and murder are hospitalized and given good care because it's felt that societal circumstances beyond their control forced them into crime. Machines are not allowed in the country for fear that they could take over the world. The hero, Higgs, meets Nosibor, a recovering embezzler, and falls in love with his youngest daughter, Arowhena. Higgs studies at the University of Unreason, where students learn anything that has absolutely no practical purpose (a commentary on British education) and meets his love secretly. When Nosibor finds out, the lovers are forced to flee to England. They marry and plan a missionary trip back to Erewhon.

Polly was moved by Shaw's recitation and was especially pleased to be given his personal copy of the book. Shaw called Charlotte an Erewhonian because she liked Handel, as did Butler and all Erewhonians, so Polly knew the message was meant to be positive. Always polite, she opened the pages to examine her gift, and an olive twig dropped softly out onto the covers.

"Oh, I'm sorry," she said, picking up the twig. "This must be yours."

"No, my dear, please keep it," replied Shaw. "It's from an ancient tree, older than any of us can ever hope to be, and it's meant to bring you long life and good health. I picked it," he said, "on Monday night." There was a silence as they remembered the long feverish day and the night that never seemed to end; then Polly smiled.

"The arrival of the doctors," said Polly, "was really a miracle, wasn't it."

"Oh, yes, it was a miracle," agreed Shaw. He said that Gene prayed and God listened. "We never know, you know, what influence prayers may have.

You can't discount them." Shaw told her that even the good Dr. Meyer, who performed the surgery, had gone to church afterwards. "He told me so himself," beamed Shaw.

Shaw cupped Polly's hands in his, warming them.

"He seemed changed," recalled Polly later. "We all were. Those were dark times — I hate to even think of them now — and yet out of that darkness came strength and new beginnings. I think it drew them (the Shaws) very close together, too." Polly felt the playwright, who so often hid his innermost feelings, was a man of great depth who could look into one's soul and see God. In this way, she thought, he was much like her husband: so open on some subjects, yet deeply private on the tender matters of faith and heart.

Four months later, Sidney Cockerell accompanied Shaw on a visit to Stanbrook Abbey, a Benedictine monastery in a pile of Victorian Gothic buildings surrounded by farms and sheep pastures, orchards and hopyards, in Callow's End, a hamlet not far from Malvern (where the first Shaw Festival would open in September of 1929 with *The Apple Cart* as its inaugural production).

Cockerell and Shaw called on the nun Sister Laurentia McLachlan. Cockerell had introduced Shaw to her in 1924, and Shaw had seen her once or twice five years before, but he did not yet know her well. They met in a small visitor's room, able to talk only through an iron grille that kept them physically separated. Cockerell confessed that on this occasion he saw a Shaw almost unknown to him. Shaw, instead of being his usual cocky self, was unexpectedly subdued. "I never saw him so abashed by anyone but William Morris," Cockerell said later.

Had the nun said something to Shaw about prayer and miracles? Or did he happen to connect her, because of the conversation, to his other devoutly Roman Catholic friend, Gene Tunney? We don't know. But it was after this visit that Shaw, in occasional letters to Sister Laurentia, began to also make mention of prayer.

"His attitude toward prayer, as expressed in these letters [to Laurentia] may have been sincere," wrote William Sylvester Smith, a scholar who specialized in studying Shaw and religion. "It would have surprised most of his associates, and is revealed nowhere else in quite the same way."

When the scholar wrote his remarks in 1981, he did not know about Shaw's experience on Brioni.

OPPOSITE: DAME LAURENTIA MCLACHLAN, THE ABBESS OF STANBROOK ABBEY, WAS A CONFIDANTE OF SHAW, AND HE WROTE TO HER OF THE MIRACLE ON BRIONI, "IT GOES TO CONFIRM THE VALUE I INSTINCTIVELY SET ON YOUR PRAYERS. SO DO NOT FORGET ME IN THEM" (STANBROOK ABBEY ARCHIVES).

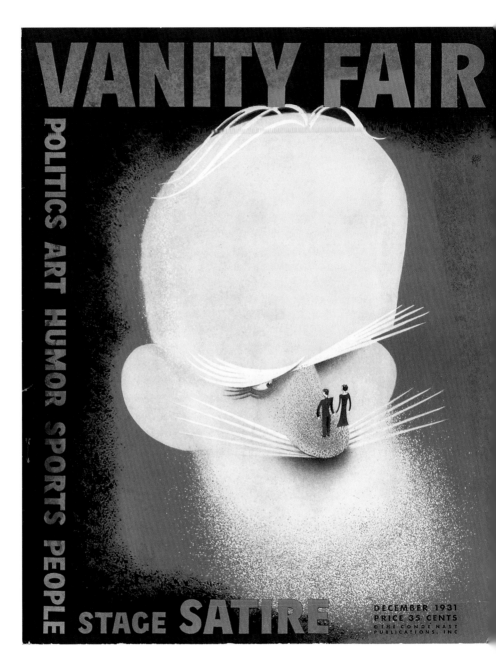

A 1931 ISSUE OF *VANITY FAIR* MAGAZINE FEATURING A COVER ILLUSTRATION BY PAOLO GARRETTO, OF G.B.S., HIS OVERSIZED LIFE FORCE ENVELOPING A YOUNG COUPLE. IT'S TEMPTING TO THINK OF THEM AS GENE AND POLLY! (USED WITH PERMISSION OF CONDÉ NAST PUBLICATIONS).

CHAPTER 16

Full Fathom Five

Far from the rabble and the cheers,
Far from the leather-covered paw,
He listens with attentive ears
To G.B. Shaw.

GRANTLAND RICE, COLUMNIST

The relationship between Gene and Shaw deepened following Polly's crisis. Their respect for one another grew as their hours together increased. "I think they were closer because they shared so much during those dark times," said Polly. "G.B.S. seemed to care for Gene as one cares for close family, and Gene certainly felt the same way toward G.B.S."

The intensity of their shared experiences, of prayer and of what they called the miracle, seemed to offer them an intuitive appreciation of one another and a mutual understanding that was more intimate, trusting and personal than the carefree, casual friendship they had shared previously. Despite the patient's 24-hour care and the attentive nurses, Gene worried about lingering medical problems for Polly and had an almost physical need to keep moving and to walk six to eight miles a day. This suited his friend Shaw perfectly. Having friends, and being a friend, were important to Gene, as they were to Shaw. Both had a wide circle of acquaintances, but true friendships were rarer.

Gene was too modest a man to purposely place himself center stage, and his reluctance to seek unwarranted attention was one of the qualities that made him seem so genuine to Shaw. (This was also the trait that made Tunney a lifelong friend to his former boxing adversary, Jack Dempsey.) Shaw found Gene's detachment from his celebrity remarkable in a man who had achieved renown and wealth by age 31, and he admired Gene's levelheadedness and his ability to distance himself from his public image and hold true to his own sense of self and values. In the few photographs taken of them on Brioni, Gene is often to the side, ceding center stage to Shaw. In others, he pulls his cap down over his eyes or turns his back on photographers completely.

For Gene, fame had become a trap. "I think unavoidably of some magnificent animal trapped in a bog," wrote sportswriter Paul Gallico after Gene retired. "And watching some such animal in his struggles to escape, one does not stop to consider how he got there or what fate he deserves; there is only a sense of pity and fascination as the terrible wrenching for freedom takes place." Shaw was the kindly hunter who set his friend free and allowed him to see the trap as an opportunity.

Archibald Kitts, a British guest called "Archie," said that the closeness between Shaw and Tunney was a subject of great speculation to outsiders who could not imagine how two such different men would get along for hours at a time and what, if anything, they had in common. He said that when they happened near other guests or sauntered on paths near the hotels, there would be a hush. And it was usually Gene who they pointed to and Gene whose autographs they sought. "Gene was gracious, but you could see he didn't much like it," Kitts remembered.

Shaw claimed it was the first time in his experience that anyone in his circle was more recognizable than himself, and he seemed to revel in his friend's discomfort as well as his fame. He frequently needled Gene about being the center of attention, recalling with great humor Gene's embarrassment. "Your publicity is greater than mine — you may remember...when I was talking to Richard Strauss nobody troubled us until you joined us, and then the cameras came with a rush."

For Shaw, the beauty of the friendship was that it informed and inspired him. Cut from the same Celtic rock as Shaw, Gene was a younger man whose character had been shaped in America, by American ideas and optimism. Yet Gene retained his Irishness, his wit and a respect for Ireland's writers. (One of Shaw's biographers said Shaw was drawn to Gene because of his "pure Irish blood.")

"I had a regard almost reverent for education and a mentality not altogether astonishing in an Irish stevedore's boy," Gene wrote. "My people were of Celtic tradition, with its homage to things scholastic. You'll find it from the Galway peasant to the Armagh cardinal. After all, isn't it the isle of saints and scholars?"

Like Shaw, he had grown up believing in his imagination and aspiring to become someone more than what was expected for him. Like Shaw, he visited Ireland, though not often, even as he acknowledged its influence on him. G.B.S. and Gene were both optimistic and believed in man's goodness and felt that for every handicap, life compensated with a helping hand.

"The art of life is the art of heroic paradox," was the underlying theme of Shaw's own life and thought, as well as that of Gene Tunney.

"You would be a great American," said Gene.

When Shaw told him that he didn't understand American idioms and dialects, Gene replied that there were hundreds. "We're a land of immigrants. Americans disagree. They welcome disagreement," he said. "Remember the Irish proverb 'contention is better than loneliness'? You would feel right at home." They laughed over a news story that said British tourists didn't like to visit the United States because there was too much razzmatazz and too many foreigners.

"But almost everyone claims to be Irish," said Gene. "You would be welcomed."

"I would be mobbed," said Shaw.

TUNNEY AND SHAW DID THEIR BEST TO AVOID THE
PRESS ON BRIONI, AND TRIED TO DUCK TOURISTS
CARRYING CAMERAS (TUNNEY COLLECTION).

Despite their cleverness in mostly avoiding the press, the playwright cautioned his friend to be more forbearing with reporters they encountered, saying that they, too, had a job to do and that not to deal with them cordially reinforced their perception of him as an arrogant champion. Gene had been disappointed that in retirement, he continued to be hounded by misunderstandings from the press. As one who had felt the whiplash of public opinion often, Shaw told Gene that the reporters' inability to accept him as he was did not matter as much as what Gene would be able to do with his life. His advice was simple: forgive and go forward and don't dwell on festering anger. The time may come, Shaw said, when you won't mind quite so much.

"Never let an interviewer put you on your guard; it's only his way of putting you off it," Shaw wrote one friend. Shaw urged him to use his celebrity for humanitarian and political purposes, to speak out on causes that concerned him and to accept the responsibilities of his position.

"We are made wise not by the recollections of our past, but by the responsibilities of our future," wrote Shaw in *Back to Methuselah.*

"The newspaper men kept coming over from the mainland," Shaw later told Professor Phelps from Yale. "They cared nothing whatever for anything I said or that Strauss could say; our opinions did not interest them. But the moment Tunney opened his mouth, the reporters took down every word. They wished to know his opinions on every subject."

The attention brought the novel *Cashel Byron's Profession* back to the forefront, because it was the only topic most people and most reporters could imagine Shaw and Tunney might discuss. A year later, in 1930, Gene would write Shaw that Hollywood had again approached him about playing the lead in *Cashel Byron's Profession,* this time in a "talkie." (A Czechoslovakian film based on the book, translated as *Roman Boxera,* had been made in 1921.) Shaw had long been intrigued with the potential of film as an art form but did not yet trust Hollywood and seemed to feel that the new offer was made to take advantage of a personal relationship.

Shaw might have sensed that Gene was interested in the opportunity to work with him. Intending, perhaps, to dissuade his friend gently but firmly, he dramatically mischaracterized his own creation:

> The Cashel Byron proposals are only blind snatches at your publicity and mine by people who don't know the book and couldn't judge it if they did. There is not a single really likable character in it: Cashel, though honest and super competent professionally, is selfish and limited; the lady is a prig and a bluestocking; his relations with his egotistical actress-mother are odious; the other girl is humiliated by her poverty and has to marry a man she doesn't respect; and the only real hero in the plot is the footman Bashville: in fact I made him the actual hero when I had to dramatize the novel in a burlesque to keep Corbett's travesty out of London.

Shaw went on to say: "They would spoil it by putting a championship fight into it. Now you are one the few men on Earth who cannot be filmed in a sham fight, because you have been filmed in no less than three real ones of the first order, and a stage one after that would be unbearable."

Gene acquiesced quickly, "Of course, I had no thought of doing it without your consent and your aid in arranging the scenario. I quite understand." As common knowledge of their friendship spread, it was frequently remarked that Shaw's novel so well described Tunney that Gene, by design or not, seemed to have modeled himself after Shaw's hero.

In fact, there were a number of startling similarities between Gene and the fictional hero. Both were Irish, both world boxing champions and both were the first to retire undefeated after holding the title for two years. Both married heiresses, both had successful careers after the ring, and later, both had four children. The coincidences seemed uncanny, and it didn't matter to most people that Gene denied modeling his life on anyone else.

The moral of Shaw's novel, however, was a reflection of Shaw's ethics, and Gene's. That is to say — while money and fame were not unimportant to either man, truth, integrity and character were paramount. In the words of Shaw biographer Stanley Weintraub, "The process of life imitating art had become complete, for Tunney the boxer became a gentleman, Cashel Byron come to life."

Gene's stay on Brioni was too much for the press as well as advertisers to ignore. "The retired world's champion, Gene Tunney, who has been spending six months endeavoring to dodge the limelight on the Dalmatian coast...has only succeeded in making Dalmatia a well-known resort," reported *The New York Times.*

Compagnia Italiana Turismo, the official agent of the Italian state railways, ran advertisements in American and European papers hawking Brioni's luxurious views and holiday accommodations: "Unheralded before George Bernard Shaw, Richard Strauss and Gene Tunney chose this beauty."

"The little island of Brioni is becoming a very popular place since the Tunneys have been there," wrote James Thurber in *The New Yorker.*

London's *Sunday Times* and *Sunday Dispatch,* updated an earlier interview based on comments Shaw had given on boxing before his holiday. "What I think of Gene Tunney," was a headline about Shaw's remarks in *The New York Times.* "Shaw chatters of boxing and his chum Tunney," bragged the New York *Evening Post.* Few of the stories had anything new to offer, and the mentions of Brioni were misleading, but the accumulated reports had the effect of keeping the friendship in the limelight.

With Polly on the mend, though still bedridden, and the doctors Meyer planning to return to Berlin, Gene hosted a dinner honoring the doctors, with G.B.S. and Charlotte as special guests. Shaw referred to his role at the dinner as "the supporting cast" and promised he would not embarrass Gene by referring to miracles as any operation in which the doctor does *not* kill the patient.

"This illness of Polly's connected Otto and me with them as well as many other guests for a few weeks," wrote Anne Marie Lenz, the doctor's wife. "Tunney became really deeply connected with G.B.S. and they were so different in life, different paths they'd led. G.B.S. was a vegetarian and had a special menu. Polly stayed in bed and got no food, but she did receive a basket of pink and red bouquets of common cyclamen."

During a feast that included local wines, antipasto with grilled vegetables, *orecchiette* with *mozzarella di bufala* and *pomodorini, scampi con fagiolini*, and veal and fresh halibut, Gene and G.B.S. had a Shakespeare-quoting contest. This continued in public a drill that they regularly enjoyed on private walks, and it lasted until the candles had burned to the wick and the homemade lemon *sorbetto* with figs and the chocolate and coffee and grappa were depleted.

Both men alternately quoted favorite passages. Shaw quoted from *The Tempest*, from Ariel's second song:

Full fathom five thy father lies.
Of his bones are coral made;
Those are pearls that were his eyes;

SHAW AND TUNNEY WITH THE BERLIN SURGEON DR. A.W. MEYER AND MRS. MEYER.
THE CRISIS ON BRIONI MADE MEYER A HOUSEHOLD NAME IN EUROPE (TUNNEY COLLECTION).

Nothing of him that doth fade
But doth suffer a sea-change
Into something rich and strange.

"But you're wrong," said Gene. "It's from Ariel's *first* song."

A pause followed, some rustling of clothes and clearing of throats. Shaw, smiling broadly, excused himself, went back to his suite, and returned with a dog-eared portable Shakespeare. He turned to the correct page and his face lit up. Looking at other guests at the table, he chuckled, "Gene Tunney might be able to lick me but he can't outquote me." Gene said he had a wide grin on his face meant to show that this was one man he didn't mind losing to at all.

Shaw said Gene quoted with "every comma in place." The two cited passages from *The Merchant of Venice*, *Henry IV*, and *Macbeth*. In illustrating a point on fighting, Gene tossed in Macbeth's words in Act v, Scene viii:

Before my body
I throw my warlike shield. Lay on, Macduff,
And damned be him that first cries, 'Hold, enough!'

Shaw then spoke of Shylock's argument for his right to dignity in *The Merchant of Venice*, Act iii, Scene i, calling it a moving reminder of the humanity of every man:

I am a Jew — hath not a Jew eyes? Hath not a Jew hands, organs, dimensions, senses, affections, passions; fed with the same food, hurt with the same weapons, subject to the same diseases, healed by the same means — warmed and cooled by the same winter and summer as a Christian is? If you tickle us, do we not laugh? If you poison us, do we not die? And if you wrong us, shall we not revenge?

Before they finished, Gene recited a passage from *The Doctor's Dilemma*, which he identified with and had memorized especially for the occasion. The play had been discussed at dinner. In introducing his selection, Gene said his recitation was dedicated to the doctors Meyer and especially to his friend G.B.S., whose poetic-artistic spirit and provocative theatre made him the man of the century. In the play, the caddish, amoral painter-artist Louis Dubedat is dying and expresses these Shavian thoughts:

I know that in an accidental sort of way, struggling through the unreal part of life, I haven't always been able to live up to my ideal. But in my own real world, I have never done anything wrong, never denied my faith, never been untrue to myself. I've been threatened and blackmailed and insulted and starved. But I've played the game. I've fought the good fight. And now it's all over, there's an indescribable peace. I believe in Michelangelo, Velasquez, and Rembrandt; in the right of design, the mystery of color, the redemption of all things by beauty everlasting, and the message of art that has made these hands blessed. Amen. Amen.

"RELAPSE!"

Only days after the Shaws departed Brioni, Polly's life appeared to be once more in the balance. "HEIRESS BRIDE NEAR DEATH"

Bold headlines in Europe and the United States followed developments in datelines from New York, Greenwich, London, Rome, Berlin and Pola. The International News Service reported the former champion's bride was again hovering at death's door. "Gene sits by bed of dying wife," said the Laurel, Mississippi, *Morning Call.* "Report Mrs. Gene Tunney being kept alive by artificial means," headlined the *New Castle* (Pennsylvania) *News.*

Polly's mother returned to the island, and Dr. Lenz resumed residence in the villa. An Italian naval medical officer was rushed by boat from Pola. An Italian doctor was called in to consult from Rovigno. Gene cabled A.W. Meyer in Berlin asking him to return. Feeding off the reports that her earlier operation had narrowly saved her life, newspapers leapt at the news, printing stories that the life of Tunney's bride was on the line.

Newspaper accounts referred to a pall of secrecy surrounding the patient's condition and quoted a friend of the family as saying, "If her life is saved, it will be because the family's wealth permits extraordinary medical attention." Newspapers re-ran Polly's engagement picture, a solemn headshot in black and white, which, in view of her failing health, seemed to emphasize the hopelessness of being isolated far from home.

In the United States, aunts, cousins and in-laws of both families were pursued by reporters for information, though none of them knew any more than those asking the questions. Cables were slow and telephone contact to the island was virtually impossible. Police Commissioner William McCabe, Gene's former confidential advisor and a man Gene kept in touch with regularly, was pelted with calls in Poughkeepsie, New York. Polly's brother George was besieged by reporters at his high school commencement, disrupting the ceremonies.

In the bedroom by the sea, Gene once again paced and prayed. Polly's fever was 104 degrees and climbing, and the piercing pains in her abdomen had returned. She had yet to regain the 20 pounds she had lost during the earlier crisis, and her slender, sweating body, curled like a child's as if to avoid blows, seemed ill-prepared to handle more surgery. The difference for Gene the second time around was that he had considerable experience with the doctors. He had been fortified in spirit by his friend Shaw, and Polly's mother lent her support to his every decision. He knew what action to take.

The surgeon Meyer arrived with a German medical assistant within 24 hours, fully prepared for the worst. The doctor was relieved after his examination of the patient to be able to tell Gene that although Polly was seriously ill, the setback was temporary.

To try to diffuse the publicity and the massive news coverage that had drawn the attention of hundreds of reporters and photographers from around Europe, Dr. Meyer, who spoke English, German and Italian, held a press conference to clarify the medical issues. Polly had come close to dying weeks earlier, he said, but there was no need for immediate surgery. He said the latest spike in fever and pain had been caused by congestion due to the temporary curtailment of the infiltration in place since the first operation and that Mrs. Tunney would visit Berlin in a few months for a follow-up operation to remove the appendix.

He urged the press to leave the Tunneys alone, allowing the husband privacy to be with his wife and the patient time to heal, away from the constant glare of publicity and public scrutiny.

In the midst of the crisis, Gene received a note from Thornton Wilder. The letter brought "sunshine into a slightly gloomy, depressed sick-room," Gene wrote back. Your "fine Thornton-ish letter! was an ideal distraction."

The Shaws heard about the relapse while on a ship sailing from Spalato to Venice. "We got a fright about you," wrote Shaw. "Just before we left Pola the captain said — quoting an Italian paper — that Mrs. Tunney had had a relapse. We both felt that we must jump off at Brioni, to offer moral support if nothing more solidly useful. But the captain then added that in the masterly hands of the Italian doctors from Trieste and Rovigno, a complete cure had been effected and an 'out of danger' bulletin issued."

When Shaw arrived in Trieste a couple days later, on May 28, dozens of reporters and photographers, aware that the Shaws had spent a month with the Tunneys, were waiting for him on the dock. "George Bernard Shaw proved today as obdurate as Major Swindon in his play, *The Devil's Disciple*, when he passed through here on his way to Venice," wrote the Associated Press, saying Shaw gave orders to the captain to keep newspapermen away from him. "He said he would not receive them under any pretext and would not discuss the illness of Mrs. Tunney. Mr. Shaw remained locked in his cabin for an hour before the ship sailed."

"I can't tell you what a relief the news about you was," Charlotte wrote Polly. "We got a horrid time when we heard the rumors...Don't you trouble to write but make Gene send a fresh load of news."

Shaw the playwright was also Shaw the boxer, and following his stay on Brioni, the strategies of the Game continued as a subject for lively discussion between him and Gene. Even before their meeting, Shaw had shared Gene's view that boxing in the ring was different from fighting. "G.B.S.'s analyses of fights are extraordinarily accurate and clear," said Gene. "He penetrates the fog and moves through the distractions for the truth and comes up with it."

Onboard ship after leaving Brioni, Shaw wrote in a letter that he had told an Italian colonel that Gene's secret to success was actually to be *afraid* of being hit on the head. "He and the whole captain's table — we were at dinner — immediately explained to me most kindly that my Italian was not correct, as I said exactly the reverse of what I meant, which was of course, that the heroic Tunney was totally indifferent to the most terrific punches on his *frontespizio*."

Shaw said he told the colonel that if you were hit on the head you were knocked out, whereas if you hit the other fellow on the head you were victorious. "He became thoughtful and said that this had not occurred to him before, and that it was true and original!"

"I wonder," replied Gene, "what he would have said if you told him I got all my fundamental ideas of dodging, feinting, sidestepping, retreating, striking and getting away without being countered from the tiny-brained, ordinary fighting chicken?... Any cock fighter will tell you that the fighting cock is capable of far more 'conscious effort' [brains] in a fight than any gladiator that ever lived. Comparing the tricks and strategies of the ordinary fighting cock with those of the ordinary boxer, it is darn hard to find a starting point to refute his argument. The average boxer is like an automaton or 'fighting machine' [brawn], and like the ordinary machine or engine, capable of doing whatever work the designing engineers planned for it to do, without 'conscious effort.'" Gene considered himself no mere "fighting machine" but rather a man with the "conscious effort" needed to attain his goals. His primary weapon was brains, not muscles.

"There is considerable speculation over the coming Sharkey-Schmeling contest," Gene wrote Shaw in May 1930. Jack Sharkey was an erratic, though powerful, heavyweight and had beaten Britain's Phil Scott a few months earlier in a fiasco.

"I believe Scott the most cowardly man I have ever seen in the ring," Gene wrote. "There is but one thing about pugilism Scott is interested in, and that is the money. He is a complete disgrace and should never attempt it again." Gene said Sharkey had the temperament of a Russian opera singer and his skill and courage depended on the ability of his opponent. "In other words, he is as good as his opponent allows him to be," he said.

Gene had never seen the German Max Schmeling in the ring but told Shaw reports of his condition and ability were not encouraging, adding that "newspaper reporters, on things pugilistic, are nearly always wrong." Of his prospects against Sharkey, he wrote, "I think Schmeling has at least an even chance to win." Schmeling beat Sharkey for the world championship in 1932.

Shaw's dialogue with Gene on boxing pleased Shaw enormously and gave him fodder for conversations. But most of Shaw's friends and acquaintances were not boxing fans, and it was inevitable that some seemed bored, peeved or indifferent. Ironically, as Gene was trying to talk less about boxing, Shaw was talking more, eager to show off his new knowledge. When Frank Harris, Shaw's former boss at the *Saturday Review*, wrote a biography of the playwright in 1931, he said Shaw's boxing novel, his description of Carpentier's fights and his friendship with Tunney, "seemed to me so out of character that I dismissed them as an elaborate masquerade to give him an air of the hardihood nature had denied him."

Calling Tunney "another of Shaw's gods, a man of action," Harris said, "Seriously, you can write Shaw's inner convictions and hidden aspirations in terms of Lenin, Mussolini and Tunney."

One of the ring debates Gene and G.B.S. never resolved was how to evaluate Georges Carpentier, the charismatic French champion whom Shaw had admired in the early 1920s. It was Gene's victory over Carpentier in 1924 that initially brought him to Shaw's attention, and Shaw always felt that Carpentier was a better fighter than Gene gave him credit for.

"You greatly underrate the interest taken in Carpentier," Shaw wrote in 1932. "You see him only when he was like a pithed cockerel after he made the fatal mistake of clinching with Dempsey in the very first exchange and being rabbit punched. If he had studied Dempsey and fought him as you fought him, he would probably have beaten him easily on points and possibly knocked him out, although his terrible right-hand punch may not have been what it once was. Up to the moment when you knocked him out, he seemed to be putting up a much better fight against you than Dempsey did...You do not see him as Europe saw him; and you even speak of him as "the little Frenchman," though he was quite big enough for anybody and was very well built for boxing."

Shaw stubbornly continued his diatribe. "Now, as you know most about it, I have no doubt that your values as between Carpentier, Dempsey and the less popular boxers who gave you more trouble, are quite right *for the moments at which you fought them*. By all appearances Dempsey was overtrained when he first met you, and just right when he met Carpentier. Carpentier had married and gone comparatively soft when he met Dempsey and seemed like a lightweight giving an exhibition spar against you, just as Dempsey with his fiddling and feinting looked like a schoolboy fooling with an instructor. But you know...what an amazing difference there is between the figure cut by one and the same boxer when he has his opponent easily in hand and when it is the other way about. Your valuation of c and d is not the same as that of the public that remembers their victories. All you know about them is that you took their measure and wiped the floor with them. You came, you saw, you overcame. By doing so, you inevitably belittled them and have taken less credit for your victories than a completely objective historian would give you."

In 1946, Gene asked a publisher to send Shaw a biography of Harry Greb, written by a friend about the only fighter who ever beat Tunney in the ring. Shaw found it "a most barbarously written biography...which describes him vividly as the foulest fighter on earth, who instructed you so thoroughly in all the tricks of the trade that he never afterwards had a chance against you." But Greb had the art of keeping many friends in the fight world (including Gene), and Shaw alluded to this in his reply.

"I tried to see H.G. Wells in his last year," wrote Shaw, "but his baroness put me off every time. We were very good friends; he had Greb's art of keeping all of them, though in controversy or under criticism, he made Greb appear an angel in comparison. On paper, he died in despair, but I cannot believe that his gaiety ever deserted him."

"He and I ended as Great Men, and you began as one."

"Is Joe Louis the wonder they say he is?" wrote Shaw. Louis, the powerful black champion who held the heavyweight title for 11 years in the turbulent period before and after the Second World War, became an American hero with his spirited defeat of the German Max Schmeling. "How black is he?" asked Shaw.

In boxing parlance, the question appears to reflect an idea held among many at the time that black fighters had exceptionally strong skull bones and could outdistance white men. Jack Johnson was the first black heavyweight champion of the world (1908-15) and was arguably the best prizefighter of his generation. Tunney's reply to this letter is one of the many that have not survived. In any case, Gene was a supporter of Louis and was proud that he

TUNNEY VISITS JOE LOUIS AT HIS TRAINING CAMP IN NEW JERSEY IN JUNE, 1935, JUST BEFORE THE MAX SCHMELING FIGHT (CORBIS).

helped devise Louis's strategy to defeat the German. (Tunney never fought a black fighter professionally, though he signed a contract to fight Harry Wills as a preliminary to fighting Dempsey. Wills, also a challenger to Dempsey, turned Tunney down.)

Two years later when Louis visited London, Shaw wrote, "It may amuse you to hear that when Jo L. arrived here, it was announced that the only people he wished to visit were myself and Winston Churchill. The whole British Press made a rush for me (probably also for Churchill) to learn the date and place and hour and minute of the visit."

Shaw was disappointed that the meeting didn't take place. After he was asked by the press why Louis didn't visit him, he wrote Gene. "I said I had not heard from Mr. Louis; but two comparatively unknown persons like myself and Mr. Churchill could not but feel flattered by a visit from a world-famous head of his profession. I have no reason to believe that J.L. knew about the stunt at all," Shaw wrote. "I am told that the tour was a failure, and am not surprised; for exhibition spars in soft gloves draw no gates here: they are out-of-date and forgotten; and our sporting crowds know nothing about boxing. What they pay for is bashing. Louis got his $100,000 (reputed) for nothing."

After Shaw left the Dalmatian coast in 1929, he stopped in Venice, where he received a sorrowful letter about another boxer, an old friend who was now destitute. Ida Beatty, the wife of the boxer/poet who had been his best friend, wrote asking if she could sell Shaw's letters to raise money to care for her beloved Paquito, now a penniless invalid. "If I had known that you had preserved them I should have advised you to sell them whilst the present boom in them lasts," Shaw replied, urging that his goddaughter Livia ("Cecilia") take them to a friendly dealer whom Shaw knew personally.

By the time the Shaws arrived home in London, news service photographs taken in Brioni and distributed by mail were appearing in newspapers. One picture taken of Shaw and Tunney at a polo match in Brioni showed up all over the world. "Bosom Friends," said the picture positioned next to an aerial view of King George's Windsor Castle. "They're buddies now," touted another paper.

Reporters rushed to ask Shaw what he and the boxing champion had talked about during their month's holiday in the Adriatic.

"Everything," said a bemused Shaw.

"Can't you be more specific?" he was asked.

"Everything from ancient Egyptian wrestling to the theosophy of Madame Blavatsky."

POLLY AND GENE VISITING A UNIVERSITY IN GERMANY IN 1931, TWO WEEKS
PRIOR TO TRAVELING TO JERUSALEM TO MEET THE SHAWS (TUNNEY COLLECTION).

CHAPTER 17

Feet on Solid Ground

From humble homes and first beginnings
Out to the undiscovered ends,
There's nothing worth the wear of living
But laughter and the love of friends.
GENE TUNNEY'S FAVORITE TOAST TO FRIENDSHIP,
IN HOMAGE TO HILAIRE BELLOC

According to Shaw biographer Michael Holroyd, in the 1920s, Shaw was "ready to dream of literary retirement," but in the 1930s, not too long after he visited Brioni, perhaps due to inspiration or by coincidence, he revived himself with an affirmation to preach and put his international fame to good use.

"At Brioni I amused myself one evening by inventing quite an amusing boxing film for you," Shaw wrote to Gene. "But it was a movie; and since then, the advent of the talkies has upset everything. I could not produce genuine American dialogue even if I had time, which will not occur for many months, as I am worked to distraction preparing a complete collected edition of my works for America, and when that is through a new play to succeed *The Apple Cart* is possibly wanted..."

Shaw started *Too True to be Good,* his first play after Brioni, as he and Charlotte left England in March 1931 for a month's holiday during which they planned to meet up with Polly and Gene. The Shaws were on a Hellenic Traveler's Club tour of the Mediterranean, sailing on the *Theophile Gautier* with a group that included the Very Rev. William Ralph Inge, Dean of St. Paul's Cathedral. The Tunneys were traveling through Egypt and the Holy Land with Jack Oliver LaGorce, managing editor of *National Geographic* magazine, and his wife, Ethel. On March 14, the Shaws and the Tunneys met in Jerusalem and were frustrated once again to find their footsteps dogged by reporters.

> JERUSALEM (AP) — George Bernard Shaw, who is visiting Jerusalem, was the dinner guest of Gene Tunney, retired heavyweight champion of the world, who is spending a week here. The fighter has long been an admirer of Shaw's writings and they have met several times.

Both had entered the Holy Land at night. "You find yourself...with strange new constellations all over the sky and the old ones all topsy-turvy, but with the stars soft and large and down quite close overhead in a sky which you feel to be of a deep and lovely blue," Shaw wrote to Sister Laurentia. "The appearance of a woman with an infant in her arms takes on the quality of a vision," he wrote. (The nuns later used this reference, and others, to discount perceptions of Shaw as a nonbeliever.)

Polly wrote home about the "marvelous sunshine and beautiful star-and-moonlight nights," and told of how she and Gene slept in a tomb in Petra and spent an evening with Bedouins on the desert. "I didn't think it was possible to crowd so many interesting experiences in so short a time." Standing on the Mount of Olives and gazing down over the dry valleys that roll through the Tigris-Euphrates basin, Polly wrote that she could imagine the soft-footed shuffle of camels between the hills.

The Tunneys and the Shaws especially liked the Dome of the Rock, which they visited together. Sometimes called the Mosque of Omar, it is the oldest Islamic building in the world. "We peeked through a mosque window down on the Wailing Wall and saw the Jews moaning and saying their prayers — a most extraordinary sight!" wrote Polly. "We walked all around the temple area and noticed the walls and the Golden Gate that Christ used to go through coming from the Mount of Olives." Shaw wrote that the mosque, in which Christ had worshiped, reflected "the charm of sanctity of Jerusalem. Omar was a man after God's own heart."

"We met Mr. and Mrs. Shaw and had such a lovely dinner with them!" Polly wrote her mother. "They are still just as sweet as ever and very cordial."

Over dinner, Shaw told them that he had picked olive leaves from the Garden of Gethsemane for Sister Laurentia, a gesture that especially touched Polly who had preserved the olive twig he'd given her in Brioni. Then, Shaw dug out of his pocket several small, smooth limestone pebbles that he had picked up at Bethlehem's Church of the Nativity. (Later, one stone, tied to a crimson pillow and set in a silver medieval-style reliquary, was given to Sister Laurentia. A second stone was tossed blindly into the abbey garden, forever lost in the sea of English stones.) They discussed Judaism, Christianity and Islam and, Polly remembered, even Buddhism.

"Mr. Shaw entertained us in his marvelous and inimitable fashion. He had some very amusing remarks to make about his correspondence with Ellen Terry but was quite emphatic on the point of the friendship being platonic," wrote Polly. "He said they exchanged at least 200 letters before they ever met."

The two couples agreed they should travel more together, and Gene and Polly extolled the virtues and quiet of long ocean voyages, which allowed privacy and time to read and talk without intrusions. "Gene and I must keep in closer touch with them," Polly wrote.

Gene wanted Shaw to swim with him in the Dead Sea; Shaw suggested instead a walk through the Old City of Jerusalem. The two tried to use a map to follow Christ's final days in the city, and sitting in an old house of worship, they discussed why the great religions could not reach an accord in a place so sacred to all of them. What is it that allows men to agree with the precepts of the Sermon on the Mount but finds them unable to put those universal teachings into practice for the greater good? pondered Gene.

In the crowded streets, there were money changers, along with merchants hawking pots and melons, and it seemed as if everywhere that Christ might have sneezed, there were booths selling cheap religious trinkets. As they stood on the street, surrounded by noisy vendors and donkey carts, Gene may have thought it was a strange place for a discussion about his future, but typically he and Shaw talked regardless of what was going on around them. He had told Shaw he was going to devote his time to study and to writing an autobiography.

"Don't you think that I could find studious effort a good substitute for the physical activity of ring fighting?" asked Gene. Shaw declined to give a direct answer and smiled as vehicles honked and people elbowed around them. "He looked at me with that quizzical expression that comes so readily to his long, bush-browed, white-bearded face and responded briefly. 'Perhaps. The life of a scholar can seem dull, and as a man of action, you may find it too sedentary.'" He let it go at that, Gene remembered, "with just a shade of the dubious."

Gene had lost money in the 1929 stock market crash and told Shaw he was deeply troubled by U.S. economic policies, the decline in business and the growing disparities between rich and poor. "Is this economic depression merely a lull in industrial growth, a momentary drawing in of the fly for a longer cast and greater prosperity?" he wondered. He worried about "bank failures, industrial operating losses and unprecedented unemployment," and he listened to Shaw enthusiastically discuss the Russian Revolution and its experiment with communism. Shaw maintained that it was high time to give Marxist ideology a chance to provide for the working man and the masses. It was a showcase for the eventual economic health of the world, he said.

Six weeks after they met in Jerusalem, Gene visited Russia after being invited by *Collier's* magazine to give his perspective on Russia's communist regime as the economic wave of the future. His conversations in Jerusalem with Shaw were clearly reflected in what he wrote. Gene said in the article he had been worried about the depression in the United States and said that initially the idealism of communism "had captured me. I was rather convinced that world communism was the next step forward. Since the war, I thought, the world had been sidestepping rather than advancing."

"Something had ripped our national moral fabric to rags; or had it been the slow methodical work of moths?" wrote Gene, citing cases of political corruption that had eaten away at the fiber of daily American life. "If it is possible that a person may be sympathetic and yet open-minded, I was both. In that attitude, I went to Russia."

Shaw would visit two months later, in July, with a large delegation, including Lady Astor, and was feted by the government with an official program of conducted tours. In contrast, Gene traveled with Henry Sell, an American advertising executive who had been asked by the Soviet tourist agency to visit the nation's pleasure spots with an eye to encouraging sightseeing. Gene was assigned an escort/interpreter and warned to watch his tongue lest he run afoul of the secret police, but as a private citizen, he visited destinations that Sell, and Shaw, didn't see.

"In Moscow you hear one theory — communism. You listen to one moral code — atheism," wrote Gene. In theatre, in plays, in newspapers, the message was the same, he said. "As virtue was always triumphant on the vanilla-flavored state of the Victorian era, so is the communist worker in the Russian play." He was deeply disturbed to realize that truth, knowledge and news were defined by the government, for government purposes. "The workers are informed that the world depression was engineered by Wall Street in order that the workers of America might be decimated by starvation and disease," he wrote. He said the workers were told of assassinations, revolutions and world revolt, and nobody contested the truth of any of it.

His saddest yet most enlightening experience was being taken outside Moscow to a smelting plant where metals were melted down to make armaments and bullets. Behind the plant, "a queer, resentful depression filled me." He found a gigantic junk pile of church bells. "There, in a bold, broad hill, lay the bells of Russia...They were the bells that I had hoped someday to hear. Some were smashed, some were being smashed, others were still intact — beautiful things wonderfully molded and engraved." Gene said he stood in silence, caught in a web of sorrow in remembering the pennies he saved from earnings at the meat market to help buy bells for his Village church. Around him, he heard the crunch of metals and the occasional clang as a bell tipped, moving into the smelter toward the fire.

"To a great extent they had been cast from metal donated by the peasants — copper, bronze, gold, silver. They had been gorgeous works of art, decorated with bas-reliefs of the saints, the apostles, of Christ, of his parables. Here was a huge brass bell on the sides of which the story of the annunciation had been told by a sculptor; and near it was another beautified with the story of Bethlehem." Six hundred thousand tons of bells taken from the churches had been returned to the metal industry, mostly to be converted to bullets, he said.

He saw bundles of icons of brass, gold, silver and platinum, candelabra, holy vessels and altar pieces, all ready for the furnace, and his mind boggled at the enormity of the state's rejection of religion. Toward the end of his visit at the smelting plant, he saw what he thought was a worker asleep amid the rubble. When he asked about the man, a workman leapt on the pile and rolled the prostrate figure over with his heel, leaving it to crash at Gene's feet. It was a great bronze figure of Christ: "A magnificent sculpture, more than life-size, had been wrenched from its huge cross." When Gene asked why it couldn't be preserved for art's sake, if not for that of religion, he was told, "We workers will no longer tolerate this nonsense. We were the slaves of the church for centuries. That's all over. We've abandoned superstition."

"I left the smelter thinking of Voltaire's 'If God did not exist, it would be necessary to invent him,'" Gene wrote.

By the time Gene's article was published in the October 1931 issue of *Collier's*, America, along with the rest of the world, was sliding into the Great Depression. The contention that the downturn had been caused by psychological factors — too much pessimism and loss of confidence — was replaced with an understanding that war loans and high tariffs were strangling international trade and sabotaging recovery. New economic and political policies were called for.

"I came out of Russia with opinions overthrown," he wrote. Gene tried to balance what he had seen and said, "Somewhere between what America is aiming for and the Russian goal is the road our children will take." He said he felt the future lay between the ideals of the two countries, not their practices. He did not think Christianity could be destroyed by atheism, nor did he think Western civilization would become robotic. "It will take more than a couple of million Communists and their mechanized followers to crush individual development; curtail the inherent urge for spiritual growth and cosmic contact; change centuries-old standards of fundamental right and wrong; or upset our conception of art."

Naively, he also did not believe that there would be a return to the inequalities that the Soviet government exterminated.

The influence of Shaw's optimism and ideological thinking was evident in Gene's article. "I see our governments of the future borrowing liberally from Communism," he wrote, "not from its culture or ideas on religion but from its political and economic philosophies." He thought he would see a Russia reborn with Tolstoys, Chekhovs and Dostoevskys "and other independent and courageous thinkers who will oppose the industrial semi-serfdom with the same violence and success with which they fought the Tsarist slavery." Individual growth, he said, is "as much a part of civilized man's inheritance as the fundamental urge of self-preservation."

In time, Gene would become vehemently anti-Communist and anti-Stalin. In 1940, Gene wrote Charlotte, sympathizing with her concerns over the war in Europe and the takeover of Finland by the Soviets, then added, "Poor Finland has gone, or should I say poor Finland, remembering G.B.S.'s admiration of Stalin?"

Over the years, Gene and G.B.S. discussed Roosevelt (Gene campaigned for him in 1932), Churchill, Eisenhower ("In a [private] two-hour conversation...I came away with the impression that he would have loved to have had the Republican nomination by draft), Truman ("no chance of being elected"), and Dewey ("I attended the Republican convention...and was interested to find the sentiment among delegates in favor of Dewey"), among others. The issue was always the same with Shaw: Who can bring change? Who can help make life better for the common man?

Shaw explored these themes in his new 1931 play. Of its working title, Polly said that "too true to be good," the reverse of "too good to be true," was a catchphrase used during their visit to Jerusalem to refer to Brioni and the opulent life there that seemed to dramatically bypass the concerns of a world spiraling into depression and grappling with a fragile peace. (Gene would express similar sentiments in a speech at the 1932 Democratic National Convention: "The bosses are tottering. Fantastic government extravagance and corruption is their platform. Without imagination, they have no conception of what our new future is going to be like.")

Too True to be Good is a serious farce about a group of people who travel a path that leads to adventure and excitement, to boredom and disillusionment; along the way they discover material *riches* and spiritual poverty, not unlike some of those on the pleasure isle in the Adriatic. Only by discovering who they are, only by giving meaning and purpose to their lives, will they find their way again. "What am I to do? What am I?" asks one character. It's a heartfelt play by a Shaw worried about the future.

As the story opens, a rich girl (perhaps a Polly?) is in bed with an oversized microbe monster (perhaps a scampi poisoning?) at her side. A doctor arrives, and the monster/microbe and the doctor discuss Christian Science. "The Christian Scientists let their patients cure themselves. Why don't you?" asks the microbe. "It's easier to believe in bottles and inoculations than in oneself and in that mysterious power that gives us our life and that none of us knows anything about," replies the doctor.

When later, a phony nurse and a burglar try to steal the rich girl's pearls, the patient leaps up and slams her foot into the burglar's solar plexus, sending him reeling to the floor, then throws the nurse across the room. "Why did you tell me that this heavyweight champion was a helpless invalid?" wails the burglar. He confides he read about the girl's jewelry in "The Lady's Pictorial," which "contained an illustrated account." (The real Polly bemoaned articles that described her wardrobe and jewelry.) The three characters conspire to take the pearls and the money and go abroad.

They consider hiding in Istria or Dalmatia on the Adriatic. "You shall have a splendid foreign title," the rich girl tells the nurse/burglar: "The Countess Valbrioni." The name itself is a subtle salute to Brioni, and the character appears to be at least partially modeled after a German countess, Vendola VonDolva, whose bohemian dress, theatrical entrances and exits and dramatic voice aroused amused attention on Brioni. In the play, Countess Valbrioni flings herself with elegance into a beach chair and speaks with a dialect that Shaw describes as an amalgam of foreign accents. (The real countess left Brioni to live "as a native" on an American Indian reservation in Arizona.)

The threesome next appears on an island with a colonel and a Sergeant

Meek (based on T.E. Lawrence). "The place is so dull," the nurse/countess says. (Shaw's view of Brioni.) "Nothing to do but be ladylike. And the one really lovable man going to waste." The rich girl masquerades as a native servant. And the burglar turns out to be a preacher. They discuss the Bible and *Pilgrim's Progress*, two books Shaw always carried with him. Shaw could be referring to himself when he writes, "And now look at me and behold the supreme tragedy of the atheist who has lost his faith — his faith in atheism, for which more martyrs have perished than all the creeds put together."

Toward the end, The Elder, based on Shaw's friend Dean Inge, appears and turns out to be the father of the burglar/preacher. They discuss atheism, losing faith and war and morality. In The Elder's final speech, he says:

> The iron lightning of war has burnt great rents in these angelic veils, just as it has smashed great holes in our cathedral roofs and torn great gashes in our hillsides...I stand midway between youth and age like a man who has missed his train; too late for the last and too early for the next...I am the new Ecclesiastes. But I have no Bible, no creed: the war has shot both out of my hands...we have outgrown our religion, outgrown our political system, outgrown our own strength of mind and character...all I know is that I must find the way of life, for myself, and all of us, or we shall surely perish.

"I have seen the play," Gene wrote after a performance in New York, saying he was "delightfully surprised to find it a first class comedy...Shavian, to be sure, but solid in every respect."

For the playwright to mine his experiences with Gene and Polly as material for his writing and regard them as inspirations for characters and dialogue as well as ideas was in itself not unusual for Shaw, who frequently borrowed from friends for his plays. But these Tunney footprints generally were not recognized. The intimacy of their friendship was not widely understood, and the Tunneys were not living in London where others might have noticed the likenesses and commented on the similarities to Shaw's characters.

The Millionairess, written in 1935, is a comedy and the last of Shaw's significant plays in which money and power are a central theme. It addresses leadership, women's roles in society and poverty. And in an affectionate gesture to Gene's friendship and his sense of humor, it has boxing as a humorous underlying motif. Shaw mentions pugilism in some form in about a third of his plays, but here, characters literally or metaphorically talk by punching, raising their fists, throwing papers and wrestling.

"Stand up, you cur," says the main character, the millionairess Epifania. "Put up your hands." There's a straight left to the chin, a savage punch with the right, a duck and counter, and even a mule kick. Gene joked that there was more punching in the play than in some boxing matches.

Epifania says she was trained in boxing because her father held that wom-

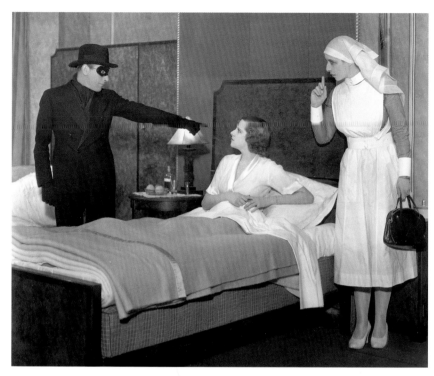

TOP TO BOTTOM: CEDRIC HARDWICKE, LEONORA CORBETT AND ELLEN POLLOCK IN SHAW'S *TOO TRUE TO BE GOOD* AT THE MALVERN FESTIVAL, 1932; MARIA EIS AND ULRICH BETTAC IN THE FIRST PRODUCTION OF *THE MILLIONAIRESS* IN VIENNA, 1936 (BOTH MANDER AND MITCHENSON THEATRE COLLECTION).

en should be able to defend themselves. "He had me taught to box. I became a boxing fan and went to all the championship fights," she says, adding that she saw Alastair, her estranged husband, win the amateur heavyweight championship. "He has a solar plexus punch that nothing can withstand." A punch in the solar plexus, a powerful jab referred to five times in this play alone, can be one of the most painful and damaging to receive and is often mentioned by Shaw in his writings. A blow to the solar plexus, a dense cluster of nerve cells located behind the stomach, can immobilize an opponent, and prizefighters build up muscles purposely to protect these tissues. (In 1897 Bob Fitzsimmons became heavyweight boxing champion by knocking out Jim Corbett with such a punch.)

No other Shaw character dominates a Shaw play the way Epifania dominates hers, writes Shaw scholar Margot Peters. "She is a dynamo whose ruthless will paralyzes the will of others. Epifania is a born boss."

In the first scene, Epifania visits a lawyer and identifies her estranged husband, Alastair. The lawyer, surprised, responds immediately with what could be a reference to Gene and Shaw's daily morning routine in Brioni:

"What! The amateur tennis champion and heavyweight boxer?" says the lawyer.

"Do you know him?" asks Epifania.

"Every morning we swim together at the club," the lawyer replies.

The millionairess then claims her husband is involved with Patricia Smith, whose pen name is Polly Seedystockings, a nod to the real Polly, whose pen name during courtship was "Miss L." Like Polly Tunney, the fictional Seedystockings has a knack for making people happy.

"Unhappy people come to me just as money comes to her," she says.

Polly Tunney was not as amused by the play as was Gene and did not like to be linked, even distantly, to a character that had inherited millions of dollars and married a boxer. This was especially so after the sensational 1932 kidnapping and murder of the baby of their friends Charles and Anne Morrow Lindbergh. Polly and Gene's oldest child, a son, was only four months old when the Lindbergh baby was abducted, and the tragedy increased her concerns of unwarranted public attention.

She loathed being identified as an heiress, had little respect for women who enjoyed the label "café society" and, unlike Epifania, did not like to talk about numbers "with zeros." ("He always wins," says Epifania. "He wins at tennis. He wins at boxing. He won me, the richest heiress in England.") Despite Gene's friendship with Shaw, no one, much to Polly's relief, connected the Tunneys to the play at all.

"You married a man because he had a superlative solar plexus punch?" asks the incredulous lawyer in the play.

"Well, he was handsome," Epifania replies. "He stripped well, unlike many handsome men." In jest, she adds that "all his ardor was in his fists."

Shaw borrowed Gene's friendship with European heavyweight Erminio Spalla to cast Alastair as a striving opera singer. To keep the Italian as a sparring partner, Gene bought records by Caruso and played arias during training. (After Gene whipped Spalla in a prizefight, Spalla returned to Italy to study music, making his debut in *Aida* at La Scala.)

In the play, Epifania says her husband received Caruso records as birthday gifts, became convinced that he could make a fortune as an operatic tenor and used her money to buy an appearance in one of Caruso's most popular roles. In one of the play's most frequently quoted lines, Epifania says money is power, security and freedom, "the difference between living on the slope of a volcano and being safe in the garden of the Hesperides."

When the estranged husband tells Epifania that he never raised a hand to hurt her, she replies as if they were sparring partners. "Yes," she agrees, "but you are like the great European powers: you never fight except in self-defense...you are two stone heavier than I; and I cannot keep my head at infighting as you can."

Writing was something Gene had always wanted to do, so when he decided to pen an autobiography, he took it as a given that a man who enjoyed words as much as he did would find this not only pleasurable but rewarding. He was confident that the willpower that enabled him to become champion would be transferable to other endeavors in life and that he could master words just as he had conquered the ring.

Working by himself, typing with two fingers on his black Remington and holed away for hours at a time in his small upstairs study in rural Connecticut, he methodically churned out chapter after chapter, trying to recount the way he summoned the willpower, ring science, training, stamina, self-denial and mental alertness needed for boxing. Shaw had talked about Apsley Cherry-Garrard, a neighbor who wrote, with Shaw's encouragement and edits, the masterpiece *The Worst Journey in the World*, about Cherry's journey to Antarctica with explorer Robert Scott's doomed 1910-13 expedition. Editorial help is a good thing to ask for, Shaw reminded Gene.

They also had often discussed T.E. Lawrence, whose best-selling *Seven Pillars of Wisdom* had been edited by Shaw, as well as by Charlotte. When not posted abroad, Lawrence had been a frequent visitor to the Shaws' home. "We were all enormously interested in Colonel Lawrence in those days, and in exploration of all kinds," remembered Polly.

"I think I would put Shaw's friendship with Gene Tunney into the same category, roughly, as Shaw's friendship with Lawrence of Arabia," said Michael Holroyd. "Both were quite different people, but they extended Shaw's experience and knowledge, active knowledge just by being themselves, really, and the graft was very good. Everybody got on well and were able to explore the others' territory and in just the right atmosphere, and I think that was a great boon to Shaw, a plus."

Perhaps out of pride, Gene chose to work alone on his book. It took a year to finish, and he chose his title from Cashel Byron's executive power speech at Mrs. Hoskyn's drawing room, naming the book *A Man Must Fight*. Once completed, he was in a rush to publish. He didn't send the manuscript to Shaw until it had been accepted by the American publisher Houghton Mifflin, which had already sold the European rights to Jonathan Cape of London.

A publishing date was set for 1932, and Shaw was asked if he would like to contribute a preface. Shaw declined, saying that because he was so well known, good sales would be attributed to him, and the result would actually smother Gene's chance for a second book. "It is the greatest insult an author can be offered to send for another author to help." It would be no act of friendship for him to write a preface for the book, he wrote Gene. "Whenever a publisher suggests that, sock him in the solar plexus."

Without a chance to consult or even suggest edits, Shaw had only one role in Tunney's autobiography: that of reviewer. One of his most humorous surviving letters to Gene concerns the book, and it's a marvel of patience for what he obviously felt was a piece of work seriously in need of editing and reworking.

> I have read the book. Have you ever read the autobiographies of George Fox, the founder of the Quakers, and Samuel Wesley, the founder of the Methodists? Perhaps not: they are not likely to have been in the library of a Catholic household. They are very remarkable books about very remarkable men (especially George, who was a magnificent fellow); and as such they must be read. But there is one difficulty about reading them without skipping. The daily work of George and Samuel was to sail into every town they met on their journeys and literally raise hell (and, incidentally, heaven) in it. George sometimes tried to pass peacefully through; but it was no use: before he could get away the church bells were sure to ring; and then, as he says, "they struck on my heart"; and back he went to "the steeple house" all out, and let them have it all in. Even a Catholic like Charles II saw as plainly as Cromwell that in some sort the spirit of God was in the man.
>
> Wesley left the steeple house alone, but took on everyone outside, from drunken bullies and blackguards to Beau Brummel, one down and t'other come on, in his fights for salvation. So far, it is all very exciting.
>
> But you are finally forced to confess that the sameness of their experiences makes you feel after a while that you are not getting any further. Only a small percentage of the meetings differ from the rest by some exceptional incident or the appearance of some interesting historical character. You brighten up when Fox is imprisoned, and are relieved when he discovers osteopathy by resetting a broken neck in America and thereby restoring a dead planter to life. Wesley becomes so unreadable that you skip to Beau Brummel. Now you may ask what the devil all this has to

do with your biography. Well, just as one prayer meeting is very like another, one fight is very like another. Just as at a certain point in Wesley's biography I wanted to skip to Beau Brummel, there was a point in yours at which I wanted to skip to Dempsey.

Shaw seemed to try to temper the effect of what he had written by saying this was his "only criticism," adding that the book will suffer "a little" in general readability by being a professional record more than an autobiography. "But at your age," he added hastily, "an autobiography is impossible: there are too many of your contemporaries alive."

Shaw allowed the ultimate criticism to come from Charlotte, with whom Gene had often discussed books. "Charlotte, who is much interested in you, and not in the least interested in boxing, declares that she cannot understand a word of it, and, I suspect, deplores your misspent and violent youth," Shaw wrote.

Whatever Gene may have thought of the letter at the time, he understood the point. Writing the book was a humbling experience and made him reassess his hopes to become a full-time author. He later wrote that Shaw's reply "was a masterpiece of shrewd criticism, a classic of its kind." When in 1962 he was told a dealer was selling a copy expensively, he replied: "the guy who offers the copy…must think I am George Bernard Shaw, Jr." In taking Shaw's advice to write less about his boxing and more about himself, he wrote a second autobiography, *Arms for Living*, published in 1941, during his five-year service in the Navy during the Second World War. The title of the book echoed Shaw's early successful play *Arms and the Man*, which satirizes warfare.

During the 1930s, Gene was in Britain at least once a year and visited Shaw at his country home in Ayot St. Lawrence, as well as in London; they also saw one another in Venice and Florida. They usually met over lunch or tea, often with Charlotte and Polly. There was speculation about Shaw's romantic encounters with other women, notably actresses, but Gene dismissed them, writing that "Mrs. Shaw, who was one of the finest women ever born, and a perfect lady, could have seen only fraudulence" in such suggestions.

In 1959, he wrote a friend saying that he had met Mrs. Patrick Campbell, the prominent actress with whom Shaw's name had been romantically linked. "As far as I was concerned, she was a little on the phony side," Gene wrote. "Of course, Shaw's letters are always exciting…particularly when he is pretending to be a lover."

It had always been understood that visits between Shaw and Gene were private. Over time, many of the famous made the journey to Ayot St. Lawrence to get their photographs taken with Shaw and often to enhance their own publicity. Shaw must have enjoyed the clamor of these visits or he wouldn't have allowed it. But Gene craved anonymity, and Shaw understood and respected him for it. There was no agenda, no one else to please, no waiting reporters or photographers at the gate. G.B.S. was flattered to enjoy Gene's company alone.

Almost always, they took a long walk together, something they both continued to enjoy and find pleasure in doing together, and they often stopped at a church. "No matter where we were, if we passed a church, we nearly always looked in. The denomination never mattered," said Gene. This was a habit of Shaw's that became ingrained in Gene. "You may read the same history of the human soul in any art you like to select; but he who runs may read it in the streets by looking at the churches," wrote Shaw. Sometimes in a church they examined artwork, and occasionally simply sat quietly to chat.

Gene never doubted that G.B.S. wanted what was best for him, and he was humbled to be included without reservation in Shaw's life. Only rarely did Gene write publicly about his relationship with Shaw, and he turned down lucrative offers to write about private visits and refused attempts by others to abuse his personal contact.

On one sunny weekday visit to Ayot, G.B.S. took Gene to the village church. It was midday, and they walked down the road from Shaw's house, playfully clambered over a farmer's fence and walked across a pasture, dodging thistles and cow pies, to reach a white Grecian-inspired chapel. While Gene sat in a pew, G.B.S. played the organ, humming through Italian opera and at least one rousing Irish ballad.

Harry S. Rayner, the postman who delivered and collected Shaw's letters for many years, remembered seeing Gene walking along the narrow, hedge-lined roads alone with G.B.S. during one of these visits in Ayot St. Lawrence. "This interested me very much, because Tunney was a great hero of mine. I was getting used to seeing Shaw by then, but Tunney was something quite new."

G.B.S. invited Gene and Polly at least four times, (1929, 1931, 1936 and 1937) to the Shaw Festival in Malvern, but they were unable to go. Gene invited the Shaws to visit the Tunneys during the winter in Hobe Sound, Florida. "Quiet and not too social," was the way Gene described their getaway. "Newspapermen and photographers are barred so that one can be entirely free from that sort of annoyance. The bathing beach is unbeatable, the water clear, blue, and temperate."

The Shaws stopped in Florida briefly in early 1936, and Charlotte wrote, "We made a great mistake that we didn't go to the hotel you recommended... then we might have seen much more of you two." She added, "We so greatly wish we could see you & your little ones all together."

More than a year later, in December 1937, apparently contemplating another visit, Shaw wrote Nancy Astor: "Gene Tunney wants us to come to Florida and spend the winter on his island. How do you get there? Do you go to New York and fly down south or sail straight to Miami?"

The births of four Tunney children during the 1930s brought congratulations from Charlotte and words from Shaw with appropriate quips. "It has often happened before but we are convinced that this one is the best ever," Shaw wrote after number one. "Keep them off the stage and out of the ring if you can," he advised, and after the fourth birth he wrote: "Four is the correct statistical number to avert the threatened extinction of the race early next century!"

G.B.S. never failed to ask about Polly's health in notes and letters, and on every visit, there was a mention of the miracle on Brioni, an experience so profound he found he could never explain it away. At one point Charlotte wrote that G.B.S. had been ill and "was saved almost, as it seemed, by a miracle — like Polly was at Brioni."

In putting together a photograph book in 1948, Shaw supplied the caption for a picture of Gene and himself, with A.W. Meyer, "the great German surgeon who arrived miraculously in Brioni just in time to save her life when Gene prayed for divine aid." In the book he sent to Gene, he wrote underneath the picture: "Whatever became of the surgeon?"

POLLY AND GENE WITH THEIR FOUR CHILDREN, JONATHAN (JAY), BABY JOAN –
NAMED FOR SHAW'S SAINT JOAN, GENE, AND JOHN VARICK (TUNNEY COLLECTION).

Years later, Shaw's longtime neighbors at Ayot St. Lawrence, Mr. and Mrs. A.W. Tuke, were interviewed about Charlotte and G.B.S. Mr. Tuke was chairman of Barclays Bank Ltd., and a member of an old Quaker family. According to Mrs. Tuke, the Shaws once recounted the story of Polly's illness; "At the end of this story, Shaw said triumphantly, 'And if *that* wasn't a miracle, I don't know what would be!'"

The author Stephen Winsten, who wrote several books on his famous neighbor, included Shaw's mentions of Tunney on occasion but seemed baffled as to why Shaw spoke of a man who seemed so far removed from Ayot St. Lawrence, the London theatre and Shaw's world in general. He asked the elderly playwright why he kept up his friendship with the boxer Tunney.

Shaw replied simply, "To plant my feet on solid ground."

In boxing, as in economics, one is up against facts, said Shaw. "Facts, facts, facts alone saved me from my superior worthlessness. I fought against sinking into the visionary, fashion-ridden theatre and loved the reality of the vestry and its dustcarts. I recognized myself as a fact and disciplined myself for action. I was always in full training." He likened himself, Winsten said, to a pugilist who could take blows and give blows. In other words, much like his friend Tunney.

Shaw's secretary Blanche Patch, who may never have met Gene, called the friendship "odd" because it didn't fit a pattern or seem to serve a purpose, as did most of Shaw's other relationships. Or maybe just as importantly to Miss Patch's sense of social priorities, Gene was a boxer, and an American.

"They loved one another," said Polly. "I think for someone who's never had that kind of relationship, especially men, that's hard to explain between two people. It must have been something Gene needed, and certainly a relationship he wanted, and so did Mr. Shaw."

TUNNEY AND SHAW
IN WHAT WOULD
BE THEIR LAST
VISIT, IN 1948
(CORBIS).

CHAPTER 18

All Souls' Day

"I have never been given to close personal friendships, as you know,
and Gene Tunney is among the very few for whom I have established
a warm affection. I enjoy his company as I have that of few men."
G. BERNARD SHAW

During the Second World War, Gene had traveled almost constantly as a U.S.
Navy commander. Now a well-dressed businessman, he walked up the familiar gravel drive in Ayot St. Lawrence, his feet crunching on the gray stones.
Suddenly, the front door of the house opened and G.B.S. appeared, just as in
the old days before the war. It was July 27, 1948, and the day after Shaw's
ninety-second birthday.

In 1943 Charlotte had died, leaving an irremediable gap in Shaw's life.
("You could not have believed that I should be so deeply moved.") During
Charlotte's cremation at Golders Green, her favorite Handel's *Largo* was
played on the organ, followed by "I Know That My Redeemer Liveth." Shaw's
secretary Blanche Patch was standing next to him. As the hymn neared its
close, she later said, he stood facing the coffin as it moved into the fire and
with his hands slightly outstretched sang the final words softly as though to
himself: "And he at last will come for me. / I know, I know, that Jesus liveth,
/ And on the earth again shall stand; / I know, I know, that life He giveth, /
That grace and power are in His hand."

After Charlotte's death, Shaw would sometimes disappear in the evenings,
only to be found sitting alone in the village church. "Passing the church, we
would hear the organ and look in to hear him playing his favorite works by
Bach and other composers," said James Thomas Williams, a neighbor.

The lost years vanished in a flash of recognition. G.B.S., all pink and
white and fresh, walked directly toward Gene, his eyes dancing and arms
outstretched in a familiar greeting. Holding tight to his walking stick, Shaw
grasped Gene by the arm. They embraced each other and stood, hardly speaking, with Gene's arms folded around the older, and now shorter man, almost
as if to protect him. "One sensed the sympathy and friendship between these
two champions in fields so widely different," wrote an observer.

On Shaw's desk in his study, visible from the entranceway, was the photograph of a younger Gene in a Rodin-inspired "thinker pose," Charlotte's
favorite picture of him.

For Gene, the return to Ayot was a coming home. He had chosen to com-
bine a trip to the 1948 London Summer Olympic Games with a visit to Shaw,
arranging to take to Ayot two friends whom he thought Shaw might like to
meet: Eddie Eagan, a former amateur boxer and chairman of the New York

State Athletic Commission, and Lester Spier, a medical doctor who liked boxing and literature.

They sat outside in the garden in folding lawn chairs, warming themselves in the welcome sunshine, Gene at 52 still fit from cutting wood on his Connecticut estate and walking three to five miles a day, looking like the successful business tycoon he was and every bit the "Gentleman Gene" his mother had hoped he would become, and Shaw in his knee breeches, brown shoes and Panama hat, his walking stick beside him. They were drinking tea and munching on chocolate birthday cake.

"You may write me off as a deader," Shaw had written. "I have only some scraps of wit left and shall soon forget the alphabet and the multiplication table and be unable to walk more than a hundred yards without two sticks." In another letter he had written, "I am damnably old (92) and ought to be dead." After Gene arrived in London, Shaw continued the theme. "I am such a pitiable old crock of 92 that it would be almost kinder of you not to see me... I'm not worth the journey." Gene saw these dire protestations as a reflection of his friend's plucky spirit, and he admired him all the more for it.

They had, of course, shared many friends over the years. Only months earlier, Gene and Polly had hosted Lady George Cholmondeley, one of Charlotte's relatives, and Kiernan Tunney, a playwright whom Shaw had backed financially to write a play on the subject of the Irish church. (Shaw mistakenly thought the playwright was related to Gene). In 1947, Shaw had appeared in an advertisement promoting Ireland for Pan American World Airways ("There is no magic like that of Ireland," Shaw wrote. "There are no skies like Irish skies.") as a favor to Gene's friend, Sam Pryor, vice president of the airline.

Afterward, Shaw wrote Sam "an emotional tribute to Gene's friendship." On a trip together in Venice, Shaw and Gene had run into the novelist Cecil Roberts, who visited Tunney in Florida. They even went into business together with the vegetarian, antivivisectionist campaigners Curtis P. Freshel and his wealthy Bostonian socialite wife Emarel, who had met Shaw in London in 1914.

At Shaw's suggestion, Gene agreed to help back Freshel with a deal to sell a vegetarian bacon-flavored yeast powder to add seasoning to food. The venture lasted years and apparently never made a profit, but it did have the effect of keeping Gene and Shaw in close touch because Freshel used the contact as an excuse to travel back and forth across the Atlantic, swapping news between them. ("I have just picked up your address from a letter you wrote to the Bakon Yeast man," Shaw wrote in 1946. Shaw was never quite certain where to write Gene, who had several homes and several business addresses. "I see Curt Freshel frequently and we talk with great admiration and affection about you," Gene wrote Shaw.)

One of the stories G.B.S. especially enjoyed concerned a society benefit staged in New York to honor Shaw in absentia, at which Gene was an honored guest. When the hotel waiters ceremoniously and mistakenly served steak, instead of the pre-ordered vegetarian entrée, Freshel's wife stood and screamed into the microphone: "MEAT! MEAT!" She shouted at the 500 guests to drop their forks, rushed to block the waiters, then with her arms waving in the air fled the ballroom, sobbing that they had all shamed the great playwright.

At the birthday gathering in the garden at Ayot, G.B.S. sat beside Gene, one hand resting on Gene's arm. Shaw was delighted to talk about boxing and the prizefight the visitors had seen in London the night before (he had listened on the radio), and also about Paquito Beatty, his old sparring partner. Shaw repeated the tale of how his "great admiration" for Gene came after watching him in newsreels defeat Carpentier. He was explaining that Gene must have had a jaw of reinforced concrete to withstand Carpentier's celebrated right.

"Gene interrupted him to say that he did only what G.B.S. had described so well in *Cashel Byron's Profession* — he rode with the punches and avoided their full impact," wrote Eddie Eagan.

At one point, they talked about the struggle to recover from the war. Shaw held that the depression in Britain, which Gene suggested was the fault of the socialist government, was due instead to the fact that Britain was not "sufficiently revolutionary." Shaw said that the American way of life was begun with a revolution and that the British of 1945 were politically in the same frame of mind as the colonists of 1775 but had missed the boat.

Shaw then resorted to praise of Stalin, with whom he had had a two-and-a-half-hour audience during his visit in 1931, mentioning in particular Stalin's humor. "I expected to see a Russian working man, and I found a Georgian gentleman," he had written. He had found Stalin frank, humorous and friendly.

Quick to speak his mind, Gene surprised his guests by bluntly telling Shaw that he completely disagreed with his assessment of Stalin, and pointed out that since G.B.S. could not speak Russian, he quite likely had not really known what Stalin actually said. Anyone could tell jokes, said Gene, adding that a world war and more than 15 years had elapsed since Shaw had seen Stalin or been in Russia.

The discussion was brief, partially because both no doubt knew that the other was intractable but also because the tenor of their private discussions might not have been appropriate for sharing. Gene also may have grown weary of Shaw's enthusiasms for the Russian and, in particular, did not want to be party to propagating Shaw's well-known views in the press. (As it happened, Gene was correct — his friends did repeat Shaw's comments, and Bob Considine wrote a column about it.)

Eagan and Spier had brought books to be autographed, and Gene produced a gold pen from his pocket as a gift for Shaw, who liked gadgets and especially pens. Gene was a director of Schick-Eversharp, manufacturer of one of the first ballpoint pens, and Shaw had never seen one. G.B.S. turned the pen over and over in his hands, fascinated, then scribbled a few lines and pronounced it "Wonderful!" Tunney insisted he keep it, and they had a good-natured back and forth over whether it should be a gift. Tunney won.

"I write this with your pen to which I have taken an extraordinary fancy," G.B.S. wrote to Gene afterward. After Shaw's house became a museum, the pen remained in his desk.

"In their conversation, one could feel the respect that each had for the other," wrote Eagan, who said though Shaw spoke to all of them, he primarily looked at Gene as if trying to memorize his face. At one point, Shaw leaned toward him and said: "Remember, Gene. Life, happy or unhappy, successful or unsuccessful, is extraordinarily interesting."

In a touching self-evaluation, Shaw said that he worried that after he was gone his plays, and the lessons to preserve the human race that he had tried so hard to convey, might be forgotten. He seemed saddened at the thought.

Brightening, Shaw placed his hand again on Gene's arm and said, "If I had another life to live, I would have liked to become a great pugilist."

Gene held Shaw's hand and smiled, replying, "And if I had another life to live, I would have liked to become a great writer."

The moment stood between them, the sentiments left hanging in the air, binding them together.

The poignancy with which Gene remembered this visit in later years affected him deeply and unexpectedly. The visit propelled him back to the young man he had once been and to the intimacy of the friendship that had defined his life by validating his choice of boxing as a way to get ahead and giving him the confidence to hold his head high in any company and carry his energies into a new business career. Perhaps most importantly, he knew that as long as he lived, he would have had the most famous playwright in the world as his mentor and spiritual father.

The visit also seemed to have given G.B.S. new strength and vigor, with the touch again of the man of action who had unconditionally bared his soul and prayed for a miracle, giving G.B.S. perhaps the greatest gift one man can give another, a window into the heart of faith. The boxer compared so often to Cashel Byron had, like Cashel, grown older. Gene now brought him stories not of bombs in Britain during the war, but of private talks with General MacArthur and Admiral Halsey in the Pacific, and of travels that Shaw could no longer undertake himself.

"I remember a night on the beach," during the war, wrote Charles McCabe, when Gene, "recited page after page of Carlyle's *On Heroes and Hero Worship* as if he were reading a page before him by moonlight. He knew the main body of English literature quite as well as most college profs."

Like Cashel, Gene created a successful life after boxing, ultimately serving on the boards of more than a dozen companies in the United States and Canada and becoming chairman of McCandless Corporation, a holding company for rubber and building material products. Gene still read books, quoted Shakespeare and never gave a speech and rarely wrote a letter without an appropriate nod to a literary figure. He had been a White House guest in every presidency since Coolidge.

For Shaw, this seemed to be a satisfying result for his man of action, a continuation of life. Remember, Shaw reminded Gene before he left Ayot, "I am old and dotty. You're the three-century man. You have time."

On the way back to London, Gene took out a business card and wrote a paraphrased quotation from Act II, Scene II, of Shakespeare's *Antony and Cleopatra*: "Age cannot wither him, / Nor custom stale his infinite variety." He slipped the card into the notebook he kept in his lapel pocket. When reporters learned that Gene had seen Shaw and pursued him for details, Gene was angry that the visit he had wanted to keep quiet was no longer private. But he kept his response simple. He had still not reconciled his public image with his concept of himself. If he had learned anything about dealing with the press, it was to say as little as possible.

"We spent the morning together and had a very pleasant time," he told an Irish reporter. "He has aged a lot since I last saw him, but that is only natural. He carries his age extremely well." When asked for details about their friendship on Brioni, Gene replied that they had gone walking together. "He could keep up with me without difficulty," he said. Gene scheduled a trip to return to Ayot St. Lawrence to see Shaw in the autumn of 1950.

G.B.S. and Gene continued to write letters and exchange books, and in 1949, Shaw wrote a ten-minute dialogue for two puppets that takes place in a boxing ring, the arena of the mind Shaw seemed to enjoy most, beside an empty church. *Shakes versus Shav* was commissioned by England's chief puppet master, Waldo Lanchester, and was performed during the 1949 Malvern Festival. In the piece, the puppets Shakes and Shav spar acrobatically and knock each other to the canvas, continuing Shaw's lifelong aim of bettering the ghost of Shakespeare.

Shortly after Gene's birthday visit, Shaw wrote a long, thought-provoking letter to Dame Laurentia McLachlan, the Abbess of Stanbrook Abbey, about the miracle he had witnessed in Brioni. He typed the letter himself, making insertions, crossing out words, and adding commas in blue ink. In writing the account, he mixed up some of the minor details, which could have been easily forgotten over time, but his sense of an epiphany, and of the holiness and deliverance from death, was as sharp as it had been during the crisis. The letter is considered by the Benedictine scholars and by some Shaw scholars as being possibly the most moving and deeply private testament Shaw ever wrote reflecting on prayer and faith.

"It is a very powerful proof...of Bernard Shaw's own belief in the reality and accessibility of a personal God," Dame Felicitas Corrigan, Abbess at Stanbrook Abbey, wrote to Gene in 1955. "So much nonsense has been talked in the newspapers of his being an atheist." The author John Stewart Collis seemed to agree that "some have thought that his letters to her suggest that he began to entertain doubt about doubt." The story of Brioni, however, was not about doubt, but about a young woman on her death bed.

"Just as your letter came," Shaw had written, "I had a visit from another very special friend whose vocation was as widely different from yours as any two vocations on Earth can be and yet who is connected in my thoughts with your subject, the efficacy of prayer." He apologized, saying that he had probably mentioned the story before and, "old men repeat their old stories mercilessly," but added that it would bear telling twice.

Shaw recounted how Polly suffered a complaint, unknown and improperly diagnosed by the doctors. "Nothing but a major operation could save her; and there was on the island only one old and useless doctor. Death within ten hours was certain. Gene, helpless and desperate, could only watch her die. Except one thing, to go back to his faith and pray. He prayed. Next morning very early there landed in the island the most skillful surgeon in Germany, the discoverer of double appendicitis. Before 10 o'clock, Mrs. Tunney was out of danger and is now the healthy mother of four children."

Then the playwright, who said all his plays were fundamentally about religion yet who railed at the constraints of creeds and church doctrine, who was called an atheist, an agnostic, a nonbeliever, and who called himself those things, wrote:

> Protestants and skeptics generally see nothing in this but a coincidence; but even one coincidence is improbable, and a bundle of them as in this case hardly credible in a world full of miracles. The prayer, the timing of the surgeon's arrival, his specialization for the rare disease, were so complicatedly coincidental that if they had been reported to me from China about strangers I should not have believed the story. As it is, I do not doubt it; and it goes to confirm the value I instinctively set on your prayers. So do not forget me in them. I cannot explain how or why I am the better for them; but I like them and am certainly not the worse.

On the late afternoon and night of November 1, 1950, the fog was the worst reporter John Roderick could remember. Killer fog, they called it, the thick, acrid pea soup that perforated the lungs like deadly gray-green gas and left layer upon layer of filth and soot on windowsills. The dank fumes of soft coal that belched from smokestacks had become unremitting, but for a nation still recuperating from war, it seemed just one more test of endurance.

As Roderick set out from Fleet Street at mid-afternoon in his small English Ford, fog had settled over the highway, turning day into night. Headlights flashed back into his face, useless. It was like driving blindfolded. Even Roderick's experience driving the fog-bound Maine coast as a youth was child's play in comparison. Ayot St. Lawrence, the picturesque village only 25 miles from London, seemed, he said, as inaccessible as the moon.

George Bernard Shaw, the great Irish wit and playwright, had fallen from a tree he was trimming at his home on September 10 and, after 24 days in the hospital, had returned home and was dying. Roderick had arrived in London the winter before, after four years covering China and the Middle East for the Associated Press, and because he enjoyed the theatre, the arts were part of his beat.

As he had to stop frequently to make sure he was still on the road and not in some pasture, the trip took hours longer than it should have. It was dark when he parked the car on the narrow lane near the gate to Shaw's home. He rang the door bell at the Edwardian house known as "Shaw's Corner," and a housekeeper who answered said there was nothing to report. She said the playwright was "still alive." Roderick bedded down for the night, his large bulk wedged pretzel-shaped into the back seat of the car.

News reports said that the pundit had been cantankerous with the physicians and nurses who attended him after his fall. He refused, then raged in anger, when doctors suggested snipping his famous beard so that he might easily be given an anesthetic. It had to be taped down instead. He curtly told his doctors it would be ill luck for them if he did not die at their hands, because, he said, doctors are noted mostly for the eminent men they lose.

At dawn on November 2, a photographer awakened Roderick in his car and said an announcement was imminent. As later noted, there were about ten reporters and photographers present when the Scottish housekeeper, Alice Laden, walked down the curved gravel drive. Without opening the gate, she looked over it with a gaunt face and in a low voice, full of emotion, read a statement saying that Mr. Shaw had passed away. Later, she recalled being blinded by flashbulbs.

The nearest house with a phone, a handsome large house, was about 30 yards away. Roderick had talked briefly to the owner after arriving the night before, and she had given him permission to use the telephone in her vestibule. She had left the door unlocked for him and was still sleeping when Roderick raced to the telephone to be first with a bulletin. Then, not content to merely be first, he kept the line engaged by reading from the telephone book while competitors from other news organizations waited outside. It would be one of the biggest stories of the day, on front pages all over the world.

AYOT ST. LAWRENCE, England (AP) — George Bernard Shaw, one of the modern age's greatest dramatists and its most caustic critic, died today at the age of 94. The white-bearded, Irish-born sage, whose wit was renowned throughout the world for half a century, succumbed at 4:59 am.

His death was announced to newsmen by his housekeeper, Mrs. Alice Laden. Wearing black, she appeared at the gates of the cottage, Shaw's Corner, and told the reporters: "Mr. Shaw is dead."

The AP story said that the famed dramatist, who professed himself both a Communist and an atheist, was visited in his last hours by an Anglican clergyman, who said final prayers for the old sage's soul. "It is wrong to say that he was an atheist," said the minister, the Rev. R.G. Davies. "He believed in God."

Since his days attending early Mass as altar boy at Saint Veronica, Gene had been an early riser. He heard the news on the radio as he was shaving at the big sink in his bathroom, looking out toward the pond at the bottom of the hill and the Connecticut trees brightening in the early dawn with scarlet and orange foliage, the prelude to a brilliant autumn day. He finished shaving, put on his walking clothes and, letting himself out of the quiet household, left for a walk along well-worn paths and old stone walls, past the rock garden with its 200-year-old statue of Saint Francis and through the rugged, rocky terrain of the surrounding countryside.

It was All Souls' Day, and Gene would remember that as a child he had been bothered — spooked, he said — because in the All Souls' Mass to commemorate the dead, the priests wore all-black vestments. He remembered it always as a day of weeping, of an angst that was particularly Irish.

When he returned home, he closed himself in his library to look through papers and letters, books that Shaw had given him, and through his large collection of rare and valuable Shakespeare and Shaw works, as well as books sent to him from Hugh Walpole, Thornton Wilder, Ernest Hemingway, John Masefield, Robert Frost, John Marquand and others. The library had special shelves for his most treasured books, and there were many authors and poets among them, but none had become so bound to his heart and mind as had Shaw.

A photograph from Brioni — the only picture they allowed to be taken of just the two of them — showed Gene standing on a path chatting with G.B.S. Now, turning it over, he wrote across the back of the picture in his bold, practiced penmanship: "The Master and the Boy." Then, as if his pen stopped in midair as he remembered his friend's wit and laughter, he added a large black exclamation point, positioned at an angle like a joyous postscript.

"Here we are," Shaw had written on a copy of the same picture the year before. "I am trying to look my size; but I did not know how to stand until Mathias Alexander treated me. Your stance is perfect. Mine is incipient pot-belly."

The play, *In Good King Charles's Golden Days*, which Shaw had mailed to him, was opened to the lines that he knew G.B.S. had wanted him to see and would have known he would understand better than anyone else, except perhaps Charlotte. ("I like this play specially much, & I am sure you will too," she had written Gene.) The words from the play were carved into Gene's memory: "It is not that I have too little religion in me for the Church: I have too much."

"One of the most precious gifts that fortune has allowed me was the friendship of George Bernard Shaw," wrote Gene. "In all our conversation and correspondence, I never knew him to say an offensive thing or to ever malign anyone's character or personality. He was a man who lived above personality in a sort of spiritual and intellectual world free from vindictiveness or malice, with a love for mankind, but a shyness that only a few people were privileged to penetrate. I am proud to have known him."

Shaw was cremated at Golders Green, as Charlotte had been, and their ashes were mingled and spread in the garden at Ayot. Cecilia Beatty, the daughter of the boxer-poet and Shaw's goddaughter, lingered behind at the service and was the last to leave, tears running down her face. "Find a life for yourself," Shaw had told her when Paquito died. "Go to Greece and start something new."

In 1955, Sister Felicitas Corrigan wrote to ask Gene's permission to reprint Shaw's letter to Dame Laurentia McLachlan about the miracle in Brioni in a book honoring their late abbess. He was glad to comply, adding that his friend Shaw should be canonized for his preface to *Saint Joan*.

"George Bernard Shaw was the saintliest man I have ever known," Gene wrote the nun. "On no occasion can I remember his using the slightest slang, let alone common profanity, nor did he ever speak ill of anyone. His approach to life was that of a benign observer, seeing all, forgiving mistakes, and helping those who could benefit by his help."

Twenty-eight years later, on November 7, 1978, James Joseph Tunney died in a Greenwich, Connecticut, hospital from complications from blood poisoning. He was 81 years old. His wife of half a century, still looking remarkably younger than her 71 years, was at his bedside, holding his hand.

Like Shaw, Tunney had asked to be cremated; services at a nearby Roman Catholic Church were private, as had been so much of his life. "Former heavyweight champion Gene Tunney remains an enigma to the boxing world in death, just as he had in life," wrote United Press International. The story said boxing "royalty" stood ready to pay a tribute, but Tunney's family, speaking through the funeral home, "refused to reveal any details of Tunney's burial service."

"He was unloved, underrated, shunned by his own people, rejected by history," wrote Jim Murray. "Still, he was the best advertisement his sport has ever had. He could outbox, outthink, outspeed any fighter of his day. His courage was incontestable. He served in two world wars, he had 76 fights... His was the cruelest sport of all, but no man ever knocked him senseless.

Only one man ever beat him, and he avenged that four times over. He was like no Irishman you ever saw, but he was the greatest Irish athlete who ever lived.

"He lectured at Yale, read Shakespeare, and was one of the few men George Bernard Shaw socialized with. He should have been a living legend."

"Gentleman Gene left a legacy of physical and intellectual stamina that should inspire us all," wrote the Boston *Herald*. "Mr. Tunney was given to quoting Shakespeare," said an editorial in the *Washington Star*. "He looked like an actor; he sailed to Europe to talk with George Bernard Shaw; he did not act like a pug. The fans would not forgive him...he died a hero. But there was never any real understanding of this man, who was too gifted, too fast and driven, to stay where the people wanted him."

Gene's ashes were buried down the road from his home in an unmarked grave near a brook in a cemetery surrounded by tall trees, birds and the sound of water running over the rocks. In winter, the snow piles up along the path through the cemetery, and footprints of deer and fox sprinkle through the snow. Polly did not want a tombstone to mark such a private place, a place she often visited, but a year or two later, after some deliberation, she agreed to accept a small cement plaque of the kind given to the families of all the men and women who served in the military. The graveside plaque listed the years of service in the Marine Corps and the Navy, through two world wars, of which James Joseph Tunney was so proud.

There was nothing on the plaque to indicate that he was known as Gene or that he had ever done anything besides serve his country in uniform.

At the same time, a far more personal and private addition was added to the gravesite, so that Polly and the family would retain the privacy they wished. For the man who cherished nature and his country walks, who had found faith again on Brioni and whose passion for privacy was matched by his passion for literature and friendship, a small stone, taken from the foot of the statue of Saint Francis in the rock garden that Gene loved, was buried near his grave.

Like the stone that G.B.S. picked up in Bethlehem to toss blindly into the garden at Stanbrook Abbey, the stone from Saint Francis would be an enduring symbol of life everlasting.

"Friendship," wrote Gene, "is the most satisfying connection in life. No man can go very far with strength and courage if he goes alone through the struggle of life. There never was constituted a human heart that did not at some time, in some long and yearning hour, long for sympathy."

POLLY'S FAVORITE PICTURE FROM GENE'S BOXING DAYS. HE HOLDS
A SPEED BAG, USED IN TRAINING, IN 1928 (TUNNEY COLLECTION).

POLLY, IN HER GARDEN, IN 1979 (TUNNEY COLLECTION).

From the beginning, the idea to do a book on our father and Bernard Shaw had been our mother's. Despite her own fierce and lifelong desire for privacy, our mother wanted the story of their friendship shared because she knew how much our father valued Shaw's friendship, and she knew Charlotte and G.B.S. were devoted to both of them. Having felt the slings of the press during their courtship, she also felt that the man she married was not appreciated as the man she knew.

In 2000, I co-wrote and presented a BBC Radio 4 program on their friend-ship called *The Master and the Boy*. For this production, Mother granted an interview, her first and the only public one since her marriage; it was heard by some 14 million listeners. The idea for a book came out of that program.

Helping with a book, however, was not an easy decision for her, and several times over the course of the research, she tried to call off the project, saying that she couldn't bear anything personal to be printed. To our mother, everything was personal. As my brother Gene said, "A good deal of Dad's reaction towards the press was really to protect Mother, because she was so horrified of being in the public eye. He kept her on a pedestal all his life and I think felt this was the least he could do for her — protect her."

One day, we were watching a video honoring boxing champions of the 1920s. There was a picture of Dad sitting in a wicker chair, his head down, absorbed in a book.

"I like that picture," said mother. "That's the way I remember your fa-ther, always reading." Then, for a split second, there appeared on the screen a long shot of her walking down the gangplank of an ocean liner, barely visible behind Dad. "Turn it off!" she demanded with all the fury of someone in her ninth decade. "That was a private moment."

Once, when I read her a section about their first meeting at Whitehall Court with the Shaws, she enjoyed it tremendously and added details with de-light — until, that is, I read a few words about how fond she was of Charlotte. "You must leave me out of it," she said emphatically. "I don't think Charlotte would want to be written about, either. Charlotte didn't like publicity or pho-tographs in the newspaper any more than I did."

And how, I asked, could I possibly write a book about Brioni and leave you and Charlotte out of it?

"I don't know, dear," said our elderly mother, suggesting that I figure it out. Weeks later, she would change her mind. "Is the book coming along? Do you have something more to read to me?"

Weekly, when we were small, my siblings and I had an appointment to ap-pear in our father's study to recite poetry assigned the week before. A perfect recitation merited a dime or a quarter and a memory lapse received a rebuke. This was not a voluntary exercise, and we had to appear alone to avoid the possibility that we would crib from each other. We memorized Shakespeare, Shelley, Keats, Yeats, Kipling and Wordsworth, among others.

"Dad was always using poetic discourse and recitations," said my brother John. None of us would have recognized the boxer who was made fun of for his reading or poetry. That person was not our father, and Bernard Shaw and our mother knew it. Like Shaw, our father believed words were the breath of life itself, and until his final days, he kept a notebook of words. It had been ingrained in him since childhood to value their meaning.

On school mornings when I was a youngster, I ate breakfast early in order to catch the bus. Coming upstairs to grab my books, I would sometimes pass our dad's bathroom about 7 am and see him shaving. Sometimes I went in, sat on the tub, and while he smeared on shaving lather, we shared guy talk. It was one of the few times in a busy household that I actually had a chance to see him by myself. I asked typically young boy questions, such as: Does it hurt to shave? Why do you use aftershave? And, one day, when are we going to Florida?

"Well, Giant," he said — he always called me "Giant" to make up for the fact that my two older brothers called me "Shrimp" — "Giant, do you deserve a trip to Florida?"

"Well, yes," I said.

"What does 'indefatigable' mean?"

I knew I was in trouble. He had caught me again, unprepared. The chance of having an enlightened, educated life, much less going to Florida, was going down the drain. I knew I had to think of something, so I guessed and told him that indefatigable meant someone who was tired.

Eyes blazing, dad turned around in his long nightshirt, his face covered with shaving cream, and told me that indefatigable meant tireless, incapable of being fatigued. "Now, don't ever forget it," he said angrily, and he told me to start a book of words and show it to him on the weekend. I have kept a book of words ever since.

Dad didn't talk about boxing at home, unless a visitor to the house asked. In the later years of his life, many of the sportswriters who had covered his boxing years, including those who had been so ravaging to his character, became good friends, a tribute to his forgiveness and maturity as much as to them. They included Paul Gallico, Grantland Rice, Westbrook Pegler and Alan Gould. Brian Bell, the wire service reporter whose initial story on reading forever changed Dad's legacy, had died of a heart attack while covering a baseball game in Washington in 1942. Dad was a pallbearer.

He had a sentimental feeling for old-time boxing professionals who encountered hard times and often wrote to them and sent checks to those in need. He advocated the establishment of a fund for their benefit, into which went three percent of the receipts of every big fight. He answered all his fan mail — and there were thousands of letters over the years — from overseas, from schoolchildren, from people who named their children after him (the actress Gene Tierney was named after him).

One day as mother approached her hundredth year, she asked if I would look in the attic for the big wardrobe trunks she and Dad used to take on sea voyages, trunks that were so large they had to be hauled by truck to the port. "I feel like I'm going on a journey," she said. "I'd love to see them again. Those journeys were wonderful." The trunks had long since been removed from the attic, but she didn't remember and I didn't tell her.

The more we talked about the book, and the older she got in the process, the more she sounded like G.B.S. She had always hated mention of her birthday, as he did. On her eightieth birthday, when her children planned a surprise party for her extended family and friends, she found out about it and canceled it the week before.

My parents' lifelong friend Thornton Wilder died in 1975. In 1935, Wilder had written *Heaven's My Destination*, a satirical novel about an evangelical fundamentalist traveling salesman. The main character, George Brush, is an earnest, humorless, moralizing, preachy product of Bible Belt evangelism — resembling members of his family, with doses of himself and his friend Gene. In one telling scene reminiscent of Dad, Wilder writes:

> It was his custom while shaving to prop up before him a ten-cent copy of *King Lear* for memorization. His teacher at college had once remarked that *King Lear* was the greatest work in English literature, and the Encyclopedia Britannica seemed to be of the same opinion. Brush had read the play ten times without discovering a trace of talent in it, and was greatly worried about the matter. He persevered, however, and was engaged in committing the whole work to memory. Now while shaving he boomed away at it.

"I am afraid not enough people know the spiritual and literary qualities of Thornton Wilder," Dad wrote to a friend in 1966. "He is one of the best writers produced in the United States during his time, which is my time. It surprised me...in talking with Ernest Hemingway, to hear him say that Thornton was not a good enough writer to do a certain thing. In my opinion, in many ways Thornton was a better writer than Ernest though, goodness knows, Hemingway was great; but so was Thornton."

The novelist Hugh Walpole died of a heart attack in service in the Second World War. Walpole had given my parents their first wedding gift, a navy blue leather-bound set of Jane Austen's works that remained on their shelves.

Our father visited Britain's Poet Laureate John Masefield, the poet whose picture he had seen in Langner's office, to reminisce about Greenwich Village. "I cannot see what others see, wisdom alone is kind to me," Masefield wrote Dad, quoting one of his own poems.

The Pulitzer Prize–winning novelist John Marquand, who wrote about the passing of slightly snobbish old Puritanical New England families and their strong ethical code in business and in life that Gene identified with, was a neighbor and frequent visitor in Connecticut.

Dad had picked up the habit of hiding books when he traveled. Once, while changing trains in Albany, New York, en route to training camp, a reporter had seen him talking to Upton Close, who had written a popular book on Asia. The reporter wound up writing about Dad's bookishness and preference for the society of writers. He didn't mention my father's trainer and sparring partner, who were also with them, and who, my father felt, would have been legitimate subjects of boxing news.

After that episode, Dad became so sensitive about being recognized and seen holding a book that he hid volumes in his luggage or locked his train compartment door if he wanted to read. "Even on shipboard, I didn't dare to indulge myself in that best enjoyment on a voyage, lounging on a deck chair and reading."

In 1936, after a trip to Europe (during which he saw Shaw), he was stranded for several hours in Buffalo, New York, waiting for a plane to go to Toronto for a meeting. He was three-quarters of the way through *Gone with the Wind* when reporters found him. He chatted at length about the possibility of war in Europe, but the front-page headline said, "Tunney Talks About Novels."

Cashel Byron's Profession, the book that launched his dialogue with Shaw, has remained in print continuously since 1886, but it was never made into a Hollywood movie.

The first U.S. Shaw Society was established August 3, 1950, in Flint, Michigan. Its members included Randolph Hearst, Marion Davies, Upton Sinclair, Lawrence Langner, Gertrude Lawrence, Albert Einstein, Gene Tunney and Curt Freshel. It seems unlikely that this group ever actually met as a body, but as a youngster, I heard Dad's discussions with Freshel about trying to pull it together, and I recall Shaw's ambivalence over it all.

Our grandmother, Katherine Rowland Lauder, died in 1957, and *Tighnabruaich*, the great, brooding Tudor mansion that had been a wedding present from her father-in-law, was torn down and the land subdivided.

Helen Ufford Butler, whose apartment had allowed love to blossom, died in 1967, and mother's devoted sister Katherine, our Aunt Kay, who introduced our parents and who retained an older sister's charm and elegance all her life, died in 1987.

Helen Sligo Pryor Rice, Mother's classmate who traveled with my parents to Brioni and who shared Tunney family holidays, weddings and friendship, died in a care home in Florida in 2001, the last survivor of the visit on Brioni, apart from our mother.

Dad's lifelong friends included Sam Pryor, who introduced him to Greenwich and the Lauders and spent the night with our father at a hotel after his last fight, and Bernard Gimbel, the merchant prince who fed dad's passion for life, whether in boxing or business, and who was unfailingly supportive. When Gimbel died in 1966, his widow returned to Dad the gloves that he had worn in Philadelphia to win the heavyweight championship and had given Gimbel as a symbol of their friendship.

Dad and Mother had tried to return to Brioni for their thirtieth wedding anniversary in 1958, and again, five years later, but were not allowed. Following the Second World War, the Istrian peninsula, which had been part of Italy, had become part of the Socialist Federal Republic of Yugoslavia. Marshall Tito, who ruled the country from 1945 until his death in 1980, made Brioni his permanent residence.

"Tito won't let anyone within 100 miles of the place. I am sore, plenty sore," said Gene. Brioni (Croatian: Brijuni) is now part of Croatia, and when I visited in the context of researching this book, Mother wanted every detail told and retold many times.

As she approached her hundredth birthday, Mother surprised us by talking about her age.

"I think I've lived longer than anyone in my family ever has," she said one afternoon. Told that there were many others who now lived to age 100 and beyond, she gasped. "But my dear, what will they ever do with us?

She was interested in the progress of the book and talked more and more about Dad and G.B.S. "I think it was awfully important that they were both Irish. People don't understand the Irish very well — they're full of gaiety and talk, but inside, they're private. Dad kept a lot of things to himself that he used to talk to Shaw about.

"I never thought of your father as a church-going person," she said, "But he was deeply spiritual. Shaw had a huge influence on him in that respect, on both of us really. I remember Mr. Shaw taking my hands in his, and looking at me with his blue eyes and being so sincere that it was like talking to a priest. He said that we had all shared a miracle."

Mention of the miracle always made her pause. You cannot come to the brink of death and not be touched and changed, she said.

"G.B.S. really was Dad's spiritual father." Maybe, she said, the only father figure he ever had. "He was closer to Dad than anyone else ever was again."

We have no pictures that show both Mother and Dad with the Shaws. Dad had never carried a camera. On Brioni, she said, they just didn't take any photographs. "Isn't that silly? But we were hounded by photographers all the time, and the last thing we wanted was pictures of us that someone could get hold of and print in a newspaper. Mr. Shaw took pictures, but even he said they never came out. Too bad."

Shaw's home at Ayot St. Lawrence is now a museum run by The National Trust. Most of Shaw's books and furnishings are as he left them. Gene's photograph, the one that Charlotte liked so much, is in Shaw's study, along with the photographs of other famous people, such as James Barrie, W. B. Yeats and Sidney Webb who, along with his wife Beatrice, was the founder of the Fabian Society.

On Christmas Eve 2007, I sat beside the bed in Mother's room. She was quiet, almost hidden, buried beneath a big green comforter pulled up to her neck. She always liked the color green and said it reminded her of nature. I had been reading some lines from Keats's *Endymion*, lines she considered too private to discuss, and abruptly she decided they were even too private for me to read, so I laid the book on the bed.

She wanted to hear more about Dad and G.B.S., a subject that remained of endless interest because it brought back the memories of first love and her honeymoon, the period when her life was just beginning.

In the living room, there was a Christmas tree from one of the meadows, its fragrance drifting up the stairs to her bed. A large portrait of Bernard Shaw by Sir John Collier hung on one wall, across the room from the portrait of Dad by Sir John Lavery, the portrait Mother had bought the day after first meeting Shaw at lunch. A tall, bronze bust of Shaw by Jo Davidson stood in one corner, near an oil painting of the Irish countryside brought back as a gift by one of her grandchildren.

It would have been impossible to visit this room at any time in our parents' lifetimes and not appreciate that the distinguished-looking man with a beard and the serious, startlingly handsome young man by Lavery were important to this family. Just like the muted green on the living room walls, the placement of the portraits had never changed. Sometimes, in her 100th year, mother would double-check and ask, "Is Dad still in the living room?" Yes, I replied. He's there with G.B.S.

I leaned over to give her a hug and was about to leave when she suddenly became agitated, as she increasingly did when she couldn't remember words. She talked about a "ball" inside her. Initially, I thought that she might be in some sort of pain. She placed her hand over her left breast. Over her heart. And I understood.

"Remember," she said quietly, so softly I had to strain to hear. "Remember to write about heart. Dad and G.B.S. had heart," she whispered. She squeezed my hand and smiled the sweet smile of satisfaction for a message delivered.

For Christmas, I had given her a shell, a beige-and-white periwinkle with a covering like old parchment that had become crinkled from dampness. It was so weightless that she didn't realize at first she was holding it in her hand. Inside there was a bit of sand and rock fragments and dirt caught in the spiral that the unidentified mollusk had once called home. I had picked it up a year earlier on the lawn of Villa Punta Naso.

There's a new villa there now, to replace the old *palazzo* that had been destroyed by bombs during the Second World War. The new one seems pleasant,
but nothing like its predecessor. Only the land and the sea around it remain
unchanged. I told her about the old steps down to the rock ledges, where they
used to sun themselves, and where Dad and G.B.S. swam, and the big cacti
and the cypress trees, some of which are still there.

She held the shell for a while, and then gave it back to me.

Put it with Dad, she said. Bury it with the stone from Saint Francis. At
the cemetery. Can you do that? You'll know when.

By the time I left, she had drifted off to sleep.

The following spring, on April 12, 2008, 12 days before her 101st birthday,
a sunny day in which gusting winds swept the pink petals of the cherry blossoms across the rolling lawn, our mother died of complications from a stroke.
She was cremated, and her ashes laid to rest beside our father. The simple
stone plaque, identical in size to our father's, was engraved with the opening
line from Keats's *Endymion*:

A thing of beauty is a joy forever.

ACKNOWLEDGEMENTS

My mother's encouragement led me to the first steps of telling the story of Gene Tunney and George Bernard Shaw, and for her candor, honesty and determination to share her intimate knowledge of their friendship, she has my eternal thanks and love. I also could not have written this book without the warm support and invaluable family memories of my siblings Gene Lauder Tunney, John Varick Tunney and Joan Tunney Cook.

My Tunney cousins Mary Agnes McIntyre Anderson, daughter of Agnes, and Rosemary Tunney, daughter of Tom, shared their recollections of stories of the early Tunney household and of our grandmother, Nana.

I am grateful to my Lauder/Rowland cousins, George Lauder and Winston Lauder, the sons of my mother's sister, Kay, who helped with vivid descriptions of *Tighnabruaich* and the schooner *Endymion*. I was also helped by the writings of my grandmother's brothers, the doctor-novelist Henry C. Rowland, and John T. Rowland (Uncle Pete).

Frank Forsberg, former U.S. ambassador to Sweden and family intimate, first pressed this project after my father's death, twenty years before I started work on it. Tappan Wilder, nephew of Thornton Wilder, and his scholar-wife Robin, were supportive friends during my research, which often bisected their own research into dad's old friend, "Thornt."

Dozens of Shaw scholars and enthusiasts shared their wisdom and suggestions through emails and letters. I twice interviewed Thomas F. Evans, long-time editor of London's *The Shavian* and editor of *Shaw: The Critical Heritage* (Routledge and Kegan Paul, 1976), and his wife Frances. Rhoda Nathan, long-time president of the New York Bernard Shaw Society, kept me focused on Shaw the human being. Among the other scholars who offered the benefit of their scholarship were Michael Holroyd, Dan H. Laurence, Stanley Weintraub, Richard F. Dietrich, Sally Peters, and Daniel J. Leary.

One of my first editors was Shaw scholar Michel Pharand. Others who improved the manuscript were Sandra Beach, Alice Rosengard, and Tom Jory. Leonard Conolly, professor in the Department of English at Trent University, Peterborough, Canada, propelled me to the finish line by finding time to comment on my book between acting as general editor of the *Selected Correspondence of Bernard Shaw* and writing his own latest book. Conolly, corresponding scholar for the Shaw Festival and Literary Advisor to the Shaw Estate, is president of the International Shaw Society.

Kate Bosley, Diane Uttley and Paul Williamson, curators for The National Trust, made me feel always at home at Shaw's country house in Hertfordshire. Barry Morse, the English actor, shared his teenage memories of Shaw at the Royal Court Theatre.

Theatre was one of my parents' greatest enthusiasms. The Shaw Festival at Niagara-on-the-Lake, Ontario, Canada, is one of the finest repertory companies in North America and the only theatre in the world specializing in plays by Shaw and his contemporaries. The Shaw Festival has been unfailingly supportive. Former artistic director Christopher Newton introduced me to Toronto's "Boxing Night" and included me on the 2000 program as a salute to the Shaw-Tunney friendship. Jackie Maxwell, artistic director since 2003, was a source of constant encouragement as were Colleen Blake, Calvin Rand, a founder of the Festival, Ron Bryden, Denis Johnston, and Sis Weld.

Tony Courier, managing director of Shaw/Chicago, and Robert Scogin, artistic director, generously shared their views of the theatrical Shaw, and of *Shakes versus Shav*, Shaw's penultimate play, which takes place in a boxing ring. Charlotte Moore and Ciaran O'Reilly, founders of New York's Irish Repertory Theatre, brought their view of the Irish Shaw vividly to the stage in productions such as *Don Juan in Hell*. Kate Farrington, dramaturge at New York's Pearl Theatre Company, highlighted Tunney's friendship with the playwright in an October 2006 talk following Shaw's *Arms and the Man*. Readings of Shaw's canon by The New York Gingold Theatrical Group's "Project Shaw," headed by David Staller, inspired new insights into much of Shaw's less-frequently performed works.

My thanks to the Roxbury, Connecticut, Minor Memorial Library staff, especially director Valerie Annis, Silky Berger, and Muriel Smerekanicz. Thanks also to David Smith, researcher at the New York Public Library, who always had time to direct me to research materials. Katherine Reagan, curator of rare books at the Burgunder Collection at Cornell University, and her predecessor Ann Ferguson, were of immense assistance, as was Darlene Wiltsie, library assistant at Ontario's University of Guelph Library, Archival and Special Collections. Valerie Komor, director of the Corporate Archives of the Associated Press, was tireless in steering me to news research.

A special thanks to Sam Pryor III, who shared his memories of the early friendship of our fathers, and to his first cousin Fred Pryor, whose mother Helen Sligo Pryor Rice was such an important part of my mother's life. Sheila Keegan, an American-Irish psychotherapist from New York, and the Reverend Rob Clements of Roxbury, Connecticut, inspired me by their instinctive penetration into the human spirit. Also thanks to my neighbors Bill Chin, John Irwin and Kathy Slivka for visiting through snow and sleet to keep my computer running, and to Craig Paige for handling voluminous mailings.

Among the many others who aided me were author Patrick Quinn of Dalkey, Ireland; Mary Caulfield, head of the Irish Byron Society; distant cousins James and Regina Tunney who located family history; theologian Brewster Y. Beach; Hugh Mulligan, whose Irish wit kept my head clear; Richard Anthony, who remembered Gene and his father, Ed Anthony, *Collier's* magazine's publisher-editor, quoting poetry; and Claude Erbsen and Ann G. Bertini, who helped with translations. Bob Saidi, from the project management department at Yale, recreated the setting for Gene's speech at the university. Julia Sniderman Bachrach, archivist for the Chicago Parks Department, dug out yellowed clippings from the Long Count fight. AP's John Roderick, who covered Shaw's death, remembered every detail of his 1950 assignment. Others who kept me on my toes were Malachy McCourt; Bruce Kippen; Alexander Kippen and his wife, Mary Ann Zoellner; Jim Houlihan; my lawyer Maura Wogan; Vernee Samuel and Isobel Williams, formerly with the BBC; Roy Rowan, Laurence R. Smith and Mary Brown Jackson.

At Firefly Books, Ltd., I am grateful to Michael Worek, Associate Publisher, who supported this book enthusiastically, and to Publisher Lionel Koffler, for his unflagging commitment to it. Scott McKowen, the book's designer, is a friend who brought his considerable talent to the finished product.

Some of those who helped me most died before publication, including my sister Joan Tunney Cook, who died in 2008, and my brother Gene Lauder Tunney, who died in 2009. To all of my friends and family, I am grateful, but most especially I am deeply indebted to my patient and insightful wife Kelly, daughter Teressa, son Jonathan, and daughter-in-law Elizabeth Tunney.

GLOVE TUNNEY WORE TO WIN
THE WORLD HEAVYWEIGHT
BOXING CHAMPIONSHIP
IN 1926 (PHOTOGRAPH
BY TERESSA R. TUNNEY).

The private Tunney Collection on which I relied for much of my primary research includes notebooks, hundreds of photographs, family movies, letters, postcards, diaries, old cablegrams, menus, cartoons, scrapbooks and piles of assorted and often undated clippings, as well as artifacts, awards and mementos of a public life. It includes several surviving letters and postcards from Charlotte Shaw and newly discovered photographs of Shaw and Tunney. In addition, I had the considerable advantage of the collection's 25 file drawers of carbon copies of Gene Tunney letters and selected incoming letters, covering the last 20 years of his life. Newspaper articles, news archives, books and library collections abound on Bernard Shaw, and I conducted author interviews with boxing historians, Shaw scholars, acquaintances of both men and many family members and others who remembered the era, including Polly Lauder Tunney.

Because Gene Tunney was my father, and because I saw Shaw as a distant though ever present family member much of my life, I initially felt that telling the story of this unique friendship would require only minimal background investigation of other sources. My father's library of some 20,000 volumes enabled me to appreciate the range of reading he enjoyed — novels, biographies, histories of ancient Greece and Rome as well as modern histories, philosophy, politics, military fare, sports and books picked up on travels in the Middle East, Asia, Latin America and Europe. There were shelves of books by authors both famous and lesser known with whom he was acquainted and multiple copies of books he especially liked, such as *The Confessions of Saint Augustine*, Samuel Butler's *The Way of All Flesh*, Shaw's *The Perfect Wagnerite*, Thomas Carlyle's *On Heroes, Hero-Worship and the Heroic in History*, books on Saint Francis, Einstein, Nietzsche, Schopenhauer, Thoreau and hundreds of dog-eared books of poetry, including all of Yeats, Keats, and Shelley, as well as multiple books on Shakespeare, and a rare 1685 Fourth Folio Edition, first issue, of Shakespeare's comedies, histories and tragedies.

Shaw gave Tunney virtually all of his own works over the years, usually with notes inside, as in F.E. Loewenstein's *Bernard Shaw Through the Camera* (B&H White Publications Ltd, 1948):

"I am not responsible for the book," Shaw wrote in the flyleaf. "I should have entitled it *Gene Tunney Through the Camera with a few minor celebrities*. Anyhow," he added, "that was what they thought at Brioni."

Dozens of books were written about Shaw during his lifetime and after, but surprisingly, our father didn't have as many of these as I had expected, apparently because he did not feel he needed to read what other people had written about his friend. In retrospect, this was typical Tunney: he rigorously made up his own mind about people's character, and the private Shaw who befriended him was rarely found in books. I reread Dad's two autobiographies, *A Man Must Fight* (Houghton Mifflin Company, 1932) and *Arms for Living* (Wilfred Funk, Inc., 1941), both of which deal primarily with his boxing career and mention Shaw only briefly.

The more I talked with my mother and others, the broader the research became. I traced the footsteps of our father and Shaw with several trips to Dublin, Dalkey and County Mayo in Ireland, to England to visit Whitehall Court, Ayot St. Lawrence, the Benedictine Stanbrook Abbey at Callow's End, and Malvern, where the first Shaw Festival was launched in 1929. I visited the Danieli Hotel in Venice, where Dad and Shaw stayed (and complained about noise) and made three lengthy visits to the Istrian peninsula, where the Shaws and Tunneys spent a month together in 1929. To be consistent with the period, I have used the Italian names for areas that are now part of Croatia: Brioni island (Croatian: Brijuni and Brijuni National Park), Pola (Croatian: Pula) and Rovigno (Croatian: Rovinj).

Ultimately, the better I got to know Shaw, the deeper my understanding became of how much the playwright influenced my father. I began to appreciate that Shaw was much more than a friend but was mentor, priest and, as my mother always said, his spiritual father and the father he never had. I appreciated anew the significance of Shaw's portrait and bronze bust in our living room in Stamford, Connecticut, and of Shaw's books and pictures in my father's New York office.

Not just a family member, Shaw was a symbol of all that was important to Gene· of intellectual curiosity, faith in the human spirit and in the great and grand opportunity to reinvent oneself with confidence, to rise from humble Irish beginnings and find one's place on the world's stage. In *Collier's* magazine (23 June 1951), the year after Shaw's death, Dad published a story called "G.B. Shaw's Letters," with edited portions of his letters from the playwright. Gene was asked by other publishers to write more about Shaw but declined. It was too personal, he said.

I never met Shaw, except through my parents' recollections. My first impression was that he was my father's business partner because both our father and Shaw had backed Curtis P. Freshel in a business venture to sell vegetarian yeast powder. Over informal weekend lunches on our sun porch, Freshel traded stories with Dad about Shaw and talked about business. I was at an age when I was at the table to listen. Freshel always wore a tailored suit with a handkerchief in his lapel, and his European manner dazzled me. The Tunney Collection of letters includes one toward the end of Freshel's life in which he lamented the loss of 200 of Shaw's letters.

He also wrote that the Shaw letter loaned to *Collier's* magazine for the story by Gene was never returned to him. The editors had asked Freshel for independent verification that Gene was a friend to the playwright, and Freshel offered them a letter on Shaw's letterhead, quoted in the magazine, in which Shaw had written to Freshel: "I have not been given to close personal friendships, as you know, and Gene Tunney is among the very few for whom I have established a warm affection. I enjoy his company as I have that of few men."

The main events of the narrative told to me by my mother over many hours of interviews (1998-2007) were confirmed by other interviews and other sources, including diaries, letters, photographs, newspaper accounts and, importantly, by a lifetime of hearing recollections of the period covered by this book from my father. Mother couldn't remember some details, especially dates, and in some instances, I have taken license to imagine how a scene might have played out. In employing dialogue to bring to life the thinking and emotions of Gene, I leaned on my memory, letters and interviews, as well as words from his books, and from the many articles he wrote over the years, including for *Reader's Digest* (February 1942), *Atlantic Monthly* (June 1939), *Collier's* (23 June 1951), *Saturday Evening Post* (1 June 1940), *Golden Book* (April 1934), *Popular Science* (December 1926), *Guidepost* magazine (*Guidepost* published a collection of author articles: Prentice-Hall, 1948) and even the *Encyclopedia Britannica*. He wrote columns for newspapers (once filling in for columnist Walter Winchell) and contributed to the local Connecticut *Nutmeg* and to the collection of essays in the *Aspirin Age*, edited by Isabel Leighton (Simon and Schuster, 1949). His comments on politics in "Feet" (Chapter 16) come from "Political Graybeards and Youth," an article written in the early 1930s (*Cosmopolitan* magazine, n.d.).

In his writing, Gene sometimes expanded on material from his books but rarely mentioned the family or included personal comments. His subject matter covered boxing, fitness, politics, morality, prayer, music, literature and, discreetly, Bernard Shaw. When he mentioned Shaw, his tone was that of an admirer. He avoided personal sentimentality and public displays of affection. There are no words in this book that my father did not write, discuss or talk about among close friends and family.

The boxing scene in "Whitehall Court" (Chapter 9) recounting the bout between Tunney and Jack Burke was often repeated by Dad and appears in various forms in much of his writing, as well as in his books. (I am left to wonder if Dad's retelling of this story was because Shaw liked it so much. Shaw's characterization of Cashel Byron in his novel *Cashel Byron's Profession* was inspired by another Jack Burke.)

In the same chapter, Heywood Hale Broun's story about his father and Gene is from *Whose Little Boy Are You?* (St. Martin's/Marek, 1983). Max Beerbohm recounts his impression of the aesthetic Gene at Shaw's lunch in *Conversation with Max* by S.N. Behrman (H. Hamilton, 1960).

The initial interview with Shaw by former amateur welterweight champion and distinguished sports judge Norman Clark was prior to the playwright meeting Gene. Later, the interview was rewritten and turned into several pieces, including at least two that take advantage of the intense interest in Gene and Shaw during their stay in Brioni: "Boxing Isn't Brutal, says G.B. Shaw" for the New York *Evening Post* (27 April 1929) and "That Peculiar Biff," for the London *Sunday Dispatch* (5 May 1929). The rewrites include Shaw's later comments regarding Tunney.

In "Coldest Place" (Chapter 10), the Hemingway punch that drew blood came during one of the family visits and is also recounted by Frank Graham Jr. in *Sports Illustrated* (4 December 1961). I set much of "He was the teacher, I the pupil" (Chapter 11) in the ruins of Brioni's Church of Saint Mary, which I knew they visited often, and I created dialogue using their words on subjects that my mother reported they had discussed by quoting from Tunney's letters and, in Shaw's case, from his writings.

Gene wrote several times about the composer Richard Strauss, including in *Arms for Living*. Family letters included the originals from Jim Fair, a friend and biographer of boxer Harry Greb, who recalled Gene's many visits to the Village and late-night walks past the house of Dr. Van Vliet. The dialogue between Fair and Greb in "Sissy" (Chapter 3) is from a Fair letter (26 July 1965).

The letters that Dad wrote in the 1920s to his close friend Samuel F. Pryor Jr., (called "Uncle Sam" in our family) were returned by the Pryor family and include Gene's first mention of meeting Polly (10 May 1926), as well as Gene's commentaries on boxing, business and his future. It was Pryor who delivered a jeweled replica of the lost pin feather broach to Polly before she sailed for Rome. A letter to television host Ed Sullivan (26 July 1965) recounts Gene's tenth birthday, a memory Dad treasured. Letters from Bill Osborne, the Marine Corps friend who owned the Osborne Inn, and from Father John Murnane, the priest in Speculator with whom Gene spent evenings discussing theology, filled in gaps.

I was also aided by my own Tunney family archival collection. For 50 years Mother mailed copies of Dad's interviews, family notes, copies of newspaper columns mentioning Dad or the Long Count and public comments of friends or copies of letters in an effort to keep us apprised of our father's activities or acclaim, even after he died. I kept these, and her written remarks often guided me in my research: "Mrs. Lucy Ferguson is a character," she wrote on a 1971 article about Andrew Carnegie's sister-in-law. "Aunt Kay and I knew her when we were very young." On a positive interview with Dad, she wrote, "Nice!" and on one she didn't like, she wrote, "Pooh." Mother also provided taped memories of the 1920s-1930s period with Vernee Samuel, a London-based BBC Radio 4 correspondent.

One of the most important interviews for the time period covered by this book was an oral history done more than three decades ago with Sam Pryor over three days at his home in Hana, Maui (16-19 June 1979), seven months after my father's death. Sam not only talked about the romance, Gene's celebrity, friends and books, but offered details of their lifetime friendship. He recalled how prudish the young Gene was around women and Bernard Shaw's favor to him as a vice-president of Pan American Airways, when Shaw allowed his name and comments to be used on a 1947 Pan Am poster promoting visits to Ireland. (A copy of this poster is one of some 4000 Shaw items in the Harry Ransom Center collections, the University of Texas, Austin.) Gene had suggested the idea, said Sam, and afterward, Shaw wrote Sam a touching letter about Gene's friendship, a letter Sam said was mailed to Polly at Gene's death. The letter has not been found. The interview initially was done as a gift for Mother, who couldn't make the trip to Hawaii but longed to hear their old friend's recollections of the early years. She listened to the recordings several times, lost some of the tapes, but luckily I had saved all the notes. Sam also introduced my parents to Lowell Thomas, the lifelong friend and broadcaster who made T.E. Lawrence famous as Lawrence of Arabia. Gene and Polly never met Lawrence, who died in 1935.

The tenor John McCormack, who sang at the wedding in Rome, was a friend not only of our parents but also of Shaw. Shaw said Charlotte liked McCormack's Irish ballads so much he would go broke buying records. For Gene's visit in Ireland ("Pursuit of the Groom," Chapter 8), I quoted from Lily McCormack's *I Hear You Calling Me* (Bruce Publishing Company, 1949).

I had a series of interviews about Shaw and Pakenham Beatty (March 2005 and April 2006) with Claudius J.P. Beatty, a generous and spirited scholar, who until his death in 2008 lived in Dorchester, England. Beatty was the grandnephew of Shaw's close friend "Paquito" Beatty, and he was a fount of Beatty family stories, including his own first memories of meeting Shaw as a child in the late 1920s at a costume party for the opening of a restaurant on The Strand, operated by Paquito's daughter and Shaw's goddaughter, Cecilia. Beatty remembered that Shaw said he would have invested more if she had made it a vegetarian restaurant.

Cecilia also told Claudius that she and her brother Bertie were models for the twins in Shaw's play *You Never Can Tell*. Claudius Beatty was the baby that Paquito suggested naming "Dempsey." Beatty wrote *Sidelights on G.B.S. and his Friend Pakenham Beatty* (Plush Publishing, 2002). He also gave Pakenham Beatty's letters from Shaw to Dan H. Laurence for inclusion in the first two of four volumes of Laurence's *Bernard Shaw: Collected Letters (Vol. 1, 1872-1897* and *Vol. 2, 1898-1910*: Max Reinhardt). These voluminous collections of letters and annotations were an enormous help but not more so than Dan Laurence himself, who enthusiastically shared his time and suggestions by telephone, by letter and in person as I researched the Shaw-Tunney years. Laurence also edited, with Daniel J. Leary, three volumes of Shaw's *The Complete Prefaces* (Allen Lane, Penguin Press).

Aside from our mother, the most helpful interviews on our parents' romance were with Helen Sligo Pryor Rice, my mother's classmate. I interviewed "Aunt Helen" often by telephone and made several trips to visit her at her retirement home in Orlando, Florida, where we pored over scrapbooks and old letters, revisiting a time that she remembered with an historian's appreciation for detail. She recalled the near lapse of being discovered at Helen Ufford's apartment, described the train trip after the Yale speech, vividly brought to life the mad race to board the ship to Italy, the wedding, the crowds, the villa in Brioni and the Shaws.

As a bystander who was close to all the participants, she also had a clear but detached view of teatime conversations with the Shaws and of the intense interest in the Tunneys and Shaws among other guests on Brioni. Her memories augmented those of our mother and enriched the story. Letters to and from Brioni friends, including Archibald Kitts in "Full Fathom Five" (Chapter 16), offered glimpses into my parent's life on Brioni, as did their own correspondence and cablegrams during this period with Helen Ufford and Polly's mother and family members. Descriptions of their Brioni home, Villa Punta Naso, came from old photographs, as well as the memories of those who lived there. Our father kept the religious icons he received in Brioni in a box, opened after his death.

Jimmy Hourihan told me in Dublin (20 November 2005) about the Mob squeeze on Dad to fix a fight. Professor Declan Kiberd, of University College Dublin, provided me with a better understanding of Cashel Byron and boxing's Daniel Mendoza, "the fighting Jew," who appears in *Cashel Byron*, and is a reference in several Shaw plays. Author Studs Terkel recalled as a youngster how much he disliked Tunney for saying he read books. (After our interview, Terkel was so excited to find out that Tunney actually *knew* Shaw, that he waved a copy of a book which mentions this during a PBS television interview. The book was Michael Holroyd's *Bernard Shaw: The Lure of Fantasy, 1918-1951*: Chatto & Windus, 1991.) Laurence F. McGivney brought to life his grandfather's memories of the boy Gene sitting in the corner of the firehouse, and Sis Jenkins Wastcoat and Robert Taylor gave me an outsider's view of our mother's family life.

The British Library's vast manuscript collections include five surviving Gene Tunney letters to Shaw and the second page of a sixth letter. The collections also include letters from Curtis P. Freshel and from Pakenham Beatty — including Beatty's hand-written poem on Shaw dated 27 November 1882, about four months before the amateur boxing championships (four verses are cited in "Rookie," Chapter 2). I was surprised to find a black-and-white picture of Gene (without identification) among the library's collection of Shaw's personal photographs. The picture shows Gene sitting in a dark tank-top swim suit on the rock ledges beneath the villa in Brioni and may have been taken by Shaw. The library has a corrected typescript of Shaw's note on pugilism, written in 1947 as a preface to a new volume for the Collected Edition that was to contain his articles on pugilism and painting. The book was not published, but I have used Shaw's words from this piece on boxing in "Rookie."

The Archival and Special Collections at the University of Guelph Library, Ontario, Canada, includes a large theatre archive, photographs, copies of news articles, including newspaper columns written by Shaw on boxing, and the largest extant collection of works about Shaw. I found here a transcript of a letter from Shaw to W.E. Stafford in Tipperary (30 March 1948), in which Shaw writes: "I know Gene Tunney quite well. He is a serious Roman Catholic with literary tastes."

Included among the thousands of letters and items of Shaviana at the Harry Ransom Center at the University of Texas at Austin is the Western Union cablegram sent to Shaw on the birth of Tunney's first child: POLLY HAD BOY TODAY GREETINGS — GENE (18 November 1931). Shaw's hand-written drafted reply reads: "Dear Gene it has often happened before but we are convinced that this one is the best ever."

The collection also includes the verses that Shaw wrote to Pakenham Beatty's infant son ("a boxer thou canst not rely on"), the Pan American Airways poster with Shaw's image, and an envelope from Beatty addressed to Shaw as "Gully Belcher Shaw."

The Brioni archives, now the Brijuni National Park Archives, were all but obliterated during the Second World War. Mira Pavletic, an archeologist and director of Brijuni's department for the protection of cultural and historical heritage, oversees the island's extensive Roman ruins and a museum on island history that covers the residency of Marshall Tito of Yugoslavia (1945-1980). The historical archives include a small number of photographs, early brochures, newsletters from the 1920s and 1930s, old newspaper clippings and, importantly for this book, the diary of Anne-Marie Lenz, wife of the island doctor. Ms. Pavletic translated the diary from German.

At Stanbrook Abbey, I was assisted by Sister Margaret Truran, the abbey archivist who as a young nun helped Dame Felicitas Corrigan with *The Nun, the Infidel and the Superman* (University of Chicago Press, 1985). The book and its softcover edition (*Friends of a Lifetime*, 1985) were updates of the friendship between Dame Laurentia MacLachlan, Sir Sydney Cockerell and Shaw as first presented in the book, *In a Great Tradition* (Harper and Brothers, 1956). Shaw's letter about Polly's illness and miracle in Brioni appears in the books in full. "Never did he make such a simple and open profession of faith in its efficacy," wrote the nuns.

The 1987 London-produced play, *The Best of Friends,* by Hugh Whitemore, was based on these books. I met Sister Margaret in the same simply furnished room with a crucifix on the wall where Shaw would have visited Sister Laurentia the only difference being that the grille which once separated the nun from her visitor had been removed. On one of my visits, Sister Margaret showed me the beautifully crafted silver reliquary with the Bethlehem stone, the letters that Shaw wrote to the nun, and Gene's letter to Sister Felicitas, in which he writes, "George Bernard Shaw was the saintliest man I have ever known." In mid-2009, driven by a need to utilize limited resources, the Benedictine order made plans to relocate to Yorkshire, and the sprawling 19th-century abbey was up for sale (stanbrookabbeyfriends.org).

The vast majority of Thornton Wilder's correspondence is housed at the Beinecke Rare Book and Manuscript Library at Yale University. This includes 15 letters and cablegrams from Polly and Gene Tunney, the picture of Wilder and Tunney on their 1928 walking tour in the Alps (on the back of his copy, Gene wrote: "Just a couple of regular tourists doing the usual thing on *Mer de Glace*, 20 September 1928") and a photograph of Gene, identical to one that Mother kept by her bedside. (Dad kept a signed and framed photograph of Wilder in his study.) The Tunney Collection includes carbons of additional correspondence and a copy of one letter sent to Wilder care of American Express in France, which was returned (8 May 1964). The Beinecke also houses the Yale *Literary Digest,* which includes coverage of Tunney's April 1928 speech at Yale on Shakespeare.

I was able to make use of the 2008 release of *The Selected Letters of Thornton Wilder,* edited by Robin G. Wilder and Jackson R. Bryer (HarperCollins). Thornton's letter to Hemingway in "Pursuit of the Groom" (Chapter 8) is from this book. I also leaned on Gilbert A. Harrison's *The Enthusiast, A Life of Thornton Wilder* (Ticknor and Fields, 1983) and Richard H. Goldstone's *Thornton Wilder, An Intimate Portrait* (E.P. Dutton and Co., Ltd, 1975). My research diverges on several points. Harrison said Hemingway introduced Gene to Thornton, but my father said it was the other way around — that Thornton introduced him to Hemingway in Paris in 1928.

It seems likely that Billy Phelps, a friend of the Wilders, put Thornton in touch with Gene, and not Hemingway. Dad rarely shared personal matters with biographers writing about friends who were still living (and sometimes not after they died), and Harrison was not someone he cooperated with. Gene wrote that he wanted to set up a lunch in London between Wilder and Shaw, whom he thought would like one another because he liked them both and because he knew that Charlotte Shaw wanted to meet Wilder.

Despite other reports, it remains unclear whether this meeting ever took place or, if it did, whether Gene attended. (Goldstone wrote that they met over lunch, and Wilder told a friend that he was offended by Shaw's smug, affected and patriarchal attitude.) Lastly, Dad asked Thornton to be best man at his wedding, but at the last moment, Thornton demurred and Carnes W. Weeks, another friend and guest, stepped in.

The Henry W. and Albert A. Berg Collection of English and American literature at the New York Public Library includes about 700 Shaw letters as well as photographs and other items. Here, I found 13 letters that Gene Tunney wrote to author Hugh Walpole. I used some of the letters in "Pursuit of the Groom" (Chapter 8) and "Whitehall Court" (Chapter 9). Rupert Hart-Davis's *Hugh Walpole* (Harcourt, Brace and World, Inc., 1952) was helpful in filling in gaps on the Tunney-Walpole relationship.

The Bernard F. Burgunder Collection of George Bernard Shaw, in the Rare and Manuscript Collections at Cornell University, houses the surviving 14 letters, plus notes and postcards from Shaw to Gene, as well as about 3000 books and several thousand manuscripts and letters pertaining to Shaw's life. Dad made the decision to give his Shaw letters a permanent home in 1964 after a large packet of letters from Ernest Hemingway was lost during an office move. Following our mother's death, in keeping with our father's wishes, the Shaw portrait by Sir John Collier and the bronze bust of Shaw by Jo Davidson from our parents' living room was delivered to the Burgunder. Also in this collection is Shaw's letter to Eddie Eagan after their visit in 1948. I have quoted from Eagan's *Sports Illustrated* account ("A Visit with G.B.S.: Fight Critic," 27 May 1957) in "All Soul's Day" (Chapter 18).

Our father also gave the university: a letter from Charlotte (5 February 1940) and a copy (16 March 1940) of one of Gene's letters to her; copies of two letters between Shaw and Curtis Freshel and a letter from Freshel to Tunney (all dated January 1948); two letters from Dame Felicitas Corrigan of Stanbrook Abbey and a copy of one from Dad to Dame Felicitas (1955); and a letter from Cecil Roberts to Tunney (28 June 1963).

The Corporate Archives of the Associated Press was the single most important news archive, with not only AP stories but the oral histories of 1920s sports editor Alan Gould and of Brian Bell Jr., son of the reporter whose story dramatically shifted Gene's image from pug to man of literature. I talked to Bell Jr. by telephone and exchanged letters with him during the course of my research.

There were letters in the AP files from newspaper editors about the Gene-Polly courtship (did they kiss?) and newspaper logs from the 1920s that include descriptions of Brian Bell sitting at ringside beside AP's Charlie Dunkley, who said Gene would lose because he couldn't "punch holes in a lace curtain." *Breaking News: How the Associated Press has covered war, peace and everything else* (Princeton Architectural Press, 2007) added information on Bell's interview with Gene. The efforts of Bernard Gimbel and Tunney to keep Gene's marriage and private life out of the newspapers were captured from Cooper's autobiography *Kent Cooper and The Associated Press* (Random House, 1959).

The newspaper databases of *The New York Times*, the New York *Herald Tribune*, the New York *Daily News*, the *Chicago Tribune*, the *Philadelphia Inquirer*, the New Orleans *Times Picayune*, the *Times* of London, the Greenwich (Connecticut) *News & Graphic* and the Stamford (Connecticut) *Advocate* helped fill in gaps missed by family scrapbooks or memory, as did a search in Pula, Croatia, of a year's worth of 1928-29 *Corriere Istriano* newspaper files, which documented Gene's presence as if he were visiting royalty. Our mother, so concerned with privacy, would have been horrified had she known how easy it was to find her picture or to follow the steps of her honeymoon through the internet at www.newspaperarchive.com — she always felt no one knew.

Gene was a collector of old boxing texts, including those Shaw likely read at the British Museum, such as *Sparring! The Art of Self Defense* (1864), *Fistiana* (W.M. Clement, 1841) and *Pancratia, A History of Pugilism* (1812). Like Shaw, he had enormous interest in the technical side of boxing, the thinking man's pugilism. They both talked about boxing as a science, and the Tunney letters reveal that Gene also liked stories of 19th-century prizefighters. I especially liked Trevor Wignall's *The Story of Boxing* (Brentano's, 1924), which recounts the earliest fights on record when the honor of victory — and not money — was the sole object, and *The Sweet Science* (Duffield and Company, 1926), which includes Dad's win over Carpentier. There were also Jeffery Farnol's *Famous Prize Fights* (Little, Brown, and Company, 1928); *From Figg to Johnson* by Barratt O'Hara, which includes an 1885 Jack Burke battle (Blossom Book Bourse, 1909); and James Corbett's *The Roar of the Crowd* (G.P. Putnam's

Sons, 1925). Paul Gallico's *The Golden People* (Doubleday & Company, Inc., 1965) was helpful, as were his many columns in the New York *Daily News*.

Since childhood, I had heard people ask Dad about the 1927 Long Count fight. I first met Jack Dempsey when I filled in for my father at lunch at Dempsey's Broadway restaurant about age 16. Until Dempsey died, five years after Dad, I kept in touch. I liked him immensely, as my father did. Dad always said Jack was the greatest fighter of his time. For this book, I interviewed boxing historians Bert Sugar (*The Great Fights*, Gallery Books, 1981), Mike Silver (*The Arc of Boxing*: McFarland and Company, 2008), conferred with Steve Lott, the expert on old boxing films, re-read many accounts of the fight, including *Dempsey* by Jack Dempsey with Barbara Piatelli Dempsey (Harper & Row, 1977), *The Long Count* by Mel Heimer (Atheneum, 1969) and *When Dempsey Fought Tunney* by Bruce J. Evensen (University of Tennessee Press, 1996). Nat Fleischer's *Gene Tunney, The Enigma of the Ring* (The Ring, Inc., 1931) and Ed Van Every's *Gene Tunney, The Fighting Marine* (Dell Publishing Co., n.d.) were helpful as early biographies. Both authors liked Gene personally but neither apparently were able to persuade him to discuss his personal life or to correct inaccuracies. *Perry Street: Then and Now*, privately published by Elaine Schechter (1972), is an expansive overview of life in west Greenwich Village.

John Jarrett's well-researched *Gene Tunney, The Golden Guy Who Licked Jack Dempsey Twice* (Robson Books, 2003) and Jack Cavanaugh's *Tunney* (Random House, 2006) both cover Dad's boxing career at length. Two of the best books for readers interested in boxing were written by women: *On Boxing* (Ecco, 2002) by Joyce Carol Oates and *Boxing, a Cultural History* (Reaktion Books, 2008) by Kasia Boddy, a lecturer at University College London, whom I interviewed (April 2006) before she finished her fascinating work. I interviewed Ulick O'Connor, a former sports essayist for *The Sunday Times* in Dublin (November 2005) and in follow-up telephone calls. The late Budd Schulberg, who often wrote about boxing, helped clarify my impressions about Dad's relations with the press. In his book about Muhammad Ali, *Loser and Still Champion* (Doubleday & Company, Inc., 1971), Schulberg says of Tunney: "He was the Gatsby who got the girl behind the orgiastic green light across the Sound." A colorful quote, but Jay Gatsby was no Gene Tunney.

Few wrote at length about Shaw's interest in boxing, though it was well known during his lifetime. Most of his contemporaries considered it an inconsequential Shavian quirk. But Shaw writes about boxing, or uses the language of the sport, throughout many of his plays and prefaces, and I have used his words where applicable. In 1901, he added a preface to *Cashel Byron's Profession* about modern prizefighting, and in 1930, he added a small postscript. In addition, he wrote at least 10 newspaper columns about boxing issues, wrapped one of his music columns around a boxing scene and covered the Georges Carpentier – Joe Beckett fight for *The Nation* (13 December 1919).

Shaw fans would not be surprised that in interviews or in writing about the sport, he was opinionated and humorous. For "Sissy" (Chapter 3), I quoted from two columns. In one ("A Warning to Betting Men," 30 July 1921), Shaw suggested the time was near when "journalists will have to obtain certificates of competence." In "Is Boxing Brutal?" (*Sunday News*, 10 July 1927), he suggests that newspapers refrain from publishing coverage of prizefights until "they had sent for a professional boxer and made the writer spar." Both of these columns are in the Archival and Special Collections, University of Guelph Library, Ontario, Canada.

Several of Shaw's notes on boxing, now in the British Library, were never published. After 1924, when he saw Tunney defeat Carpentier, he usually included Tunney the boxer in his written comment. But after he met Gene, it appeared that Shaw was satisfied with the real life boxer, with whom he could and did converse in great detail, and his public commentary on the game ebbed.

The British broadcaster, critic and Shaw advocate Benny Green (*Shaw's Champions*, Elm Tree Books, 1978) wrote of Shaw's friendship with Beatty and Shaw's admiration for boxing heroes. The prolific Shaw scholar Stanley Weintraub discusses boxing in *Shaw, An Autobiography 1856-1898* (Weyright and Talley, 1969) and includes a chapter on boxing in *The Unexpected Shaw* (Frederick Ungar Publishing Co., 1982). Sally Peters' *The Ascent of the Superman* (Yale University Press, 1996) includes a chapter suggesting that boxing allowed Shaw's inner self to emerge "in a strikingly romantic guise — supremely vigorous and powerful, moral and courageous — in short, as a superman." Peters also contributed a chapter on "Shaw and the Seamy Side of the Ring" to *Unpublished Shaw*, edited by Dan Laurence and Margot Peters (Penn State Press, 1996). Richard Farr Dietrich comprehensively writes about *Cashel Byron's Profession* in his scholarly and unique *Bernard Shaw's Novels, Portraits of the Artist as Man and Superman* (University Press of Florida, 1996).

There have been hundreds of books devoted to various aspects of Shaw's multi-faceted life. Shaw assisted several biographers, in his way, and wrote occasionally on his own life. There have been so many books and works, in fact, that the word "Shavian" is an adjective to be found in the dictionary. The gold standard is Sir Michael Holroyd's four-volume biography, which took 17 years to research and write. (*The Search for Love, 1856-1898*, *The Pursuit of Power, 1898-1918*, *The Lure of Fantasy, 1918-1951* and *The Last Laugh*: Chatto & Windus). An abridged version of all four is available (*Bernard Shaw*: Vintage, 1998).

I also used Holroyd's *The Genius of Shaw* (Holt, Rinehart and Winston, 1979), a collection of essays from which I quoted "Religion and Philosophy" by John Stewart Collis. Sir Michael was a great resource for me personally. I interviewed him in 2000 for my BBC program *The Master and the Boy*. His interest in details about the friendship between Shaw and Tunney and his insights into Shaw the man confirmed my own understanding that our father had both a student-teacher relationship with G.B.S. and a binding friendship based on mutual respect. Holroyd notes in his writing that Shaw looked at almost everything in life as a shadow boxer — that is, the art of hitting without being hit. Gene was a ring master at shadow boxing.

Other works that I found helpful and which led me to realize how similar many of Tunney's ideas were to Shaw's and to better appreciate the playwright's influence on the boxer included: Hesketh Pearson's *A Full Length Portrait* (Harper and Brothers, 1942) and his later *G.B.S., A Postscript* (Collins, 1951), Maurice Colbourne's *The Real Bernard Shaw* (J.M. Dent and Sons, Ltd., 1930), *George Bernard Shaw* by G.K. Chesterton (Hill and Wang, 1956; the book was first published in 1910), *Bernard Shaw: The Man and the Mask* by Richard Burton (Henry Holt and Company, 1916), *Bernard Shaw: His Life, Works and Friends* by St. John Ervine (William Morrow and Company, 1956) and *George Bernard Shaw: Man of the Century* by Archibald Henderson (Appleton-Century-Crofts, Inc., 1956).

Gene met Henderson, a professor from North Carolina, in the early 1930s. Henderson wrote that Shaw "especially admired" Tunney and "sought out his acquaintance" partly because Gene was of "pure Irish blood." None of this came from Gene, who did not wish to be interviewed on his friendship with Shaw. When Frank Harris, Shaw's former boss at the *Saturday Review*, wrote *Bernard Shaw* (Victor Gollancz Ltd, 1931), he said that all Shaw's heroes were men of action, and "You could write Shaw's inner convictions and hidden aspirations in terms of Lenin, Mussolini and Tunney." Also helpful was J.L. Wisenthal's *Shaw's Sense of History* (Clarendon Press, 1988), the update of Eric Bentley's *Bernard Shaw* (Applause, 2002) and *Bernard Shaw: A Life*, by A.M. Gibbs (University Press of Florida, 2005).

To better understand my father's fascination with Saint Augustine and to clarify my own notions of how being Irish and Catholic affected the friendship, I reread Irish history, including *Emigrants and Exiles* by Kerby A. Miller (Oxford University Press, 1985); *The American Irish* by William V. Shannon (The Macmillan Company, 1963); *How the Irish Saved Civilization* by Thomas Cahill (Doubleday, 1995) and scoured *The Recorder*, journal of the American Irish Historical Society, edited by Christopher Cahill.

At least three North American universities publish a series on Shaw, adding greatly to the scholarship and, in particular, making Shaw more accessible to the public. The multi-volume series from the University of Toronto Press called *Selected Correspondence of Bernard Shaw* includes *Bernard Shaw and Nancy Astor*, edited by J.P. Wearing (University of Toronto Press, 2005), a lively collection of letters between the two friends. In it, I found Shaw's note to Nancy about departing London for Brioni (13 April 1929) and Shaw's rhyme about plenty of room in the box for more socks, as well as his later query about how to get to Tunney's place in Florida. The University Press of Florida is the scholarly publishing arm of the state university system under the editorship of Richard F. Dietrich and includes a wide range of work, including Michel W. Pharand's *Bernard Shaw and the French* (2000), which helped refine my thoughts about Gene's favorite Shaw play, *Saint Joan*. The Penn State Press has published *SHAW: The Annual of Bernard Shaw Studies* since 1981, and the books include general articles, reviews, notes, the bibliography of Shaw studies and a continuing checklist of Shaviana. I contributed to three of these volumes (2003, 2005 and 2009).

In addition, the Shaw Festival in Niagara-on-the-Lake, Ontario, (www.shawfest. com) has published a series of books about Shaw. The Festival's library contains copies of all past programs, which include insightful essays by scholars on Shaw's work. I also reviewed back copies of *The Shavian*, a journal published for members by the Shaw Society in London, and *The Independent Shavian*, published by the Bernard Shaw Society in New York City.

In order to appreciate Shaw's life in Ayot St. Lawrence, Hertfordshire, I read the "neighbor books." These include books by Steven Winsten, who once asked Shaw why he was friends with the boxer Tunney, to which Shaw replied, "to plant my feet on solid ground." In the same book, Shaw also tells Winsten about the Brioni miracle (*Shaw's Corner*: Hutchinson & Co, 1952). In *Days with Bernard Shaw* (Vanguard Press, 1949), Winsten quotes Shaw as saying that on Brioni, no one took notice of Strauss or himself when they walked with the more famous Tunney. *Shaw the Villager*, by Allan Chappelow (Macmillan, 1962), includes neighborly recollections of G.B.S. and gave me the Tukes, who said G.B.S. talked about the miracle, and the postman, who remembered seeing Gene and G.B.S. walking together alone on a country road. And in *Recollections of George Bernard Shaw* by R.J. Minney (Prentice-Hall, Inc., 1969), we read of Alice Laden, Shaw's housekeeper, who remembered that after Charlotte's death, Shaw frequently went alone to the church, where she found him meditating.

Much of what is written in these books fits with my parent's recollections of G.B.S. and Charlotte as caring, sympathetic friends. I found support for Mother's memories of Charlotte in *Mrs. G.B.S.* by Janet Dunbar (George G. Harrap & Company, Ltd, 1963). Our father was interviewed twice for that book. Dunbar told Dad that Charlotte, who was 50 years older than our mother, affectionately referred to Polly as "little Polly." In *Thirty Years with G.B.S.* (Victor Gollancz Ltd., 1951), Shaw's secretary Blanche Patch recounts the letters written by the Shaws on Brioni about the weather, Polly's illness and the activities of Gene and G.B.S. In *Arms for Living*, Gene wrote about Shaw asking him to call him G.B.S., rather than Mr. Shaw. He also wrote here about his talk with Shaw and his plans to devote his life to writing (I placed this conversation in Jerusalem because of the time frame and because Mother said they discussed personal matters together there).

I learned from Lawrence Langner's *G.B.S. and the Lunatic* (Atheneum, 1963) that it was Gene who suggested in October 1926 that he act in the role of Cashel Byron. Our mother dismissed such a possibility, and the press brouhaha between Gene and G.B.S. was not something she wanted to discuss. Coverage of their first contact through the newspapers was, fortunately, easily found in news archives, notably that of *The New York Times* and the Associated Press.

Creating a revisionist history, Dad always gave the impression that Hollywood, not himself, initially broached the idea that he act in the role of Cashel. William Lyon Phelps, who invited our father to speak at Yale, wrote about the July 28, 1928, dinner in London with James Barrie at which he first met Shaw in *Autobiography With Letters* (Oxford University Press, 1939) and described Gene in newspaper columns and also in *Gene Tunney Shows the Way* (The Butterick Publishing Company, 1929). Donald V. Mehus, a writer, music critic, teacher and Shaw devotee, guided me through Shaw's great enthusiasm for Wagner, Strauss, Beethoven and others, and I coupled this with my own knowledge of opera and music. Particularly helpful for quoting Shaw were Eric Bentley's *Shaw on Music* (Doubleday Anchor Books, 1956) and Shaw's *Music in London as Heard by Corno di Bassetto, later known as Bernard Shaw* (Vienna House, 1973).

Shaw, in saying he wanted to set the record straight, also wrote his own history in *Sixteen Self Sketches* (R. & R. Clark, Ltd., 1949). He wrote about his childhood faith and described his move to London as an Irishman (in "Rookie," Chapter 2) as "the most foreign of all foreigners." Rebecca West's remarks on Shaw's response to crisis in "Tipping Point" (Chapter 14) are from the London *Daily Telegraph* (3 October 1965). West was an intimate of Shaw's friend H.G. Wells.

From Shaw's *On Going to Church* (John W. Luce & Co., 1905), I used the playwright's own words about having to sit still in a pew, and dreaming at night that he was dead and gone to heaven, to create the sense of Shaw's shared moments with Gene at Saint Rocco's Chapel. *The Religious Speeches of Bernard Shaw*, edited by Warren S. Smith (McGraw-Hill Book Company, 1965), record his public utterings. Despite what Shaw said about Man as God immanent, G.K. Chesterton saw the spiritual Shaw, saying that in "a sweeter and more solid civilization he would have been a great saint." My father agreed.

Material quoted from the letters and writings of Thornton Wilder is used with the permission of Tappan Wilder. Use of Charlotte Shaw's letters is done with the kind permission of the trustees of the will of Mrs. Bernard Shaw. The words of George Bernard Shaw are used with the generous permission of The Society of Authors and Jeremy Crow, Head of Literary Estates, on behalf of the Bernard Shaw Estate.

Many of the pictures are from the private Tunney Collection. Particularly helpful has been AP Images at the Associated Press, and the Chicago History Museum which made available its excellent collection from Gene's boxing days, including pictures just prior to, during, and following the September 1927 Long Count fight. The photograph of Dame Laurentia McLachlan, the abbess of Stanbrook Abbey, is used with the generous permission of the abbey's archivist, Sister Margaret Truran. Maria Elena Rico Covarrubias granted the kind permission to reprint the caricature by her uncle, Miguel Covarrubias, showing Tunney and Shaw with reporter Jim Tully.

Every effort has been made to list all sources used for this book and to contact the owners of copyright material reproduced herein. The author and publishers apologize for any inadvertent omissions, and will be pleased to incorporate missing acknowledgements in any future editions.